ROUTLEDGE LIBRARY EDITIONS:
LIBRARY AND INFORMATION SCIENCE

Volume 38

FINANCE, BUDGET, AND MANAGEMENT FOR REFERENCE SERVICES

FINANCE, BUDGET, AND MANAGEMENT FOR REFERENCE SERVICES

Edited by
RUTH A. FRALEY AND BILL KATZ

Routledge
Taylor & Francis Group

LONDON AND NEW YORK

First published in 1988 by The Haworth Press, Inc.

This edition first published in 2020
by Routledge
2 Park Square, Milton Park, Abingdon, Oxon OX14 4RN

and by Routledge
52 Vanderbilt Avenue, New York, NY 10017

Routledge is an imprint of the Taylor & Francis Group, an informa business

British Library Cataloguing in Publication Data
A catalogue record for this book is available from the British Library

ISBN: 978-0-367-34616-4 (Set)
ISBN: 978-0-429-34352-0 (Set) (ebk)
ISBN: 978-0-367-37428-0 (Volume 38) (hbk)
ISBN: 978-0-429-35446-5 (Volume 38) (ebk)

Publisher's Note
The publisher has gone to great lengths to ensure the quality of this reprint but points out that some imperfections in the original copies may be apparent.

Disclaimer
The publisher has made every effort to trace copyright holders and would welcome correspondence from those they have been unable to trace.

Finance, Budget, and Management for Reference Services

Edited by
Ruth A. Fraley and Bill Katz

The Haworth Press
New York • London

Finance, Budget, and Management for Reference Services has also been published as *The Reference Librarian*, Number 19 1987.

The Haworth Press, Inc., 12 West 32 Street, New York, NY 10001
EUROSPAN/Haworth, 3 Henrietta Street, London WC2E 8LU England

Library of Congress Cataloging-in-Publication Data

Finance, budget, and management for reference services.

Includes bibliographical references.
1. Reference services (Libraries) — Management. 2. Reference services (Libraries) — Fees. 3. Library finance. 4. Library fines and fees. I. Fraley, Ruth A. II. Katz, William A., 1924-
Z711.F55   1988   025.5'2   88-2679
ISBN 0-86656-691-0

Finance, Budget, and Management for Reference Services

CONTENTS

Now That We Are Talking About the Budget   **1**
Ruth A. Fraley

THE PROCESSES, PROCEDURES AND CONUNDRUMS OF REFERENCE BUDGETS

Reference Planning and Budgeting in the New Technological Era   **5**
James A. Benson

Introduction   6
An Integrated System   8
What to Do Until the Network Arrives   10
Reference Service and the Brave New World   12

What Reference Librarians Should Know About Library Finances   **15**
Dale S. Montanelli

The Resource Request Process   16
Managing Resources   23

Changes in Attitudes, Changes in Latitudes: Reference/ Information Services Management in a Time of Transition   **27**
Edwin S. Clay III

Office of Evaluation and Information Development   28
Quality Control   30

On-Line Services 31
Training 32
Change 33
Budget 34

**Budgeting at the Library Department Level: A Middle
Manager's Perspective** **39**
Tamsen Dalrymple

Understanding the Environment 40
Budget Calendar 41
Budget Systems 42
The Economy 43
Be Prepared 44
Documentation 45
Selling It 48

**Budgeting for Reference Services in the Academic Library:
A Tutorial** **53**
Gloria S. Cline

Step One: Study the Literature on Budgeting 55
Step Two: Become Acquainted with Types of Budgets 56
Step Three: Examine University and Library Goals and
Budgets 60
Step Four: Identify Factors Influencing the Design of
the Reference Services Budget 61
Step Five: Identify Reference Services Programs, Assess
Their Needs, and Set Goals 62
Step Six: Prepare Line-Item Budget 63
Step Seven: Present and Defend the Budget 67
Step Eight: Monitor the Budget 68
Step Nine: Assess the Success of the Division's Budget 69
Conclusions 69

**Budgeting for Reference Services as Part of a Library's
Financial Planning** **75**
Joan S. McConkey

Budgeting Systems 76
The Total Library Budget 78
The Reference Service Budget 81
Conclusion 84

Statistical Data as a Management Tool for Reference Managers, or Roulette by the Numbers   **87**
Bruce Morton

Introduction   87
Of Numerphobes and Numerphrenes   89
Reasons for Collecting Statistical Data   90
National Surveys: The Tails That Wag Reference Managers   98
Conclusion   103

Budgeting and Financing Reference Services: Managing the Unexpected and Unpredictable   **111**
Gerard B. McCabe
Constance E. Gamaluddin

Introduction   111
Administrative Budget Development   112
Adding Information Technology   118
Coping with Budget Reductions   123

SOME SPECIFIC SITUATIONS INCLUDING REVENUE GENERATION

To Charge or Not to Charge: No Longer a Question?   **125**
Sally F. Williams

Services Eligible for Fees   129
Guidelines for Fees   131

The Reference Department Budget in the High Tech Era: An Endangered Species?   **137**
Kathleen Coleman
Linda Muroi

Literature Review   139
Surveys: New Technology in Reference Departments   141
Discussion   153

Integrating Electronic Information Systems into the Reference Services Budget   **161**
Nancy L. Eaton
Nancy B. Crane

Introduction   161
The Automated Reference Center   162

Cost Analysis 163
Funding Sources 175
Conclusions 176

Budgeting for Reference Services in an On-Line Age **179**
  Charles R. Anderson

Analysis of Print Source Use 181
Alternative Reference Sources 183
Cost-Effectiveness of On-Line Searching vs. Manual 188
Cost Analysis Validity 190
Alternative Budgeting Patterns 192
Conclusion 193

Multiple File Computer Searching: Can Trends in Use
Be Predicted? **195**
  Jean E. Crampon

Background of SIU-SM Library Services 196
Data Collection 198
Summary of Searching 200
Patterns in Searching 203
Applications for the Administrator of On-Line Searching 205

Financing and Managing Technology-Based Reference
Services in the Undergraduate University Library **209**
  Rodney M. Hersberger

Introduction 209
Traditional Approach 210
Introducing New Technology in Reference Services 211
Collection Development—Ownership vs. Access 221
Conclusion 222

InfoTrac: Is It an Appropriate General Reference Tool? **225**
  H. Julene Butler
  Gregory M. Kortman

Introduction 225
Methods and Procedures 226
Presentation of Findings 231
Conclusions 235

Fee-Based Business Research in an Academic Library   **239**
    Mary McNierney Grant
    Donald Ungarelli

  Origin of the Center for Business Research (CBR)   239
  CBR — Physical Description   244
  Scope of Service for Fee-Based Research   251

High Priced or Over-Priced: They're Every Library's
Problem   **257**
    Nancy R. Posel

  Are Libraries Being Priced Out of the Information
    Business?   258
  Need for Library/Publisher Dialogue   259
  Protests Which Don't Work   262
  Dialogues with Publishers Produce Results   263
  Other Publishers Need to Join the Dialogue   265
  Are Librarians Too Busy or Too Passive to Beard
    the Lion?   266
  Conclusion   266

MANAGING THE RESOURCES

Managing Difficult People: Patrons (and Others)   **269**
    Helen M. Gothberg

  Interpersonal Communication as a Tool   270
  Difficult Situations   271
  The Assertive Librarian   272
  Rights and Responsibilities   275
  The Difficult Person   276
  Conclusions   282

The Realities of College Reference Service: A Case
Study in Personnel Utilization   **285**
    Terrence Mech

  The Study   287
  The Colleges   289
  The Libraries   289
  Results   297
  Observations   302

**In Search of Insight: Library Administrators Work the
Reference Desk**   **309**
Ralph E. Russell

Why Do It?   311
Some Disadvantages   313
Is It Worth It?   314

**Unobtrusive Evaluation: An Administrative Learning
Experience**   **315**
Patsy J. Hansel

Background   316
What We Learned   320
Conclusion   324

**Reference Service vs. Work Crews: Meeting the Needs
of Both During a Collection Shift**   **327**
Susan L. Seiler
Terri J. Robar

Cataloging the A&I Collection   328
Introduction to Methodology   330
Conclusion   339

**A Scenario of the Reference Librarian in a Small
University Library**   **341**
Beatrice E. Flinner

Personality Traits   343
Professionalism   343
The Reference Interview   344
The Patron   347
The Reference Desk   349
Communication   349
Policy Manuals   350
Responsibilities   351
Bibliographic Instruction   353
On-Line vs. Manual Searching, or Technology vs.
    Reference Librarians   354
Education: Formal and Informal   355
Evaluation of Reference Librarians   356
Collection Development, Evaluation and Weeding   356
Conclusion   357

Marketing the Library in a Time of Crisis: Rewriting Public Policy Statements   **359**
    Ruth E. Turner

Introduction   359
Library Policy Statements   360
Charging Fees   363
Librarian Performance   366
Conclusion   367

Letter to the Editor   **371**

Now That We Are Talking About the Budget

Ruth A. Fraley

The question of the library budget cannot be discussed and dissected enough because it is the document, more than any other that controls and shapes the development of not only each individual library or group of libraries but ultimately the profession. Unfortunately, the reference department is one of the areas most difficult to explain to a nonlibrary person who often controls the library purse strings. On one hand, this is the department usually housing the most expensive part of the collection and it is the area of the library, in most places where most of the personnel costs are concentrated. If the library departments are compared, the reference budget is a sizable chunk.

Explaining the budget, therefore, becomes a task of explaining not only the collection but also the services and the processes in place for managing the fiscal resources. Gothberg's article about effectively dealing with people is intended to help the reference librarian deal with patrons and other staff members but contains descriptions of "people types" often encountered when explaining the library budget. While each library budget process will differ slightly from those described in detail by Montinelli, McConkey, Clay, and Cline, they remain similar in that the library administrators are responsible for making articulate presentations of the needs of the library and convincing the parent agency or organization to provide adequate support. When budget presentations are not successful, for whatever the reason, the library should have in place some clear priorities written in such a man-

Ruth A. Fraley is Chief Law Librarian, Office of Court Administration, Empire State Plaza, Agency Building #4, Albany, NY 12223.

ner as to reflect the goals of the library so that the impact of the lack of resources may be presented in the next round. No budget operates in isolation from history or from the future. A library cannot claim a goal of providing quality reference service, decide to rotate purchasing needed materials, or cut the staff hours on the reference desk and report complete success in the following year.

Net purchasing losses created by gaps in library collection budget increases and book price inflation will have an impact and that impact should be stated. Posel cites specific title price increases and suggests activities with publishers to try to change pricing policies. Any comparison of standard title prices based on actual costs to a library over a period of time will tell a very effective story. In fact there have been instances when the increase was so large that the accuracy of the library figures was questioned. If, as in the case of the libraries surveyed by Mech, the resource allocation creates a responsibility for heroic reference desk hours or no reference service at all, then this should be pointed out with a statement of the impact. It might be that the library has determined it is more important to provide access to information than to have all of the collections needed on site and up-to-date. If so, this decision would be reflected in the budget and alternative information sources would also be included.

Without technical standards or some uniformity, each of the new services or resources such as compact discs or end user searching becomes a major expenditure. Coleman and Muroi, Butler and Kortman, and Hershberger report results of local investigations into the costs and the advisability of adding compact disc systems to the reference resources. They do not reach the same conclusions. Anderson has developed and tested a cost algorithm to help determine if a resource should be retained in online or print format. A decision about continuing the print resources must be part of the decision to acquire each of the alternative resources. Costs are a major part of the process.

The fiscal or budget process is difficult not only because of the need to explain what we consider obvious—Clay's anecdote about the well-intentioned budget analyst who decided no book trucks could be purchased because the next step would, inevitably, be to request drivers illustrate the problem. This same analyst will probably understand the problem if it is explained in terms of statistics or numbers. The need to quantify services and project costs and demands increases consistently. The same analyst who objected to the trucks might understand the fact that one person can efficiently transport 125 volumes with one trip using a book truck and without the truck several trips would have to be made and some seating would be lost while the books were placed in an interim location.

Morton talks about interpretative statistics and points out the lack of a national data resource for libraries. While it is true that there are no good sources for national data it is also true that there is a great deal of disagreement about how we should measure library services. The ANSI Standards (Z39.7) were discussed in the ALA Statistics Section for years and the results were a true compromise, almost everyone was unhappy with some of it. The Outcome measures work of the ALA Public Library Association is being used more and more often while other ''type of library'' organizations are moving toward development of similar guides. The Association of Research Libraries produces statistics but the comparison is often helpful in only libraries whose mission is to serve as a research library. In the meantime, the budgets must continue to be developed, defended and controlled.

One area of the library budget receiving increasing attention is revenue generation. Traditionally libraries do not generate revenue and this is not yet a major item in many agendas. However, if fees are under consideration, Sally Williams provides an overview of factors to be considered in determining the fees and developing the projections.

Technology is not separate from operations, the management control system presented by Benson outlines a system that will enable the person in charge of budget preparation in the reference department or for the library to have, in place a system to quickly and efficiently produce the information required to prepare and monitor a budget. It can provide meaningful information painlessly and this is becoming more and more important in library management.

THE PROCESSES, PROCEDURES AND CONUNDRUMS OF REFERENCE BUDGETS

Reference Planning and Budgeting in the New Technological Era

James A. Benson

SUMMARY. Institutional environments are moving us toward more complex budgeting systems. Technological changes have increased the number of automated sources and services available for reference work. Changes in budgeting and planning systems have increased the demands for quantitative data describing reference work and for sophisticated analysis of that data. These developments will force changes in the conduct of reference service and administration will occur in the next few years. Local area networks are a probable consequence of the proliferation of separate automated information systems used in reference work. These networks have the potential to assist us in meeting the data gathering requirements of planning oriented budgeting systems. Service must survive these changes. We must maintain the privacy of library patrons and staff on which such systems may infringe.

James A. Benson is Associate Professor, Division of Library and Information Science, St. John's University, Grand Central and Utopia Parkways, Jamaica, NY 11439.

INTRODUCTION

Technological changes in library service are moving us toward more automated activities, services, and sources. Institutional environments are moving us toward more complex budgeting systems. These changes are affecting reference departments. Technological changes have increased the number of automated systems available for reference work. Changes in budgeting and planning systems have increased the demands for quantitative data describing reference work and for sophisticated analysis of that data.

Technological Change

Currently various reference departments are using technologies such as mainframe computers, minicomputers, microcomputers, laser printers, modems, and telecommunications networks. We use these technologies to access online catalogs, acquisitions systems, remote online services, CD-ROM databases, 12 inch optical disk databases, and locally generated databases on hard disks and floppy disks. We upload searches to online services, download the results of online searches, word process reports and user aids, access computerized personnel records, build local databases, and analyze data with spreadsheets. This automated portion of our already complex work environment appears to be expanding regularly and rapidly.

In general, each of these automated systems are separate and distinct. One of our pressing needs is the integration of these systems. We use one terminal for the library's online catalog, another to look up personnel records, another to access the shared cataloging utility. We use one microcomputer to access Dialog, another to search the WilsonDisk CD-ROM. Staff and patron alike need to be able to access the various systems without moving from device to device. We need to be able to communicate with one another and with patrons while using these devices. Additionally an integrated system should enhance our ability to plan and budget services, if we are able to integrate data gathering elements into the system.

Budgeting

We are facing new budgeting systems in library after library. Sometimes they are imposed by our funding agencies. Sometimes they are adopted at the library's initiative. Sometimes we must cope with entirely new budgeting systems. Sometimes we merely face incremental additions to the existing budgeting process.

The traditional line item budget was simply a chart of categories with projected expenditures attached to each category. Categories in a reference budget included such items as personnel, materials, online services, and supplies. Each of these broad categories might be divided into subcategories. For example, online services might be subdivided by vendors used. Often our primary responsibility was requesting new money as needed because of inflation or new programs.

The degree of direct involvement in budgeting and accounting varies widely among reference departments. The forms of budgets and accounts vary widely among reference departments (and indeed in libraries). Some responsibility in this area must be assumed by the reference manager. In collegially managed departments, this responsibility is more dispersed among the members of the department than it is in hierarchically managed departments.

The degree of responsibility may be limited to requesting funds for the budget and assuring that monies received for such activities as online searching are properly recorded. In departments where more responsibility is assigned, we might expect that budgeting and accounting functions would be intertwined with formal planning and evaluation procedures.

The new budgeting process will often include identifying programs of service, establishing objectives for each program, setting priorities, and measuring performance toward the achievement of the objectives. Projected expenditures would be distributed among the programs. Increasingly we must closely monitor actual expenditures against the projected expenditures. Additionally, such questions as the cost/performance ratio for each program might be raised.

In organizations which use performance budgets or PPBS budgets, we would expect that the reference department would have an evaluation process tied to the budgeting process. Under such circumstances the department would be expected to accomplish the following: identify programs of activity; identify output measures for each program; allocate resources among the programs; and evaluate performance. As a product of such a process, the department should be able to: identify strengths and weaknesses; modify the allocation of resources; and improve services.

One of the clear implications of the new budgeting is the demand for more and better data about operations. There are demands to know the unit cost of various services. For example, we may need to know the cost per search for a new CD-ROM database. To calculate that cost we have to know how many searches were conducted. Once that data is supplied, we may be asked questions such as: what categories of users search the database; how much staff time was consumed assisting the users; and how satisfied were the users. The new budgeting requires more systematic planning and evaluation.

We have had these new budgeting responsibilities placed upon us at the same time reference work itself has increased its complexity because of the introduction of new automated sources and services. If we chose to implement the new technology on a cost recovery basis, we also face new accounting responsibilities. Bills and receipts are issued and funds are received. These developments combine to create significant new responsibilities.

AN INTEGRATED SYSTEM

We have a variety of unconnected automated systems which we must use, monitor, and evaluate. We must budget for them. We must chose among the available ones. We must do all of this while continuing nonautomated activities and maintaining levels of service. Clearly we need to marry the new technology to the new budgeting processes. If this marriage is not achieved, we will spend excessive amounts of time gathering and analyzing the data demanded by planning, budgeting, and evaluating. We face an imperative to integrate our automated systems and incorporate into that integrated system a data gathering and analysis subsystem which will facilitate our planning and budgeting process.

At the present time, the integrating technology would appear to be a local area network with microcomputer-based workstations. Ideally the network would consist of workstations at any service point and at individual work locations. Thus, there would be workstations throughout the reference department, if not throughout the library. They would be in patron carrels, at the reference desk, and at the desks of the individual reference librarians. Many of the workstations would probably be fully functional microcomputers.

The workstations would all be interconnected by the network. Any workstation should be able to interrogate any subsystem and be able to communicate with on-duty reference librarians. That is, any workstation should be able to access end-user search systems, the online catalog, the acquisition system, CD-ROM databases, and send and receive messages to and from the reference desk. Subsystems for staff use only and private files should be protected by security procedures such as passwords. The network should be able to monitor use of the subsystems and automatically gather data concerning patron-librarian communication. Thus, the network should record the fact that a patron accessed an end-user search system, completed a search, and downloaded the results to floppy disk. Reference questions submitted by a patron over the network should be automatically logged. Because of privacy concerns such automatic data gathering must not be tied to patron name.

Ultimately what is contemplated is the complete migration of reference service to a computerized environment with the various elements linked in a network. One component of that network would be a reference department management information system. The Reference MIS would be capable of answering ad hoc queries about the department's operations and usage patterns. A reference librarian should be able to ask the system such questions as what databases do high school students access most frequently. Such queries should not require specialized programming by the librarian or assistance from a systems analyst in order to obtain the answer. Data from the MIS subsystem should be capable of being easily downloaded for further analysis.

WHAT TO DO UNTIL THE NETWORK ARRIVES

The system as envisioned does not exist today. Components, do, however. We have microcomputers, some linked into local area networks. We have a variety of automated services, some able to monitor usage and collect data. We have a variety of analytical tools, such as database management systems, electronic spreadsheets, financial modeling software, and project management software.

We may be able to capture data from some of our automated systems. For example, H. W. Wilson's Wilsearch program will keep simple statistics about use of the system and BRS' Accounts file can be downloaded for analysis in a spreadsheet. We can explore the problems of transferring that data to analytical programs such as Reflex and Lotus 1-2-3. The data may be stored as ASCII data in a separate file. Such data may be copied, and edited into a format that can be loaded as a Lotus file. Indeed we should insist that vendors provide modules to gather and record such data, and that it be easily transferable to analytical programs.

Once the data is in a usable format, we can examine that data to determine the utility of what is now being gathered. We can present the data in a variety of formats to determine which are most meaningful to our staffs. We can display the data as percentages. We can graph the data. We can conduct statistical tests. The object is to determine: what forms of data are most meaningful to us; which forms will communicate best; and which ones will provide the best assistance in decision making. For example, we might find that reference desk activity by hour is best communicated by a bar graph.

We can integrate the data and analysis into our reports without rekeying, thus reducing the burden of report writing. If we recommend a change in our staffing pattern, we may be able to directly incorporate that bar graph into the report. As we explore such possibilities we will be developing specifications for the capabilities of our fully integrated system.

We can use these same tools to build budgets, keep accounts, analyze manually gathered data, and attempt to build a broader basis for our decision making.

We can experiment with automated data gathering forms for our present transaction data. We can attempt to define new and perhaps more appropriate statistical units of analysis.[1]

If we presently wish to answer questions such as what class of patrons ask questions of particular types we typically use survey instruments. To gather data appropriate to such questions as part of our normal reference record, the data gathering form would be complex and error prone. If there is such a form for each transaction, we become buried in a paper blizzard and are intimidated by the prospect of transferring the data to a form suitable for analysis.

If there is a single statistics sheet for recording such data for a day's transactions, it is a maze of complex rows, columns, lines, headings, subheadings, and check marks. Complex reference statistics sheets can take longer to determine where to record the data than to answer some reference questions.

With a microcomputer workstation at the reference desk, however, we might be able to design a prompted interactive form that would be easy to fill out. The data would be captured in machine readable form. The data could be directly accessed by a favorite analytical program. We could: present the data quickly in aggregated form; cross-tabulate the various categories of data; could convert the data to percentages with a few keystrokes; present the data in graphical form; and, do all of this more rapidly than manually tabulating the simplest data.

These components may be used to enhance the budgeting and planning process in reference departments now. In addition to implementing the already available tools, we must also begin to develop the future system.

Technological change may make it possible to gather more reliable data without placing the collection burden on the reference staff. In order to exploit the new technology we must insist that vendors include mechanisms for recording use information and for easily capturing that data in formats suitable for analysis programs. We must also begin to explore the possibilities of interconnecting the disparate elements of the emerging reference technology.

REFERENCE SERVICE
AND THE BRAVE NEW WORLD

The system envisioned here is not without hazards. We must maintain service, staff acceptance, and privacy. The suggested system will use quantitative data to facilitate decision making and budgeting process. Many librarians have reservations about such techniques. Implicit in the data gathering techniques suggested is the possibility of privacy loss.

Care must be taken to maintain the privacy of patrons and staff. Usage data must not be linked to individual patron records. Data gathered must not so comprehensively describe the patron that identity may be inferred. Data gathered about staff activity should often be similarly proscribed. Clearly, private files and internal operating files must be protected by a network security system. There must be levels of security. Some files may be accessed for obtaining data, but may not be altered. Other files may only be accessed for any purpose by those with authorization.

Reference librarians are dedicated to the provision of service, although there are legitimate disagreements among them about relative priorities among the array of services and about the approaches to the delivery of services. Such commitment can make management concerns seem intrusive. Every report, every data gathering effort, consumes jealously guarded time which might otherwise be devoted to service.

Many reference librarians are skeptical of the validity and/or reliability of quantitative measures and analysis. This skepticism may be based on an understanding of the limitations of present statistical reporting techniques applied to reference activities;[2] or it may be based upon a lack of experience and training in the use of mathematical and statistical tools. Whatever the reason, such skepticism seems widespread.

The introduction of complex accounting and budgeting procedures to facilitate planning and evaluation must include provisions to overcome objections based upon concerns such as those enumerated above.

If techniques such as PPBS or a complex chart of accounts are introduced, they will be resisted if they will be used to diminish the relative priority of service. The goal of such procedures must be to enhance and improve service. If total resources are declining, the goal must be to maintain or improve the effectiveness of service while increasing efficiency.

Data gathering and analysis must not assume a disproportionate share of the department's time. Just as one does not spend $10,000.00 to save $100.00, planning, and the activities which support it, must not outweigh the programs being planned.

The uses and interpretation of information gathered to support planning must be consistent with the reliability and validity of the data and analysis underlying that information. Data must be gathered in a fashion not susceptible to falsification or grossly inaccurate recording. The analysis of that data must generate information which will facilitate discussion and resolution of meaningful problems.

It is tempting to suggest that analysis of data should always directly answer important questions concerning the operation of the department. Quantitative analysis, however, will at best frequently serve only as an organized framework for studying a problem. Solutions come from human creativity, not from the mechanistic application of formulas.

These criteria for the data gathering and analysis component of a budgeting and planning system for reference departments suggest several further points.

1. Decision making needs should be identified by the department in a participatory fashion.
2. Data to be gathered should be clearly relevant to the department's decision making needs.
3. Data gathering should be a reference system by-product rather than a procedure dependent upon self-observation by staff.
4. Data analysis should be designed to facilitate understanding and discussion by the department's staff.

Clearly, significant changes in the conduct of reference service and administration will occur in the next few years. Technological change and new planning and budgeting requirements are among the forces which will assure these changes. Local area networks are a probable consequence of the proliferation of separate automated information systems used in reference work. These networks also have the potential to assist us in meeting the data gathering and analysis requirements of planning oriented budgeting systems.

These changes are inevitable. We must take care to ensure that service survives them while we use and fully exploit the advantages offered. We must also take care to maintain the privacy of library patrons and staff on which such systems may infringe.

NOTES

1. Clark & Benson, for example, have suggested that the appropriate unit of analysis for reference statistics is the individual patron rather than the transaction. Without analytical tools such as spreadsheets, this type of change would be burdensome and complex. "Linkages Between Library Uses Through the Study of Individual Patron Behavior," by Philip M. Clark & James A. Benson, *RQ*, Summer 1985; 24(4):417-426.

2. Clark & Benson, 425-426.

What Reference Librarians Should Know About Library Finances

Dale S. Montanelli

SUMMARY. The two most important things reference librarians need to know about library finance are how to obtain financial resources and how to manage the funds once they are obtained. To obtain resources it is necessary to determine the parent institution or community's receptivity to the request and to develop an appropriate request. Included in this process are: testing the social/political/economic climate, fitting the needs of the particular library unit into the library's priorities, and timing the request appropriately for the institutional budget process. Some specifics of developing a budget request and documenting library needs are reviewed. Alternative funding sources are identified. Finally, procedures for managing resources once they have been received are described.

It is often the belief among library school students that library directors are the only librarians who must deal with the issues surrounding library resources. This idea is fostered by talking about resources (and how to get them) only in classes on library administration, and then only briefly between discussions of personnel administration and public relations. Yet, as Richard Talbot[1] and Ann Prentice[2] point out in their articles on library finance and budgeting, the library's budget is a statement, in monetary terms, of institutional intent concerning the library's programs and priorities. It is simultaneously a statement of goals and objectives for the library and a promise to carry out those objectives if funding is provided. In many institutions, for the library and the larger social structure of which it is a part, the

Dale S. Montanelli is Director of Administrative Services, University Library, University of Illinois at Urbana-Champaign, 1408 West Gregory Drive, Urbana, IL 61820.

annual (or biennial) budget is the only formal, up-to-date statement of institutional policy which exists. Therefore, it is important for all librarians, not just directors, to recognize the budget planning and request process for what it really is — a crucial political and social interaction between the library, its parent body and the constituencies which are served — and use this process for the maximum benefit of the library and its patrons.

THE RESOURCE REQUEST PROCESS

Since reference librarians provide a primary link with the patrons, and are therefore on the forefront of detecting both user needs of and community feelings for the library, reference librarians serve a central function in the development of programs and services which in turn must be funded through the budget request process. Reference librarians are also responsible for implementing the programs and services once they are approved, and therefore must be able to manage the funds for such projects once they are received. Getting resources is a two-part process which involves determining what can be expected and developing an appropriate request.

Needs Assessment

The first step in acquiring resources needed to execute a particular program or do a special project is to assess the needs of the community for whom the service is intended and to determine the library's perceived role in the community which it serves. It's important to know the audience to which the budget request will be addressed and to gain community support for the services which will be available if the budget request is funded. One way to do this is develop a concept paper, a brief written description of the proposed program and why it is needed.[3] Using this concept paper as a "trial balloon," the library can determine if its proposed program will find support directly or if modifications are required before support for funding the proposal can occur.

Define library needs and purposes in useful and pragmatic terms that can be expressed in the budget and at local, regional, and national levels. The budget process is not only a way of providing dollars, it is also a way of defining and obtaining support for the definition of the role and function of the library in the larger institution. In addition to understanding the library's role in the large community, it is important to know and understand the role of the reference department within the library. What kind of requests will appeal to the library administration? How do reference department goals fit into the overall library goals? If the reference department's budgetary requests fit into the overall plan which the library has adopted for its growth and development, the budget request will be received much more enthusiastically.

Timing the Request

Equally important in acquiring resources is understanding the budget cycles for the institution or agency. When do you ask for the money? How far in advance must the intention to ask for funds be announced? What is the format for a budget request? Each institution or agency has its own budget cycle, so there is no one prescriptive set of instructions that can be applied here. For publicly funded higher education a major budget request must be made almost two years in advance of the date on which a new program or project is to begin because the campus review and development process can take up to a year and the state legislative review and appropriation process takes almost a second full year. In a private institution, the ability to begin a major new program may depend on fund raising efforts as well as the regular budget allocation process, which may be as brief as three months.[4] A fund raising plan may take two to five years to come to fruition, depending on the amount of the funds to be raised. In the public library sector a budget request may be presented as little as four or six months before the beginning of a new fiscal year, and corporate budget requests will depend largely on the individual corporation's budgeting cycle.

It is important to learn the timing of the budget cycle of the parent institution and the point in the cycle at which the library administration must present its budget request. It is also necessary to determine how much in advance of these dates units within the library must present budget proposals to the library administration in order to have them included in the library's budget request. There is nothing as unwelcome as a request for resources which arrives on the library director's desk after he/she has submitted the library's budget request to the parent institution. Therefore, of all the characteristics or variables involving getting resources, timing is both the simplest and the most crucial.

Format of the Request

The budget proposal should be presented in a format that meets the needs of the library and the larger institution of which it is a part. Historically, the budgeting process has been one of adding simple increments to the lines for personnel, materials, and operating expenditures. Often, these increments have been based on things like the Consumer Price Index or the Higher Education Price Index and reflect the general inflation of the economy. In the 1970's public agencies became increasingly interested in developing budget processes which tied dollars to specific programmatic activities and built budget requests, not on an incremental basis, but rather on a programmatic basis. Although the maintenance of existing programs and activities can normally be funded through incremental budgeting, programmatic budgeting in any one of its various forms may prove useful in developing and presenting a budget for a new service or a radically altered version of an old service.

Since the advent of the program budget concept there have been a variety of "refinements" to the basic idea which have provided a bewildering alphabet soup (PPBS, MBO, ZBB) without changing the real content of a programmatic budget. No matter what set of initials the process is wearing, programmatic budgeting involves defining the specific program by listing its goals and objectives, and by defining an evaluation procedure to see if the specific objectives have been met. Each objective and its evaluation is then tied to the costs for the activity. These costs will include the personnel required, the supplies and equipment required, any special expenses (such as a lease payment for property rental, use of copyrighted information, or a turnkey automation system), and the overhead costs to the library (the director's time, the business and personnel office's time, increasing demand on mail or janitorial services). The costs of the program are built up from zero based on the actual time, materials, and overhead needed. A typical assumption is that none of the existing resources of the library will be used to support the program being described. If existing resources are available, they, too, are prorated and converted to a dollar figure which is then added to the request for new funds to show the total cost of the new program.

It is important to determine the type of budget process being used at a particular institution. This enables the development of the best presentation of the budget to the parent group. Judy Drescher, when she was Director of the Champaign Public Library, discovered that the members of the City Council were familiar with the budget requests of the Police and Fire Departments. Those units presented their budgets in terms of cost per call. The City Council found this a very acceptable way to deal with these agencies and they didn't get bogged down in administrative overhead, but, rather, how many calls were made per year. Drescher, having learned what her audience was like and the format in which they preferred to evaluate budgets, developed budget requests for the Champaign Public Library and Information Center which were similar to those of the Police and Fire Department. She calculated library operating costs on a cost per service basis, much like the Fire and Police Departments, and found this a very successful way to present the budget to the City Council.[5] It is frequently the case that if one is making a request to expand or make minor improvements in existing programs, that an incremental budgeting process is acceptable and suitable. But if one is developing major new programs or moving existing programs into new areas such as providing an existing service to a new population, the most effective request for funds is outlined in a program budget format in which the dollars to provide the service and documentation of benefits of such a service.

Alternative Funding Sources

Up to this point it has been assumed that the resources being requested would come from an appropriation or allocation from the parent body (state government, city council, corporate headquarters, school district, etc.). However, there are programs for which it is appropriate to seek funding from sources other than the parent body. These funds may replace or supplement institutional funds or they may provide an opportunity to demonstrate the advantages of a new program which can then be incorporated into institutional funds.

Programs which have large "start up" costs, but relatively low maintenance costs (low enough to be absorbed in the units existing budget), programs which support a transition from one mode of operation to another (automating circulation, for instance) and programs which have a clearly defined and limited life span (an exhibition of specific library collections, perhaps) are ideal candidates for the type of resources which are available through state and federal granting agencies or private foundations. Programs which have *permanent* funding requirements (such as providing services to the handicapped or running a state-wide delivery system) which will extend after the outside agency funds are gone are not good candidates for outside funding unless the library administration (or the parent institution) is willing to commit to the required level of funding to maintain the program once the outside agency funds are no longer available. The federal government is particularly concerned about the continuation of projects for which they fund start up costs, and failure to maintain such a program may well affect the library's ability to acquire grant funds in the future.

There are many granting agencies, both public and private, which can be investigated as appropriate sources for library resources. The key for obtaining funds is to find an agency which has an interest in funding the type of program which the library wishes to carry out. Fortunately, there is a great deal of helpful information available to direct the librarian seeking outside funds to a potential granting agency. The second edition of Emmett Corry's *Grants for Libraries: A Guide to Public and Private Funding Programs and Proposal Writing Techniques*[6] is particularly useful in that over half of the volume focuses on federal and state grant sources for school libraries, college and university libraries, public libraries, and library and information science education. The information outlined by Corry can be supplemented by more location specific information such as that found in "Funding for Libraries and Their Services," *Illinois Libraries*[7] which describes the grant opportunities from state and federal resources in Illinois, the state libraries goals for the programs, and the timetable and other submission details.

For those libraries seeking funding through foundations and other nongovernmental sources, in addition to Corry's book, Carol M. Kurzig's *Foundation Fundamentals: A Guide for Grantseekers*[8] is recommended. *The Foundation Grants Index Annual*,[9] also published by The Foundation Center, a not-for-profit service organization which coordinates and shares information about the 25,000 foundations currently making awards, is a good source for finding a match between the library's proposed program and those interested in funding it.

As was the case for traditional fund sources, when developing a funding proposal for a state, federal, or private foundation grant, it is important to determine the agency's timetable. Is preliminary notification of intent to submit a grant required. If so, when? Does the agency offer to review draft proposals before submission? On what date, with what proof of mailing, must the proposal be sent or delivered to the agency? How long is the review period? How soon after notification of the award are the funds actually available? What are the reporting requirements once the grant is received and what is the schedule for the reports? Equally important is the determination of the appropriate budget format and budget documentation. Grants are almost always program budgets but the level of cost justification for each component part of the request varies from one agency to another.

Documenting Needs

No matter what funding source is involved, the unit requesting the funds must document the need for the program being requested. How do you make what you want to do seem important and needed? First, it is important to take advantage of information that is routinely gathered by libraries. Federal, state, and local statistical reporting is a source of documentation that librarians may use in comparing their programs and their resources to other comparable units. It is important to select a peer or comparison group quite carefully, taking into account the larger society in which the library finds itself. A public library often must compare its resources to those of other libraries of similar size performing similar functions as well as to the other services provided through the city government such as the city fire and police departments. In an institution of higher education the library must compare itself not only to other similar libraries, but also to other departments within the campus.

It is also important to make sure that the peer group that you define is one that is acceptable to the larger institution of which you are a part. For example, the University of Illinois Library at Urbana-Champaign makes frequent comparisons of itself to Harvard, Yale, California-Berkeley, and UCLA. However, the institution at-large has found itself most successful in making comparisons to other institutions within the Big Ten, not because all the institutions within the Big Ten are comparable but, rather because the state legislature sees that as an appropriate peer group. Therefore, one must be sure that one's peer group is also perceived to be one's peer group. Data gathered by the Association of Research Libraries, the Association of College and Research Libraries, the Public Library Association, the Special Library Association, and the Integrated Postsecondary Education Data System (IPEDS) (formerly HEGIS), are all sources of publicly available data on library staffing, expenditures and services which can be mined for effective comparisons.

In addition to using the existing data which is widely collected by librarians throughout the country, it is equally valuable to create data which show the library in a favorable light in terms of acquiring needed resources. Examples of this approach are data showing historical comparisons of levels of service for various activities, patron groups, or collection use. One can look at service units per size of population served and compare the past with the present. One can analyze the number of reference questions answered per the deflated dollars it costs to answer those questions. For materials increases, one can look at cost per volume, controlling for inflation. One can identify new fields in which it is now necessary to collect and the net costs of adding these fields in spite possible reductions in other areas of collecting. One can describe the impact of societal change (such as the increase in the number of "latch-key" children using the library on their own after school) and tie these changes to the costs for the increased and/or special services which are generated. Whenever possible, array the information from these comparisons in graphic and tabular form. This is a case where a "picture" speaks louder than words in getting the library's message across. Robert Burgin's 1987 article on "Creative Budget Presentation" contains additional suggestions for supporting budget requests.[10]

MANAGING RESOURCES

Managing Staffing

Once a budget request has been funded, it becomes the librarian's responsibility to insure that the funds are used as efficiently as possible to accomplish the program for which they were received. There are two main areas in which most librarians have traditionally had some budget management responsibilities: supervision of hourly or part-time staff and acquisition of library materials. In both of these areas, having a past history of the library's use of the resource is an invaluable help in planning for the future. In planning for staffing needs and allocation of staff over the course of a given year, it is particularly useful to find out what cyclical patterns of patron demand exist in the population. Are longer hours needed at some times of the year than others? Do vacation schedules have to be accommodated (vacations of the staff and normal vacations times in the institution or agency in which the library is located)? It may be the case that, in a corporate library, library demand is heaviest during periods of new product development or during annual report writing time.

If the librarian knows this and keeps in touch with the management of the corporation about plans and activities, he/she can then ensure adequate staffing at the peak times. In academic libraries peak demand frequently arises when students prepare to write their term papers and drops off significantly during the university holidays and break periods. Staffing patterns can be matched to this schedule for the most efficient, economic use.

Managing the Materials Budget

When one looks at the careful management of a library materials budget, there are several variables, the chief of which is the continuing commitment to periodicals and other serials, which represent the major ongoing expenditure of most library resources. There are two types of new materials that must be dealt with, new materials which are superceding old materials and are replacing outdated information with up-to-date information, and new materials which represent new areas of scholarship or interest in the community which have not existed before. Planning to fund these new collections is frequently something that can be addressed in programmatic budget requests.

In terms of the timing of purchases for library materials when managing one's funds, its important to identify whether or not there are times of the year which are peak times for ordering. In an academic institution this might be early in the fall when the faculty return and are planning their course work and research efforts for the year. In the public library it may depend more on the patterns of publishing in a particular area. For instance, the great bulk of children's books come out in the fall before the Christmas shopping season. A children's librarian might well want to plan to make major fund expenditures during that time period and purchase very selectively at other times of the year.

Project Management

When managing the resources for a new program, or a major revision of an existing program, historical activity and spending patterns are inadequate to provide sufficient information for the project management process. Bryce Allen[11] recommends that large grants be divided into smaller, discrete projects, with the responsibility for each of these smaller projects delegated to appropriate staff members. Each of these subprojects should encompass a discrete activity, of limited size, capable of being accomplished in a clearly defined time period. The actual costs associated with each component should be identified, and the staff person delegated the responsibility should keep the project within the time limits set and the funds available. This procedure has the fringe benefit of involving more of the library staff in the responsibility for the success of the project.

Additional techniques for having the project and the budget "run out" at the same time may be borrowed from the literature of architecture and business. These techniques, Critical Path Method (CPM) and Program Evaluation Review Technique (PERT), provide a method of planning, to make sure things do not get overlooked; communication, to make sure all members of the project team know what has to occur and when; controlling, to make sure that staff concentrate on those activities which are important for keeping the project on schedule; and training, to provide a framework for bringing new employees up to speed on the project as quickly as possible.[12] In addition, they serve to identify those subprojects within the larger project which are crucial which "lie along the critical path" for all aspects of the project to be accomplished within the time frame required.[13]

NOTES

1. Talbot, Richard J., "Financing the Academic Library," in T. Galvin & B. Lynch (eds.), *New Directions in Higher Education: Priorities for Academic Libraries*, no. 39, San Francisco: Jossey-Bass, September 1972, 35-44.

2. Prentice, Anne E., "Budgeting," in Charles R. McClure & Alan R. Samuels (eds.), *Strategies for Library Administration: Concepts and Approaches*, Littleton, CO: Libraries Unlimited 1982, 175-95.

3. Corry, Emmett, *Grant for Libraries: A Guide to Public and Private Funding Programs and Proposal Writing Techniques*, Littleton, CO: Libraries Unlimited 1986, 196.

4. Williams, Sally F., "Budget Justification: Closing the Gap Between Request and Result," *Library Resources and Technical Services*, 1984, 28(2) p. 129-35.

5. Drescher, Judith, Lecture to Doctoral Seminar, February 15, 1984.

6. Corry, Emmett, 1986, ibid.

7. "Funding for Libraries and Their Services," *Illinois Libraries*, 1986, 68(2), 107-114.

8. Kurzig, Carol M., *Foundation Fundamentals: A Guide for Grantseekers*, New York: The Foundation Center, 1980.

9. The Foundation Center, *The Foundation Grants Index*, New York: The Foundation Center, 1985.

10. Burgin, Robert, "Creative Budget Presentation: Using Statistics to Prove Your Point," *The Bottom Line*, 1987, 1(1), 13-17.

11. Allen, Bryce, "Administration of Grant Funds—the Project Approach," *Collection Management*, 1983, 5(3/4), 175-184.

12. Moder, Joseph J., Cecil R. Phillips & Edward W. Davis, *Project Management with CPM, PERT, and Precedence Diagramming*, New York: Van Nostrand Reinhold, 1983.

13. Horowitz, Joseph, *Critical Path Scheduling*, Malabar, FL: Robert E. Kreiger, 1980.

Changes in Attitudes, Changes in Latitudes: Reference/Information Services Management in a Time of Transition

Edwin S. Clay III

SUMMARY. Jimmy Buffet didn't have public library administrators in mind when he sang of "Changes in attitudes, changes in latitudes." His words do, however, describe the current state of reference/information services management. This article first attempts to define several of the major changes happening in reference/information services. Next it briefly addresses why these changes are occurring. Responses to these changes on the part of one public library system are then detailed. Finally, the budget implications of these changes receive review.

The author contends that the key to the provision of quality information/reference services in a time of change is solid management data. Decisions and/or modifications to services need to be based — as much as possible — on quantifiable data. This data must also serve as the basis of agency budget requests. While this approach demands that considerable agency resources be devoted to it, the author argues that a system can afford no less.

"Discover reference librarians. They are the modern inhabitants of the temple at Delphi. They know everything or else they know where to find it. These wonderful professionals make their living looking up information for people like us. These people delight in figuring out how to find anything out. Lucky for us."

Edwin S. Clay III, is Director of the Fairfax County Public Library, 11216 Waples Mill Road, Fairfax, VA 22030.

So states Dick Levin in his publication *The Executive's Illustrated Primer of Long-Range Planning.*[1]

And indeed, lucky for library administrators that such individuals on our staffs wish to devote their talents and energies in the pursuit of information. I wonder, however, if library administrators are as eager as our reference/information staff to secure information that allows us to plan for, evaluate and budget for information/reference services within our respective systems.

OFFICE OF EVALUATION AND INFORMATION DEVELOPMENT

When I came to the Fairfax County Public Library in 1982, I joined an excellent system. As a part of its organization it had an Office of Information Services. Primary duties of this Office centered upon the examination of new reference/information tools and the loose coordination of system information/reference services.

I was delighted to discover this Office, for I believed it had the potential to ask my favorite question—"Why?" Furthermore, the Office, after asking "Why?", could discover the answer to the question and then provide whatever techniques, methods, steps and/or other strategies the research demonstrated would improve the situation under review.

Accordingly, I rechartered and renamed the Office to the Office of Evaluation and Information Development. Its mission was, and is, as follows:

1. Establish a plan for ongoing measurement and evaluation of basic library functions.
2. Establish a 12-month plan for measurement and evaluation which addresses "one-time" projects.
3. Implement these plans. Implementation will include literature searching, developing data gathering mechanisms, training staff to gather data, analyzing data, and communicating results to all affected persons.
4. Establish and maintain a central file of data gathered through the system, together with procedures that encourage its use in decision making.

5. Work as requested with persons or groups making decisions or policies based upon the data developed by this office.

Data for decision making is the goal of this office. All too often we as administrators make a decision because we "think" something, or "believe" something to be true, or we "feel" something is needed.

Establishment of the Office of Evaluation and Information Development has produced wonderful and painful results. Wonderful in that we have good, solid data upon which to make corporate decisions. Painful in that some of my cherished library assumptions have been disproved.

Because of the evaluation focus we have a new perspective of ourselves and what we do as a system. We have management data that has been of tremendous assistance in developing budget justifications. We have increased credibility with other county agencies in the products that we forward to them making a case for whatever it is that the Fairfax County Public Library needs from them.

More importantly, we have expanded our way of thinking. We ask "Why?" and find the answer. It may not be what we like or expected, but we always learn from the exercise.

My bias, in addition to an addiction to "Why?" is that the provision of information/reference services is the function that validates the "worth" of the public library to today's and tomorrow's funding agencies. Because of this bias, the Fairfax County Public Library has expended considerable effort and time in evaluating and focusing upon information/reference services. We have done so because we want to provide the best reference/information services available to our public.

With this background in place, I would like to discuss the changes that have come about in the provision of reference/information services, the reasons for these changes, and the budget implications of these changes. I suspect that many public library systems have felt similar pressures for change. My example, however, will be the FCPL.

QUALITY CONTROL

Personnel issues received the major change emphasis—and for obvious reasons. Reference/information staff members themselves are facing a public that requires new information avenues. They must confront and learn to deal with information in totally changed formats, and reexamine the way in which they do "business." Underscoring all of these issues is the question of training.

A move toward specialization and away from generalization is the thrust of the biggest change at FCPL in the provision of reference/information services. Heretofore the corporate philosophy was that staff members would be trained in all of the public services. This was to allow for the maintenance of interest in one's position and to allow for, so it was thought, more promotional opportunities.

The result of this policy was reference/information staff that made few, if any, distinctions between "professional" and "nonprofessional" activities. Depending upon the time of day and the branch one utilized, a patron had no guarantee that the reference/information staff person was trained adequately in the service being provided. We had, in three words, "no quality control." This was unacceptable.

Through an extensive training and restructuring effort, reference/information staff positions are being refocused. Career paths within reference/information have been established. Staff members were taught to refer patrons and/or questions to the appropriate department and/or individual. No more answering reference/information questions at the Circulation desk.

In order to assist staff members with these changes, an *Information Services Guideline*[2] was developed. These guidelines articulated the mission statement of information services at FCPL: to provide accurate information or materials in response to user requests in an efficient, courteous, impartial, pleasant and timely manner.

The purpose of the guidelines was threefold: to ensure that users throughout the system receive the same levels of service based on uniform procedures; to make information services procedures clear for staff; to provide a basis for training and evaluating staff performance.

The philosophy of service is as follows:

— Users of all ages and circumstances are to be treated with equal attention and with sensitivity to their particular needs.
— All requests for public information are legitimate.
— The basic function of the information staff is to provide information, not opinions. Questions should not be answered on the basis of personal experience. It is the staff's responsibility to provide information in an impartial and businesslike manner even when the information is contrary to personal beliefs.
— Information staff personnel subscribe to the librarians' Code of Ethics.
— Information staff depend upon management to provide adequate staffing, training and resources to ensure excellent service.
— All questions should be either answered or redirected.

The guidelines are divided into seven sections: General Guidelines, In-House Information Services, Telephone Information Services, Referrals, Requests for Special Information, Circulation of Reference Materials and Complaints about Library Materials, Staff, Services, etc. They define the scope of system information/reference services, and the system's approach to the provision of these services.

ON-LINE SERVICES

New information formats — specifically on-line services — required special attention. Staff and administration felt that since there were so many new issues surrounding the integration of on-line services into "regular" information/reference services, another set of guidelines was warranted. Accordingly, we published *On-line Information Services Guidelines*.[3]

On-line services are viewed as an integral part of FCPL public information services. Our position is that online databases can provide information when the printed resources of the library are insufficient to meet the patron's needs in terms of time expenditures necessary to search the printed materials, complex subject needs that involve combining two or more terms or concepts in the search for information, and currency or availability of information about the subject in the library.

The *On-line Information Services Guidelines* provide a philosophy of services (as previously stated), deal with levels of service, define staffing for on-line services, establish procedures for conducting on-line searches and suggest methods of reporting procedures. These guidelines will be updated once a year.

TRAINING

Because of the coupling of the redefinition of information/reference service positions with the development of new information formats, the issue of training became of paramount importance. Information/reference personnel have had to undergo so many changes that training procedures needed revision. The heart of these revisions is the *Training Checklist for Information Services Staff.*[4]

Prepared by a staff task force, the checklist was written with three beneficiaries in mind:

First, it serves the interests of FCPL as a whole by providing the training that will ensure a consistently high level of service across the county. Furthermore, the system concept demands that each staff member must be able to function as an information professional in any branch at any time. This kind of staff flexibility is only possible if all employees have received the same basic training. Before the creation of the checklist, training methods and content varied from branch-to-branch, and this inconsistency imposed added difficulties when staff members were asked to serve at branches other than their own.

The second beneficiary of the training checklist is the trainer. The constraints of day-to-day branch operation and hours of work aside, there is a limit to the human ability to absorb new information. The checklist will be a guideline as to how much and how fast the training of new staff should progress, as well as a reminder of specific items to be covered. The checklist also provides a logical order or framework for the transmission of information. It should help the trainer to keep track of your progress and pinpoint the areas in which you may need added help or in which your background has already prepared you adequately.

Finally, and most importantly, the checklist was designed to benefit you, the new information services employee. We hope that it will give you a concrete strategy for acquiring the skills, tools, and self-confidence that you will need to deal with the majority of situations that you will face in your initial period of employment. The checklist provides you with self-administered assignments for your first few weeks, tasks which you can tackle on your own before you are assigned the extra off-desk duties which will be part of your job. It will help you to use your first few months wisely and to channel your efforts into those areas that you and your trainer have identified as being most crucial. By reinforcing your professional and educational background with information peculiar to FCPL, the checklist will help you function quickly and efficiently, minimizing "start-up" time for you and your employer. Be aware, however, that the checklist is just a beginning. We've tried to give you a sturdy foundation — the rest is up to you. Be sure that your understanding of these basics is solidly grounded, and that you continue always to build on them according to your needs and in your own preferred style.

It then goes on to address public service at the information desk; specifically, basic information desk procedures and forms, important documents, branch and community characteristics, basic reference sources, adult and juvenile reader's advisory, and specialized system resources. It concludes with sections on collection development and collection merchandising.

CHANGE

Yet another major issue/change that has been addressed by the system is that of single-service information desks. That is, we have consolidated the children's information/reference desk and the adult reference desk into the single-service information desk. This consolidation has been completed in 19 of our branches to date.

Staffing problems originally initiated this serve change. One community branch had difficulty in staffing both a children's information/reference desk and an adult information/reference desk. After a trial of consolidated service in this branch and a thorough review of and evaluation of the results of the single-service concept, it has been adopted throughout our system. The one major question, i.e., would children's information/reference services suffer? has been answered in the negative. (FCPL is now pursuing the interfiling of adult and juvenile nonfiction and, in test sites, the interfiling of adult and children's nonfiction along with reference materials.)

Since 1982, our information/reference services have undergone some dramatic changes. We feel that we have met the challenges of these changes and that our responses have been thoughtful and always to assist the information/reference staff member to be able to efficiently and effectively deliver information/reference services.

As the FCPL system has brought about and at the same time reacted to (we are not sure, in some instances, which came first—the chicken or the egg), significant changes in the way in which it provides reference/information services, who provides these services, how they provide these services, and how the services are evaluated, FCPL has also had to reexamine the methods by which it budgets for reference/information services. As the public service aspect of reference/information has modified significantly, so, too, have the administrative support systems.

BUDGET

Fairfax County, Virginia, has an annual budget (including capital expenditures) in excess of $1 billion. Obviously, a very complex budget process is required to coordinate the financial needs of the county's agencies and to maintain the county's prized AAA bond rating. For all its complexities and sophistication (the budget process is now an on-line system), the county's, and hence, the library's budget, is essentially a line item budget grouped into cost centers.

FCPL has three cost centers: administration, library operations—all costs associated with operating the branches, and technical operations—funds required for cataloging, acquisition, materials selection, automation and research. Its FY 1988 budget, including capital construction, is $27 million ($14 million operating, $13 million capital). FY 1988 staff levels will include approximately 800 individuals.

Reference/information costs are identified in each of the three cost centers. The bulk of the cost of services — personnel — is contained in the library operations cost center; supplies, etc., are located in the administrative cost center; and reference/information materials, i.e., books, periodicals, etc., are housed in the technical operations cost center. Not a particularly effective way to budget, but one that is dictated to the library system by county administration.

The county's Office of Management and Budget (OMB) has overall responsibility for preparing the county's fiscal plan. Each agency submits its annual request to OMB where it is "reviewed" (a euphemism if there ever was one) and based upon the review, a funding level is recommended to the County Executive who, in turn, recommends an amount to the Board of Supervisors.

A key player in the budget game is the Budget Analyst. This individual, who works directly with the library system, is the person who "reviews" the agency request, and is the person who recommends a funding level. By design this individual changes every other year.

Given the procedure and the key players in the FCPL budget process, our strategy regarding budgeting for information/reference services has been to base our requests, whenever possible, upon statistics and the results of system analytical studies. The foundation upon which this approach is based is that the budget analyst has no idea what a public library is all about, let alone the role and function of information/reference services.

Lest one think that ignorance on the part of a budget analyst is bliss, a quick example to the contrary: several years ago we requested funds to replace a number of book trucks that had worn out. Our request was denied, with the comment from the budget analyst that if this request were approved, "book truck drivers" would then have to be hired at yet an additional expense.

Accordingly, our budget requests are constructed as if the budget analyst knows nothing about the service. We sometimes ask members of other county agencies to read the request, and if they can understand it, we feel we have a chance.

Most significantly, however, is the information that we quantify in order to support a request. This is particularly important in the area of additional staff. Our major tool to justify addition staff is the increased business. For example:

—The number of information transactions handled by FCPL staff increased by 43% from 1,233,900 in FY 1984 to an annual estimate of 1,767,000 for FY 1985.
—The number of reference questions handled by FCPL staff increased by 48% over the estimate reported for FY 1984. This estimate means that FCPL staff handled 1.2 reference transactions per capita in FY 1985.[5]

These percentage increases are in turn tied to historical data to demonstrate the "staggering" growth in service in this area, and the per capita reference questions compared to per capita questions of other area library systems of comparable size "clearly demonstrate" that we need additional staff.

The issue of the number of staff required to provide quality reference/information services is a universal one. There is no one answer or formula that one can plug data into to come up with the right answer. What has been effective for FCPL has been the comparisons of workload efforts of FCPL information/reference staff to other library systems. In addition, we have reached a "gentleman's agreement" with our Office of Management and Budget that our estimates of personnel required to open a new library serve as a baseline against which requests for additional staff are judged.

Budgeting for materials to support information/reference activities has undergone a transformation. One aspect of this change was the result of our *Information Services Profile Study*.[6] We determined that our branch reference collections were too large. We discovered through a rigorous monitoring procedure that in more than one-half of our branches less than 25% of the reference materials were used by reference/information staff during the one month test period. The result of this study, which has been revalidated in later studies, is to cause a change in the number and type of reference materials that are purchased for the system.

The new information formats, however, have created a number of policy issues that result in financial issues that will, at some point, need to be addressed in the budget. Some examples:

— What database and on-line services will FCPL subscribe to?
— What branches will offer what array of services?
— Will all reference/information staff have on-line search responsibilities?
— What are the training implications of the answer to the previous question?
— As more and more information sources are available on-line, what print sources will we no longer acquire?
— What percentage of the on-line search costs should be borne by the system? By the patron?
— What on-line information/reference experience should the system expect to find in individuals applying for a reference/information position?

Since 1982 FCPL has added more than 100,000 square feet of public library service area. This translates into two new regional libraries and a renovated/expanded existing regional library, plus a new minilibrary and a kiosk library. Approved for future construction (by 1990) is a new regional library, two new community libraries, and the expansion of two community libraries and one regional library. All of this construction has had implications for reference/information services in the area of what is the perfect design of the perfect information/reference station that accommodates all of the present and future on-line information tools?

Construction equals money. Accordingly, staff and I have spent considerable time studying information/reference station layouts, design, etc., in an attempt to develop a cost-effective, serviceable design — a design that needs to meet the needs of the staff, the public, and present and future information services technology.

FCPL makes no claims to having discovered the "one way" to information/reference heaven. What we have discovered, however, is an approach to information/reference service based upon management data and common sense.

The provision of quality reference/information services is vital to the future of the public library. The challenge to the administrator is to ensure that these services are funded adequately, that the staff is equipped with the tools to allow it to meet the changing demands of technology and patrons, and that management and/or decisions pertaining to information/reference services be based upon the best data available.

None of these requirements is easy. Each takes tremendous time to accomplish. The results, however, an efficient, effective information services staff eager to meet the public demand no less.

NOTES

1. Richard Levin, *The Executive's Illustrated Primer of Long-Range Planning* (Englewood Cliffs, NJ: Prentice-Hall, 1981) 37p.

2. Jane G. Goodwin & M. Lydia Patrick, *Information Services Guidelines* (Fairfax, VA: Fairfax County Public Library, Office of Evaluation and Information Development, 1986) 21p.

3. Jane G. Goodwin, *Online Information Services Guidelines* (Fairfax, VA: Fairfax County Public Library, Office of Evaluation and Information Development, 1986) 10p.

4. Elizabeth Quay, *Training Checklist for Information Services Staff* (Fairfax, VA: Fairfax County Public Library, 1985) 93p.

5. Jane G. Goodwin & M. Lydia Patrick, *Information Services Profile* (Fairfax, VA: Fairfax County Public Library, 1985) 98p.

6. Eleanor Jo Rodger, *Information Services Profile* (Fairfax, Va: Fairfax County Public Library, 1983) 35p.

Budgeting at the Library Department Level: A Middle Manager's Perspective

Tamsen Dalrymple

SUMMARY. "Budget time" can be a stressful and mystifying experience for the reference administrator. This article describes specific planning strategies middle managers can use to be better prepared for budget issues. Reference administrators must understand the budget environment, incorporate strategic planning techniques into the budget cycle, and develop relevant policies and procedures to assist in budget allocation. They must also develop techniques for more effective budget presentations.

As library middle managers, administrators of reference services often share a popular misconception: that the upperlevel administrators in the library actually control the budget. In reality, top managers in libraries are not only in the same position relative to *their* superiors — legislators, board members, or corporate comptrollers — when dealing with budgets, but they must also weigh requests from other middle managers seeking support for programs and services.

In many respects, heads of principal departments in libraries have a much greater opportunity to "sell" their budget proposals than do administrators at higher levels. Middle management librarians' supervisors are usually librarians themselves, who have an understanding of both the "hard" costs of doing library business and the difficulty of measuring the impact of services. Similarly, middle managers often have a better grasp of the perspec-

Tamsen Dalrymple is a product manager in the Electronic Publishing and Information Delivery Division at OCLC, 6565 Frantz Road, Dublin, OH 43017-0702.

tives and priorities of their immediate supervisors than those same supervisors may have of their libraries' governing unit, be it the Provost's Office or the City Council.[1]

This is not meant to imply that one can get blood from a turnip or that budgeting at the middle-management level is easy. However, reference administrators can take steps to make budget management less arduous and the results more successful, both for themselves and for their supervisors. This article will review key elements in budgeting and will outline specific strategies for managing with "worst case" or — however unlikely — "best case" situations in the budget process. To paraphrase the real estate maxim, the three most important things in budget administration are planning, planning and planning.

UNDERSTANDING THE ENVIRONMENT

Middle managers too often overlook the fact that almost all libraries operate as part of a larger organization. Before fitting the reference department into the library environment, one must first learn how and where the library fits into the overall picture of the parent organization, be it academic, municipal, or corporate. The library's written "mission statement" should address this issue. If the library has no written statement of purpose, middle managers must do their best to deduce it on their own, the most useful approach being conversations with people knowledgeable about the institution.

One must keep in mind that even a written mission statement may not accurately reflect the true nature of a parent institution's value system in relation to the library. A city council may pass proclamations of praise for the library, but if the recreation department, however unacclaimed, wins the budget battle year after year, the true priorities are clear. To understand the "big picture" and lots of little pictures, too — "following the money," by studying what has been the case in the past, will show what is truly valued in an organization.

BUDGET CALENDAR

Once one grasps a basic understanding of the parent institution, one can assess the role of the library as an entity within it. At this point, the successful manager will develop a budget calendar that highlights the important dates that make up the budget year.[2] Besides serving as a "tickler" file to remind one of deadlines, the budget calendar can serve as a tool to keep departmental planning on track.

In almost all cases, each organization — and its corresponding "global" environment — has a budget cycle, occasionally a multi-year affair. Some states, for example, operate with biennial budgets, and some library systems have five-year plans. In these cases, consider how these longer periods of budget management will affect the middle manager's situation, especially in looking ahead to the second or later years of the cycle.

Further questions: What is the library's fiscal year? To whom, successively, is the budget submitted for review? For action? When is the budget due? (And when is it really, *really* due?) Are requests for staff, materials and equipment made at the same or different times throughout the year? Is the book budget request due the same week as evaluations for salary increases? When are requests for periodical subscriptions and other open-ended commitments due, and what's the last day one can change a request? When do they "close the books" on book orders? Is there a "spend it or lose it" budget system? All of these questions, and more, depending on the idiosyncrasies of the institution, must be answered and noted by the reference administrator to provide a planning timetable not only for the budget, but also for the overall operation of the unit.

Discovering the answers to these questions will demonstrate the interdependent nature of the budget process. As an administrator, one must rely on basic facts from a variety of internal and external sources. Part of the process of developing the budget calendar must be identifying areas where this fact-gathering process may break down. For example, data may be provided late, or not at all. In such situations, laying the blame on others will not enhance the success of the reference department's budget request. One must be prepared with reasoned estimates and informed guesses.

BUDGET SYSTEMS

Clearly, a reference head has no practical say about the nature of the budget system that is used by the library, often a system prescribed by the parent institution or a legislative body. In any event, the type of budget system used by the library as a whole will affect the format and nature of the department's budget request. Whatever system the library uses—the traditional line item, or more recent formulations, such as zero-based budgeting (ZBB), program budgeting, Planning Program Budget System (PPBS)—one must thoroughly understand the system, why it was chosen and, particularly, its advantages and disadvantages. Several recent works review the many sources on budgeting available for collection managers or deal specifically and in-depth with systems currently in use.[3,4,5] Most likely, a given library will not use a "pure" version of any single system. It may, for example, superimpose a program budget onto a line item budget. Of course, some budget systems that are useful for planning may be difficult to apply in practical terms.[6]

Perhaps the most common budget system used in libraries, as in many organizations, is the line item budget. Line item budgets are often treated incrementally; that is, increased each year by more or less across-the-board annual percentages for personnel, library materials, supply, equipment and other accounts.[7] This system is easy to comprehend insofar as the amount of money committed to different *categories* of expenses. Such a system is geared, however, toward preserving the *status quo*[8] making it especially difficult to add a new or innovative program.[9] Several library managers have suggested that this type of incremental budgeting is no longer appropriate for libraries.[10,11] This can be especially true in reference departments, as online databases, CD-ROM's and other "nontraditional" resources proliferate, and librarians face the task of supporting both old and new technologies. In other words, budgeting for *change* in a line item system takes more planning and more political skill than is necessary in other systems.

Whatever system the library uses, managers should familiarize themselves with techniques used in other approaches to budgeting. Certain aspects of ZBB and PPBS systems, for example, can assist in evaluating present services. ZBB, in particular, can be useful in making tough decisions and many of its tools of analysis can be applied, in an informal way, to the budget cycle as a whole.[12]

THE ECONOMY

In addition to understanding the library's "microsystem," reference managers must also come to understand the "macrosystem" of the economy — local, national and global — that will affect the library's income, buying power and demand for services. Fluctuations in the economy trigger those windfall/exigency budget years that are so trying to librarians attempting to sustain and improve collections and services. Managers cannot be expected to be financial wizards, but at least a rudimentary knowledge of relevant economic issues can greatly aid in planning.

In most cases, one should keep an eye on the legislative body that controls government dollars — are they changing the tax base? shutting off a funding source? providing *new* grant monies? Similarly, reference administrators need to keep tabs on inflation. Here the Bowker price indexes, *CPI Detailed Report* and other similar sources are obviously of great benefit. Depending on the scope of the collection, for example, foreign exchange rates can have a dramatic or negligible effect on the budget.

In the case of economic matters, in particular, it is a mistake to think that someone else — the library director, for example — is responsible for comprehending and managing the "big" issues, like taxes or legislation or a devalued dollar. One of the most essential things in assessing the library's environment is understanding the environment in which top library administrators are trying to function. Without a clear notion of the pressures on *them*, middle managers are too prone to make requests that appear, at best, naive, at worst, irresponsible.

BE PREPARED

Once the reference department is seen in the contexts of its environments, the manager can begin planning for the budget. Planning is a continuous process, not just an occasional exercise undertaken to produce a final budget document. Year-round planning is a necessary part of management; by making it routine, reference administrators can reduce the pressures of "budget time."[13]

The too easily used excuse that there is no time to plan contributes to a cycle of "crisis management" that managers must break.[14] Integrating planning into the management routine is intended to lead to informed, not panic-induced, decisions. Planning is not predicting, and it should not produce a rigid blueprint.[15] Plans must be flexible, not only because situations — income, prices, curriculums — change, but also because people change, and people must implement the plans and spend budgeted resources.

One way to keep plans flexible is to use such techniques as "SWOT" analysis. SWOT (*S*trengths, *W*eaknesses, *O*pportunities and *T*hreats) identification is a key component in developing a strategic plan for the use of an organization's resources.[16] Possibly, a strategic approach to management is used in the library system as a whole. If not, strategic management techniques can still be employed within a department, even informally, so long as department personnel are informed about and involved closely with the process. SWOT's are almost self-explanatory, but a few examples in each category will help clarify them:

Strengths — strong community support, productive staff, willingness to accept change;

Weaknesses — eroding tax base, outdated equipment, weak in [subject area];

Opportunities — online information systems, unit reorganization, a new mayor, provost or board president;

Threats — decaying facilities, noncompetitive salaries, inefficient automated systems.

Note in these examples that weaknesses, successfully addressed, should become strengths, and threats, opportunities.

The main point of the exercise is to identify issues in each of these categories and to rank them in priority order. This process, in and of itself, should serve several purposes that are crucial to budgeting.

First, it demonstrates the relationship of the reference department to its environment. Second, it involves the entire staff in planning and allows for innovative thinking and the exchange of ideas. Finally, it articulates for both the manager and staff a range of possibilities and suggests directions to be taken should certain events occur. No matter how negative the final list of SWOT's may appear, the best preparation for austerity is "a state of readiness for the unwanted."[17]

DOCUMENTATION

It should be noted that the SWOT analysis itself does not produce a "plan." In fact, the goal of this type of strategic management should not *be* a written plan. Instead, it should provide a flexible framework for action. For the reference department, this framework may be used in forming policies and in detailing procedures, most of which are commonly understood, but not always written or seen as aids to budget management. The documents listed below are always much easier to write if the library *system* has them, but even without such umbrella guidelines, the reference administrator should try to have them in place, up-to-date and at hand.

1. A mission statement for the department.
2. A reference services policy.[18] This is a critical document to define levels of service provided, and the writing of it will require a rigorous analysis of the department's priorities. Used in budget work, it can help identify services that could (must) be cut back or areas of weakness that should be addressed first if funding for an upgrade of services becomes available.
3. A collection development policy.[19] This statement must be specific and must describe clearly what is included in and excluded from the reference collection. It should take into account the reference department's interaction with other units of the library, particularly in the areas of collection

overlap and duplication. Especially important is the percentage of the materials budget that is given over to periodical subscriptions or continuations. While libraries must obtain regularly those works that are dependent upon their timeliness, committing too much money to continuations greatly diminishes budget flexibility. On the other hand, maintaining a "manual continuations" system, in which updated editions are ordered irregularly, is very time-consuming for staff in both reference and technical services departments. In short, the decision to commit funds over the long term is a very important one.

4. A minimum equipment list. Continually updated, this list should include the bare essentials, such as new or replacement shelving, microform cabinets, and index tables that the reference department must have for its collections and patrons. This basic list should not neglect office furniture and equipment required for a productive reference staff, even though justifying these needs to higher-ups is often difficult. (Remember, too, these basic equipment needs are even more difficult to communicate *further* up the ladder.) In addition to the "minimum" list, the reference department head should have a five-year projection that includes the equipment that might be needed to enhance existing or begin new services. The five-year plan should have a replacement schedule for older equipment. Equipment budgets, perhaps more than any other category, are subject to "last minute" expenditures. When the boss asks for a list of equipment needs *by the end of the day*, it's in the department's best interest to be ready to provide order information—with catalog numbers and *re-checked*, up-to-date prices.

5. A preservation/storage plan. Preservation is a hot topic in librarianship these days, but the reference librarian in this instance need not address the complexities of deacidification. Rather, this plan should focus on more traditional, but rapidly changing, technologies. How much money will it take over, say, the next five years to acquire microfilm to

replace deteriorating backruns of periodicals? How much for binding? How do CD-ROM's fit in? Note that large purchases of microform, in fact, most media, usually require large purchases storage, reading and copying equipment. Where is *that* money going to come from?

6. A staffing plan. This plan should be developed in conjunction with the reference services policy, and should consider the need for support staff as well as librarians, temporary as well as permanent employees. Many communities have summer youth employment programs, for example, and library schools may offer practicum students. Being ready with well-defined projects and job descriptions will enhance your chances of benefiting from such programs. For example, a thorough knowledge of the potential strengths and current weaknesses of the reference desk schedule can take the headaches out of adding even a part-time librarian.

In addition to these documents, other information will be required as part of the budget planning process. Price index and other financial data have already been mentioned, but it's important to have access to data that support the extraordinary, such as evidence of what another price increase of silver might do to microform costs. In developing and working with such data (and especially in producing some of the five-year plans mentioned above) access to a microcomputer and expertise with spreadsheet software can be invaluable.*

Also important are the inevitable "wish lists" that all librarians have on hand. Don't leave desiderata files unexamined until the end of the budget year, though; keep them up-to-date and in priority order. Be prepared to make several—or a few—small purchases as well as a single large one. When called upon to spend money quickly and responsibly, preparation is the only way to make good decisions.

---

*If you do not have a microcomputer, now is the time to put it in your budget request. Keep asking. Also, consult Philip M. Clark's *Microcomputer Spreadsheet Models for Libraries* (Chicago: American Library Association, 1985) for excellent help in preparing budget templates as well as on preparing statistics spreadsheets that can assist in the planing process.

SELLING IT

One of the key day-to-day tasks of a reference administrator is "justifying."[20] This responsibility cannot be over-emphasized. Every budget request one makes — routine or otherwise — will be viewed in light of the efficiency and effectiveness of the reference department's daily operations. Similarly, and perhaps too obviously, "a claim for additional resources is more likely to succeed if [the department] has a reputation for delivering the goods."[21] This adds up to knowing the necessity of each activity in the department and taking creative approaches to improving the way things are done now.[22]

To be sure, all this is easier said than done.** The process becomes more and more difficult as a high level of efficiency is achieved and involves one particular danger: that patrons' (and administrators') expectations will rise more quickly than service actually improves.[23] Stretching the department thin may be one way to draw attention to the plight of the reference department, but pushing staff to the limit (especially when many of them perceive they are already there) is demoralizing and counter-productive if the real chances for relief are slim.

A number of approaches to evaluating public services have been outlined in the literature, among the best "What *Are* You Doing?" by Anthony Ferguson and John Taylor.[24] All of these approaches come down to insuring that the services provided in the department are consistent with the goals and objectives of the organization.[25] Similarly, budget requests must be driven by the goals of the library as a whole.

In justifying specific requests, one has to see the broad implications of the proposal. Have you anticipated the entire cost? Have you included on-line training expenses as well as the database subscription?*** Software as well as hardware? Be espe-

---

**The "easiest" approach is to ask for more money as a requirement for accomplishment. When the money is not forthcoming, one has a built-in excuse for having made no progress.

***The need to spend money on training is often a very difficult point to "sell." How many libraries have plunked down microcomputers for their staffs and expected instant productivity? Unit heads must do their best to convince administrators that foregoing training is false economy.

cially careful in counting on supplementing the budget with grant monies. Consider *before* applying what will happen if the grant doesn't come through or what to do when the grant money runs out.

The following list of steps apply to the actual submittal and discussion of a budget request. While many are self-evident, even elementary, they can make or break (usually break) a budget proposal:

1. Follow procedures
2. Don't miss deadlines
3. Be brief, keep it simple, neatness counts
4. Sell your case on its own merits; don't belittle someone else's project to make yours look good
5. Include plans for some projects that don't cost much (any) money *and put them into action*
6. Present all the facts****
7. Use comparative statistics and standards with caution; instead, relate most things to the specific institution[26]
8. Choose your battles and don't cry wolf
9. "Be persistent, with patience and principles"[27]
10. *Be ready to make a choice when one is offered*

When all is said and done, even the most conscientious head of reference may still receive a disappointing budget allocation. Indeed, cutbacks and "cost-of-living" budget increases are the rule rather than the exception. In terms of the reference department, specifically, "the best justification process may still do battle with library priorities if services are not considered the primary reason for the library's existence."[28] Still, careful planning and year-round preparation allow reference administrations to allocate resources judiciously in times of feast or famine.

****Gerard McCabe suggests, in "Austerity Budget Management," that "requests should be submitted in terms of library objectives and present both affirmative and negative results" (p. 228). One library manager put it another way: "It is not my policy to run around at the last minute asking questions of people who have failed to make a case for themselves."

NOTES

1. Winkworth, Ian, "Acquiring and Allocating Resources: A Pragmatic View," *Library Acquisitions: Practice and Theory* 6 (No. 3, 1982): 305-312.

2. Prentice, Ann E., *Financial Planning for Libraries*. Metuchen, NJ: Scarecrow Press, 1983.

3. Sanders, Nancy P., "Review of Selected Sources in Budgeting for Collection Managers," *Collection Management* 5 (Autumn/Winter, 1983): 151-59.

4. Ramsey, Inez & Jackson E. Ramsey, *Library Planning and Budgeting*. New York: Franklin Watts, 1986.

5. Chen, Ching-chih, *Zero-Base Budgeting in Library Management*. Phoenix: Oryx Press, 1980.

6. Prentice, *Financial Planning for Libraries*.

7. Vasi, John, *Budget Allocation Systems for Research Libraries*. Washington, DC: Association of Research Libraries, 1983.

8. Prentice, *Financial Planning for Libraries*.

9. Allen, Kenneth S., *Current and Emerging Budgeting Model Budget Analysis Program of the State of Washington*. Seattle: University of Washington, 1972.

10. Martin, Murray S., "Budgeting—the Practical Way," *Canadian Library Journal* 39 (October, 1982): 299-302.

11. Adamany, David W., "Research Libraries from a Presidential Perspective." In *Issues in Academic Librarianship*, edited by Peter Spyers-Duran & Thomas W. Mann, Jr., 5-20, Westport, CT: Greenwood Press, 1985.

12. Crowe, William J., "Zero-based Budgeting for Libraries: A Second Look," *College & Research Libraries* 43 (January, 1982): 47-50.

13. Cherrington, David J. & J. Owen Cherrington, "The Role of Budgeting in Organizational Improvement." In *The Management Process: A Selection of Readings for Librarians*, edited by Ruth J. Person, 156-62, Chicago: American Library Association, 1983.

14. Martin, "Budgeting—the Practical Way."

15. Nitecki, Joseph Z., "Creative Management in Austerity," In *Austerity Management in Academic Libraries*, edited by John F. Harvey & Peter Spyers-Duran, 43-61, Metuchen, NJ: Scarecrow Press, 1984.

16. Yalif, Anat, "Strategic Planning Techniques," *The Magazine of Bank Administration* 58 (April, 1982), 22-26.

17. McCabe, Gerard B., "Austerity Budget Management," In *Austerity Management in Academic Libraries*, edited by John F. Harvey & Peter Spyers-Duran, 225-35, Metuchen, NJ: Scarecrow Press, 1984.

18. Katz, William A. & Anne Clifford (eds.), *Reference and Online Services Handbook: Guidelines, Policies and Procedures for Libraries*. New York: Neal-Schuman, 1982.

19. Futa, Elizabeth (ed.), *Library Acquisition Policies and Procedures*. Phoenix: Oryx Press, 1977.

20. Neville, Sandra H., "Day-to-Day Management of Reference Services," *The Reference Librarian* 3 (Spring, 1982), 15-27.

21. Winkworth, "Acquiring and Allocating Resources."

22. Martin, "Budgeting—the Practical Way."

23. Winkworth, "Acquiring and Allocating Resources."

24. Ferguson, Anthony W. & John R. Taylor, "What *Are* You Doing? An Analysis of Activities of Public Service Librarians at a Medium-Sized Research Library," *Journal of Academic Librarianship* 6 (March, 1980), 24-29.

25. Williams, Sally F., "Budget Justification: Closing the Gap between Request and Result," *Library Resources & Technical Services* 28 (April, 1984), 129-35.

26. Winkworth, "Acquiring and Allocating Resources."

27. Williams, "Budget Justification."

28. Neville, "Day-to-Day Management."

Budgeting for Reference Services in the Academic Library: A Tutorial

Gloria S. Cline

SUMMARY. Academic libraries are under pressure to improve their weak budgetary practices as parent institutions emphasize accountability. Several have adopted various versions of program budgeting which result in spreading part of the responsibility for budgeting beyond top management to division heads and others. Additional libraries will undoubtedly be encouraged to do the same. The program budgeting effort is difficult, frustrating, and time-consuming, yet it forces the library to assess its services in terms of effectiveness and efficiency. This paper examines the steps required to implement in the Reference Services Division a version of program budgeting that combines goal statements with a line-item budget.

Budgeting in any organization is a complex process that is often shrouded in mystery and its product, the budget, a document rarely seen or discussed by employees, even at the supervisory level. This occurs because budgeting normally takes place at top management levels, far removed from the lower echelons. In recent years there has been a movement in many organizations to involve more people in budgeting, probably because of the need to tighten belts in the face of economic hard times. However, top management always retains its prerogative to make final decisions because it is they who must take the consequences of those decisions.

Like most organizations, libraries also strongly support the principle of budgeting by top management. Standard 8 of "Stan-

Gloria S. Cline is Assistant Director for Public Services, Dupre Library, University of Southwestern Louisiana, 302 E. St. Mary Boulevard, Lafayette, LA 70503.

dards for College Libraries, 1986'' specifies that the library director shall bear the responsibility for preparing, defending, and administering the library budget.[1] Yet, despite the soundness of the principle and its widespread application in libraries, budgeting is still perceived to be one of the weakest areas of library management. Rarely can a library director or budgetary officer account for exactly what is spent by various departments such as Reference or Cataloging. Why is this? Roberts focuses on six reasons why budgeting is so weak in libraries.[2] Briefly, they are:

1. Libraries usually are not corporate independent legal entities but instead are part of a larger organization, e.g., a university, and thus are not subject to the same financial discipline.
2. The lack of obligation to prepare detailed budgets leads to almost total lack of action in the area of financial accountability.
3. The tradition of financial accountability has not grown up in or been nurtured in libraries. The typical library budget is usually constructed for the library as a whole rather than broken down into detail on a program by program basis.
4. The lack of a definable product or final output in most library activities makes it difficult or impossible to determine unit costs.
5. There is an inherent barrier to objective measurement because librarians do not hold a materialistic view of their work but rather permit their emotional bias to influence economic rationality.
6. Librarians believe that final delivery of service to the patron is the most important outcome of their work regardless of the level of performance achieved.

While many librarians may challenge the validity of some of these reasons, it is clear that Roberts paints an ugly picture of the typical librarian's performance as financial manager, pointing, as he does, to apathy and poor attitude toward budgetary matters. He concludes the discussion of these weaknesses by saying:

Although the library may not have direct financial control over all resources used (e.g., staffing), internal management needs dictate that surrogate control is exercised. That is, the manager must have full information and data on all resources (including staff costs), so that all decisions about allocation and of an economic nature can be taken in the light of the fullest possible management information.[3]

Obtaining the fullest information is a complex process requiring more time than most library directors can afford to spend on it. For that reason some libraries are hiring budget specialists, appointing committees, or dividing the responsibility for data gathering among department heads. Some are experimenting with different types of budgets; for example, several large libraries are using program budgeting internally.[4] This trend toward new methods and the involvement of more people mandates that all librarians, especially department heads, acquaint themselves with budgeting theory and practice.

This paper is intended to provide practical information for academic reference librarians, especially Reference Division Heads, who have had little or no experience in budgeting. Step-by-step instructions hopefully will supply a framework for the preparation and presentation of a divisional budget. Completion of the activities presented in each step will require time, probably a great deal of time, and much effort. However, the results will be rewarding and the mechanisms required for data-gathering will be set in place for the future.

STEP ONE:
STUDY THE LITERATURE ON BUDGETING

Although nothing can quite equal experience in any endeavor, its best substitute is reading and studying. It is best to stick with current information as much as possible because practices change over time, and what was in vogue 10 or 20 years ago may be discredited today. Keep in mind that books usually provide basic information applicable to libraries in general while journal articles present information specific to individual libraries or library functions such as bibliographic searching, allocation formulae, personnel, etc.

Standards and statistical data should not be overlooked as sources of information since they can provide an important point of reference for comparing what is with what is recommended or exists elsewhere.[5] While most of the information available on library budgeting does not deal specifically with Reference Services, reading and studying it nonetheless builds knowledge, understanding, vocabulary, and even some appreciation for the headaches and frustrations experienced by budgetary officials.

STEP TWO:
BECOME ACQUAINTED WITH TYPES OF BUDGETS

The librarian should emerge from his study with knowledge of what a budget is (a planning tool, an estimate of future needs) and what it does (constraints, controls). Obviously, if a budget restricts or controls those under it, it will not please everyone. Stan's Law of Budgeting humorously states that, "Effective budgeting is the uniform distribution of dissatisfaction."[6] Wildavsky says that budgets only "satisfice," i.e., satisfy and suffice.[7] As the librarian begins to understand the nature of budgets, he should also begin to recognize types of budgets commonly used in libraries, the most important of which are line-item and program budgeting. Zero-base budgeting is a relative newcomer often mentioned in the literature but of limited value to libraries. It will be discussed with program budgeting.

Line-Item Budget

The line-item budget undoubtedly is the most commonly used budget type. In it expenditures are categorized by type of item or service purchased. A simplified line-item budget for an academic library might look like this:

A. Personal Services (salaries)	$1,200,000.00
B. Materials (books, periodicals, etc.)	900,000.00
C. Contractual Services (rentals, maintenance, etc.)	97,000.00
D. Supplies (consumables)	20,000.00
E. Capital Outlays (equipment, building repairs, etc.)	63,000.00
Total:	$2,280,000.00

The line-item budget has several advantages over other types — it is easier to prepare because it requires a limited number of calculations; it relies on readily available historical data; and it presents a clear picture of overall budgetary matters. Its disadvantages include the fact that it is incremental, i.e., the current year's budget is based on last year's plus (or minus in hard times) a small increment; it is not tied to goals and objectives; and it does not promote sound decision making since it is fragmented into areas such as personnel or maintenance rather than specific service areas. Line-item budgets are usually viewed as restrictive because the sums listed in each line often receive individual approval and cannot be transferred from one category to another at the administrator's discretion.

The line-item budget above can be contrasted with a "lump sum" budget wherein the library would simply be allotted a lump sum of $2.28 million to be distributed at the discretion of the budgetary officer. On the surface, the lump sum budget seems preferable to the line-item budget because of its flexibility. However, there is danger that one area could be emphasized at the expense of another. For example, personnel reductions might be effected in order to increase book purchases, but the end result could be that there are too few employees around to handle the purchase, processing, and circulation of those books.

Program Budgeting and Zero-Base Budgeting

Although sharply different in most respects, program budgeting and zero-base budgeting (ZBB) have several elements in common, e.g., both strongly emphasize goals and objectives; both show how much an agency spends on individual programs rather than what it spends as a whole on goods and services; and both are controversial, garnering as they do either strong support or strong opposition.

Program budgeting, commonly referred to as PPB (Planning, Programming, Budgeting) was a major budgetary experiment of the federal government in the 1960s and early 1970s. Instead of presenting budget requests in line-item form, PPB made its presentation in terms of end products which required an elaborate framework of goal statements. It failed because it was impossible to put a price tag on goods and end products, and was abandoned in the 1970s.

ZBB was developed by Peter Pyhrr[8] in the late 1960s for use in private industry and was introduced into the federal government in the late 1970s. ZBB required that each program or activity be justified from the ground up or point zero each year, and that each activity be divided into subactivities until a hierarchy of activities was created. Although ZBB was found to be useful during periods of retrenchment when shrinking funds were used to support only important programs at the top of the hierarchy while programs at the bottom were eliminated, starting from point zero each year proved to be too costly and time-consuming for most agencies, thus ZBB did not prove to be a popular budgetary system.

Wildavsky described ZBB as working vertically from zero to base while PPB works horizontally across programs to relate their objectives. He blasted them both by saying:

> Though one has died [PPB] and the other [ZBB] should, their experiences teach about better budgeting by negative example. Whatever they do, the rule is, should not be done. . . . ZBB and PPB embody extreme (though different) forms of comprehensive calculation . . . ZBB insists on making all possible vertical calculations . . . PPB covers at least all major horizontal relationships . . . PPB is ahistorical . . . ZBB doesn't so much ignore as set out to abolish history; the clock is always set at zero.[9]

The gist of Wildavsky's criticisms is that neither PPB nor ZBB can be done. It is impossible to perform the comprehensive calculations required in an organization of any size, just as it is impossible to formulate and rank rational objectives and then make budget categories out of them.

If these budgeting systems are so deficient and traditional line-item budgeting is still preferable, why are many agencies, including some libraries, in favor of experimenting with them? The answer, of course, relates to the continuing emphasis on accountability in budgeting. As mentioned earlier, libraries need to strengthen fiscal management practices, and program budgeting in its various versions can provide a means of doing so. Trumpeter and Rounds have proposed that libraries adopt a version of program budgeting that appears to be a cross between line-item and PPB.[10] It requires six basic steps which, briefly stated, are:

1. identify the programs and their goals;
2. project changes in each program for the budget year;
3. prepare a line-item budget for each program;
4. rank the programs by order of importance;
5. compile the program budgets into a final budget for the entire library;
6. evaluate both the budgeting process and whether the funded programs accomplished their goals.

At this point, the librarian charged with preparing a divisional budget request can compare the type of budget adopted in his/her library with the types already examined. Without doubt, the adopted budget type will be a version of program budgeting. If it closely approximates that recommended by Trumpeter and Rounds, several areas of concern should be addressed. First, how stringent is this budgeting system? Will it be necessary to develop goals and objectives and tie cost figures to them, or will goals and objectives be only loosely tied to the line-item budget? Second, which of the complex, time-consuming tasks will be reserved for top management and which delegated to division heads and others? Certainly top management will reserve for itself the tasks of ranking the programs, preparing the final budget, and evaluating the budgeting process. Division heads, in consultation with top management, will probably be charged with developing goals and objectives, preparing a line-item budget, and at the end of the fiscal year, evaluating whether the goals were accomplished. When their charge is received, division heads will in turn delegate various tasks to program supervisors, thus more and more people will be involved in the budgeting effort.

STEP THREE:
EXAMINE UNIVERSITY AND LIBRARY
GOALS AND BUDGETS

Once the requirements of the budgeting system adopted by the library are known, the next step is to examine both university and library goals and budgets as preparation for formulating Reference Services' goals and budget. The university's goals may appear in formal statements in the college catalog, a mission statement, reports to the governing board, and/or to accrediting agencies. The library may or may not have written goals, but if no written goals are found, consultation with the director will provide insight into the direction he/she wants to move the library. These goals should be kept in mind when examining budgets for the past two to three years, because goals and objectives are necessarily tied to financial resources. There can be no ends without means.

The university and library budgets undoubtedly will be in line-item format devoid of goal statements but readily understandable. In the university's budget, look for answers to these questions: what were the total financial resources of the university; did the resources increase, decrease, or stand still over the years; how were the resources allocated (e.g., was the greatest portion of the funds allocated to personal services); how much was allocated to overhead costs such as building maintenance, insurance, utilities, etc.; were individual salaries listed; how well was the library supported when compared to other departments; and finally, was the library allocated approximately six percent of the university's educational and general budget as recommended by standards?[11]

Examine next the library's budget for the past two or three years. It probably will be a separate document available in the office of the director, budgetary officer, acquisitions librarian or library accountant, and oftentimes in the library's annual reports. If it also is a line-item budget, it will reflect the categories of expenditures used in the university's budget but in greater detail. For example, instead of a gross amount for contractual services, the budget will list, line by line, the contracts maintained with various vendors for rental and maintenance of equipment and services. The portion of the budget dealing with materials will reveal gross expenditures for books, periodical subscriptions, standing orders, etc., as well as a list of allocations made to academic and library departments. Note that individual salaries may not be part of the library's budget as this is sensitive information which usually is not readily available. Note also whether overhead costs for building maintenance, utilities, etc., are included in the library's budget. Academic libraries usually do not account for these hidden costs.

Finally, look for answers to these questions: where were most of the library's resources spent (undoubtedly on personal services and materials); did the budget increase, decrease, or stand still; did the library overspend or underspend its allocations; what academic and library departments received the largest allocations; and what percentage of the materials budget was spent on serials, standing orders, etc., as opposed to books? Unfortunately the answers to these questions will not provide the specific data needed to formulate the Reference Services budget because few items in the library's budget pertain solely to Reference Services. However, just as surely as personal services and materials account for most of the university's and library's budgets, so will they account for most of the Reference Services budget. Preparing the line-item budget for Reference Services will necessitate pulling together information from both the university and library budgets, as well as from other sources.

STEP FOUR: IDENTIFY FACTORS INFLUENCING THE DESIGN OF THE REFERENCE SERVICES BUDGET

Once university and library goals have been ascertained and their budgets thoroughly examined, it is time to focus on factors that influence the library's budget and ultimately, Reference Services' budget. Today the two most costly items in the academic library's budget are personnel and materials, both of which directly relate to the library's organizational structure, i.e., whether it is centralized or decentralized. Although there are pros and cons to both, the fact remains that decentralization requires more staff and more materials while centralization controls staff size and duplication of materials.

Reference services are affected by many of the same factors, and answers to the following questions should be obtained before the budget is designed: how many programs comprise Reference Services—information desk and telephone assistance (centralized or decentralized?), bibliographic instruction, on-line bibliographic searching, catalog assistance, interlibrary loan, and/or government publications; do some services operate on a cost recovery basis, e.g., interlibrary loan and on-line searching; if so, do the funds collected actually cover the amounts invoiced; where is each activity physically located; how many employees are needed to staff each area; how many hours of service does each maintain; how busy is each, i.e., how many questions are answered, how many interlibrary loan transactions completed, how many documents processed; and what equipment and on-line services are utilized in each program? These factors strongly impact the budget. It is no wonder then that in recent years, many libraries have centralized reference services, shortened hours of service, and done other such things to effect savings in personnel and materials.

STEP FIVE:
IDENTIFY REFERENCE SERVICES PROGRAMS, ASSESS THEIR NEEDS, AND SET GOALS

Three discrete tasks of varying difficulty are included in step five. Identifying the programs in Reference Services will undoubtedly be the easiest task, requiring only that the programs carried out within Reference Services be identified separately, e.g., interlibrary loan, on-line bibliographic searching, etc. If any of the programs have immediate supervisors other than the Head of Reference Services, this should be noted and responsibility for assessing the needs and setting the goals of each program should be delegated to or shared with the supervisors. The needs of each program should be identified and ranked in order of priority. Although needs possibilities are endless, they usually boil down to people, materials, space, and/or equipment. If additional staff are needed, what level of expertise is required—professional, clerical, student assistants? If more space is needed, what kind — shelving, office, work, storage? It is important to assess and rank needs carefully because goals and objectives derive from need.

The task of goal setting is a particularly difficult assignment. Recall that PPB foundered from the inability of its users to set meaningful goals and attach a price tag to them. Thus it seems wise for libraries to adopt a version of program budgeting that is less stringent than the original PPB. Goals and objectives definitely should be set, but they should be meaningful and realistic, reflecting the resources likely to be allocated to the division.

STEP SIX:
PREPARE LINE-ITEM BUDGET

As noted earlier, the line-item budget forms the core of the version of program budgeting suggested by Trumpeter and Rounds.[12] When program budgeting is implemented for the first time in the library, no readily available data on specific expenditures for Reference Services are likely to exist to aid in developing the line-item budget. Although it may be extremely difficult to gather together that data, it can be done in large measure. Cost information for the most important and expensive elements of Reference Services, personnel and materials, definitely can be ascertained, while other less critical categories of expenditures such as supplies can be estimated. The data for all categories of expenditures should be collected for at least the past two to three years as well as estimated expenditures for the current year in order to forecast the upcoming year's needs. Arrange the data collected into tables and footnote any unusual expenditures.

Listed below are the categories of data usually required to prepare the line-item budget, along with comments and suggestions for possible sources of information:

Personnel

The single most important element of Reference Services is competent personnel, including professional librarians, paraprofessional and clerical staff and student assistants. Salaries of reference librarians should be in line with those of other professionals within an institution and within the profession as a whole, as well as with salaries of teaching faculty with comparable credentials and in comparable areas such as the Humanities and Social Sciences. Individual salary information, though sensitive, is essential for the preparation of the line-item budget and can be obtained from library or university budgets, or from the director, budgetary officer, or personnel director. Tracking the data on salaries for two to three years will reveal ever increasing amounts on personal services as raises are given and beginning salaries edge upward.

Employee benefits such as retirement and insurance usually are not budgeted for in academic libraries because they are known only at the end of the fiscal year and only as a line-item for the entire library staff rather than for individuals. Though benefits amount to a great deal of money, in academic libraries they essentially remain hidden costs along with other overhead expenses and should not be included in the line-item budget. The same situation holds true for wages of student assistants in many libraries, thus their wages may not be required for the line-item budget. If data are available, however, include them.

Materials

The reference collection is of almost equal importance to the reference librarian and should rank high among the library's priorities. Not surprisingly, the cost of maintaining the reference collection is high, and in fact rivals the cost of personnel. The library's budget may already reveal expenditures specifically for Reference Services materials, but if it does not, it will be necessary to obtain the costs of all reference materials, including serials and standing orders; monographs and other separates; and special forms of reference materials, e.g., indexes in microform and on laser discs.

Binding expenditures should also be included in the total cost of materials for Reference Services. Predicting the cost of materials for the upcoming year would be simpler if the reference market were static, but it is not, and excellent, usually expensive, new materials appear daily, and the availability of new materials should be considered when preparing the budget. Materials incur many hidden costs, e.g., housing, maintaining and repairing them, thus costs should be controlled as much as possible by continually weeding obsolete materials and cancelling unneeded subscriptions. Compile reference materials expenditures for two to three years, looking at the rate of increase in the cost of those materials, and then predict the current and upcoming years' costs accordingly.

Travel

Reference Services staff must attend workshops, conferences, and other meetings which incur registration fees, transportation, meals and lodging expenses. These should be covered in large measure by the library. It will be necessary to obtain the data based on the travel of individual Reference Services staff. Usually the data can be found in the office of the director or budgetary officer. However, prior travel costs may prove to be unrelated to the current and upcoming years' budgets, since costs vary greatly from year to year and city to city where meetings are held. Reference staff should be queried regarding the meetings they plan to attend in the upcoming year, and the budget request for travel should be tailored to those requests.

Contractual Services

The correct equipment, properly maintained, enhances Reference Services immeasurably. Contractual services usually encompass equipment rental and maintenance contracts, repairs, printing, communications (telephone), and advertising. Obtaining the costs of contractual services as they apply solely to reference probably will be troublesome since equipment and network utilities may be shared with other library divisions. Begin by creating an inventory of all equipment used in Reference Services, including network utilities such as OCLC (for searching and interlibrary loan); other on-line bibliographic services, e.g., DIALOG, BRS, etc. (membership dues, minimum charges, etc.); computer services including mainframe and personal computers; printers, typewriters, and microform reader/printers; and telephones (number of lines and long distance charges).

Printing costs for guidebooks, bibliographies, etc., that assist patrons in the use of the library are usually attributed to Reference Services, as is advertising of Reference Services positions. Discussions with the library accountant (or whoever pays the bills) in addition to close examination of the invoices received for the past two to three years will reveal expenditures specific to Reference Services. Based on past usage figures, the current and upcoming year's expenditures can be calculated. Where rental and maintenance contracts are involved, it is wise to call the vendors for quotes on prices to be charged for the next year. Be aware, however, that they may not honor the quoted price. Contractual services costs seldom decrease, but instead like everything else, usually creep up in price yearly.

Supplies

Supplies are usually defined as consumable items such as pens, pencils, paper, file folders, etc. There often is a ceiling on the per item cost of supplies, e.g., $100.00. As with contractual services, it may be hard to gather accurate figures on this category of expenditures. Again begin by creating an inventory of supplies regularly purchased for Reference Services. Keep in mind not only general office supplies but special supplies as well, e.g., a special type of printer paper, specific printer and typewriter ribbons, mailing bags and boxes for interlibrary loan. Remember also that items such as software packages often can be purchased as supplies because of their low costs. A close estimate of the costs of supplies is desirable, because although supplies usually are not the most expensive items in the budget, their costs do add up to a considerable amount nonetheless.

Capital Outlays

Capital outlays involve expenditures for permanent rather than consumable items. Equipment, furniture, new buildings, additions, or renovations are types of capital outlays. Obtaining and tracking the data on capital outlays for Reference Services for the past two to three years should be readily accomplished as these major expenses will be easy to identify. However, these data will probably have limited usefulness in predicting future expenditures because capital outlay allocations vary widely from year to year. Estimates of costs for capital outlays in the upcoming year may be obtained by consulting vendors for quotes on equipment or furniture. Always remember to specify exactly the features desired or model numbers if they are known. Larger expenses for building changes usually will be handled by the director since they affect the library as a whole and require much time to prepare for and accomplish. However, some minor building changes such as removing or adding walls or dividers are capital outlay expenses that can be accomplished by university personnel in the maintenance department at minimal cost to the library. Sometimes minor renovations can markedly enhance reference service.

When all of the data on expenditures for Reference Services for the past two to three years have been gathered, they should be compiled into tables similar to Examples One or Two in Appendix A. The data in these tables present a clear and fairly accurate picture of past expenditures on which projections for the upcoming year will be based. However, since a program budget has been adopted by the library, the next step will be to project needs from the goals and objectives set for the upcoming year, estimate costs, and lay out the budget. The format of the program budget might be similar to either Example One or Two in Appendix B. It is apparent from comparing the examples in Appendices A and B that program budgeting is much more difficult to accomplish than straightforward line-item budgeting. Nonetheless, because goals and objectives are stated (usually in priority order), the program budget provides a better vehicle for accountability.

STEP SEVEN:
PRESENT AND DEFEND THE BUDGET

At this point all of the financial data for Reference Service programs have been tabulated and now it is time to prepare the budget information for submission to the director or budgetary officer. The written document should include background information, a brief discussion, the program budget itself, and as supporting evidence, the line-item budget that tracks expenditures for the past two to three years should be attached.

The oral presentation probably will take place at an informal meeting between the Head of Reference Services and the director or budgetary officer, although it may occur at a more formal meeting between division heads and the director. Whatever the environment, if there has been sufficient communication between the Head of Reference Services and the director or budgetary officer, there should be no surprises in the budget presentation. If care has been exercised in the data gathering phase, the division head should feel confident of the accuracy of the data, and should be prepared to answer any questions and defend any special requests.

STEP EIGHT:
MONITOR THE BUDGET

Budgeting is not a once-a-year activity but is ongoing throughout the fiscal year. Once the budget for Reference Services has been approved and allocations set for the upcoming year, it will be necessary to monitor expenditures to ensure that adjustments are made as needed, and that allocations are spent in a timely manner and are neither under- nor overspent. However, in academic libraries fiscal affairs are normally limited to only a few people who are authorized to purchase services, goods and materials, usually the budgetary officer and the Acquisitions Librarian who work closely with the accountant to monitor the total library budget and prepare regular reports (at least monthly) listing expenditures, encumbrances, and free balances for the various line-item categories. The division head may want to monitor the division's budget in some of the same ways, setting up a ledger that shows monthly expenditures for various categories (see Appendix C for an example). There are benefits in doing so, not the least of which is that the data needed to produce next year's budget will be forthcoming at the end of the fiscal year.

Too, if funds can be shifted from one expenditure category to another, the division head can take advantage of this flexibility early on as it becomes apparent that one category is being overspent while another still has reserves. The more closely the budget is monitored the stronger budgetary control is exercised.

STEP NINE:
ASSESS THE SUCCESS
OF THE DIVISION'S BUDGET

The time to assess the success of the Reference Services budget is near the end of the fiscal year when most of the division's allocations have been spent. Several questions should be asked. First and most important, were the goals and objectives of the Reference Services Division met? If not, why not? What were the strengths and weaknesses of the budget? What are some ways these weaknesses can be improved or corrected in the future? Finally, were the results worth the effort?

CONCLUSIONS

Academic libraries have been battered by inflation, decreased revenues, and increased expectations of users. These and other pressures have intensified the need to examine and improve the library's traditionally weak budgetary practices. The emphasis now is on accountability and the library is being forced to account not only for how much it spends but where and how wisely it spends its funds. Various versions of program budgeting have been adopted in a growing number of academic libraries because it stresses goals and objectives. This paper examined a version of program budgeting that includes in its core the line-item budget, and stepped through its implementation in the Reference Services Division. While program budgeting requires a great deal more effort and planning than traditional line-item budgeting, the benefits are numerous. Library staff as a whole are involved in the process and consequently come to appreciate the costs involved; real costs are determined; and genuine examination of efficiency and effectiveness takes place.

NOTES

1. "Standards for College Libraries, 1986," *College & Research Libraries News* 47 (March, 1986), p.199.

2. Stephen A. Roberts, *Cost Management for Library and Information Services* (London: Butterworth, 1985), p.2-4.

3. Ibid., p.5.

4. "Preparation and Presentation of the Library Budget," *SPEC Flyer*, no.32 (April, 1977).

5. See, for example, various ACRL standards such as "Standards for College Libraries," *ARL Statistics*, published annually by the Association of Research Libraries; and *ACRL University Library Statistics*, published annually by the Association of College and Research Libraries.

6. Lawrence M. Matthews, *Practical Operating Budget* (New York: McGraw-Hill, 1977), p.17.

7. Aaron Wildavsky, *The Politics of the Budgetary Process*, 4th ed. (Boston: Little-Brown, 1974), p.12.

8. Peter A. Pyhrr, *Zero-Base Budgeting: A Practical Management Tool for Evaluating Expenses* (New York: Wiley, 1973).

9. Wildavsky, p.219.

10. Margo C. Trumpeter & Richard S. Rounds, *Basic Budgeting Practices for Librarians* (Chicago: American Library Association, 1985), p.19.

11. "Standard for College Libraries, 1986," p.199.

12. Trumpeter & Rounds.

APPENDIX A

Example 1: Line-Item Budget

Reference Services Division

Category	Year			
	1984–85	1985–86	1986–87 est.	1987–88 proj.
Personal Services	$311,700	$324,200	$340,400	$350,612
Materials	98,340	101,300	105,000	110,250
Travel	2,000	2,200	2,500	2,500
Contractual Services	15,700	16,050	17,000	17,000
Supplies	600	700	650	700
Capital Outlays	1,400	1,200	10,000	3,500
Total:	$429,740	$445,650	$475,550	$484,562

Example 2: Line-Item Budget

Programs of Reference Services

Program/Category	Year			
	1984–85	1985–86	1986–87 est.	1987–88 proj.
Reference Desk				
Personal Services	$155,850	$162,100	$170,200	$175,306
Materials	98,000	100,000	104,000	109,000
Travel	700	850	800	1,200
Contractual Services	2,200	2,000	2,000	2,300
Supplies	125	110	110	150
Capital Outlays	---	---	1,200	3,000
Subtotal:	256,875	265,060	278,310	290,956
Online Searching				
Personal Services	23,000	23,920	25,150	25,900
Materials	340	380	340	400
Travel	500	150	300	500
Contractual Services	3,300	3,000	3,500	3,800
Supplies	200	150	200	200
Capital Outlays	3,500	---	3,700	---
Subtotal:	30,840	27,600	33,190	30,800

APPENDIX A, continued

Program/Category	Year			
	1984-85	1985-86	1986-87 est.	1987-88 proj.
Interlibrary Loan				
Personal Services	29,500	30,680	32,214	33,180
Materials	---	---	---	---
Travel	---	150	225	300
Contractual Services	2,100	2,300	2,400	2,350
Supplies	200	250	250	280
Capital Outlays	---	1,200	3,700	---
Subtotal:	31,800	34,580	38,789	36,110
GRAND TOTAL:	$319,515	$327,240	$350,289	$357,866

APPENDIX B

Example 1: Program Budget
Line-Items without Goals and Objectives[a]
1987-88

Category	Program			
	Ref. Desk	Online Searching	ILL	Biblio. Instr.
Personal Services	$175,306	$25,900	$33,180	$25,600
Materials	109,000	400	---	500
Travel	1,200	500	300	600
Contractual Services	2,300	3,800	2,350	800
Supplies	150	200	280	100
Capital Outlays	3,000	---	---	---
Total:	$290,956	$30,800	$36,110	$27,600

[a]Goals and objectives form a separate document as illustrated below.

Goals and Objectives
Reference Services Division
1987-88

I. Reference Desk

    A. Goals:

        1. To improve public access to the reference collection.

           a. Objectives:

               (1) To remove three 12 ft. non-supporting walls surrounding closed reference stacks.

               (2) To add one 8-section range of steel shelving.

        2. To increase hours of reference service on weekends.

           Objective: To employ a qualified librarian to work 20 hours per week, including hours on Friday, Saturday and Sunday.

II. Online Searching

III. Interlibrary Loan

Example 2: Program Budget
Goals and Objectives with Line Items
1987-88

| Program | Goals | Category of Expenditures | | | | | |
		Pers. Serv.	Materials	Cont. Serv.	Supplies	Capital Outlays	Total
Reference Desk	—To improve accessibility[a] of reference collection.	$175,306	$109,000	$2,300	$ 150	$3,000	$289,756
	—To increase hours of reference service on weekends.[b]						
Online Searching	—						
Interlibrary Loan	—						
Totals:							

[a]Capital outlays allocation to be used to remove three 12 ft. walls surrounding closed reference stacks, and add one eight-section range of steel shelving.

[b]Personal services includes $12,000 to hire a qualified librarian for 20 hours per week.

APPENDIX C

Example of Monitoring Aids

1. Personal Services (Expenditure Code: 2100)
   Allocation: $340,400.00

Month	Item	Expended	Running Total	Free Balance
July	Staff Salaries	$ 3,400.00	$ 3,400.00	$337,000.00
	Faculty Salaries	21,000.00	24,400.00	316,000.00
	Staff Salaries	3,400.00	27,800.00	312,600.00
August				
September				

2. Materials (Expenditure Code: 2700)
   Allocation: $105,000.00

Month	Item	Expended	Running Total	Free Balance
July	Chemical Abstracts	$ 8,400.00	$ 8,400.00	$ 96,600.00
	Biological Abstracts	2,950.00	11,350.00	93,650.00
	Readers' Guide	220.00	11,570.00	93,430.00

   [use inventory of serials and standing orders to determine that no titles
   inadvertently go unpaid.]

	Books	600.00	12,170.00	92,830.00
August				
September				

3. Contractual Services (Expenditure Code: 2300)
   Allocation: $17,000.00

Month	Item	Expended	Running Total	Free Balance
July	OCLC (ILL)	$ 224.00	$ 224.00	$ 16,776.00
	DIALOG	1,300.00	1,524.00	15,476.00
	Printing	800.00	2,324.00	14,676.00
	Telephone	55.00	2,379.00	14,621.00
August				
September				

Budgeting for Reference Services as Part of a Library's Financial Planning

Joan S. McConkey

SUMMARY. Changing patterns for reference service are having an impact on budgeting as new programs vie with existing ones for funding. In developing a budget for reference services, the reference manager should be familiar with library budgeting systems and with the institutional mission, goals and objectives. Budgeting is an integral part of library planning efforts. The more complex budgeting systems, such as the program-planning budgeting systems (PPBS) and zero-based budgeting (ZBB) share elements with strategic planning and are particularly useful in times of change. Evaluation and performance measurement are essential parts of this financial planning. The reference manager should be able to forecast reference service direction for the library and to provide cost-benefit estimates for varying levels of service as a contribution to library strategic and financial planning.

Changing patterns for reference service in the automated library is one of the major topics in library literature today. The relative importance of the traditional reference desk function, on-line services, bibliographic instruction and various special reference services is being debated extensively. An important aspect of the discussion focuses on ways to fund the newer types of reference service. An entire literature on the "fee or free" on-line services issue has developed.[1] The cost of reference tools is forcing difficult decisions about whether, or how rapidly, printed reference materials should be replaced or supplemented by on-line or CD-ROM services and their accompanying hardware expenses. Articles such as "Reference beyond (and without) the

Joan S. McConkey is Assistant Director for Administration, University of Colorado at Boulder, Campus Box 184, Boulder, CO 80309.

Reference Desk''[2] and ''Replacing the Fast Fact Drop-In with Gourmet Information Service''[3] reflect an interest in using the more specialized skills the reference librarian may already have or should acquire. This could lead to an increase in reference salaries, traditionally the largest percentage of the reference budget.

It is obviously time for the reference manager to consider Marcia Pankake's challenge: ''The budget should be seen as the tool to seek additional funds to support new services rather than as yesterday's leftover pie to be divided into smaller and smaller pieces.''[4] In developing a reference service budget, it is important to consider the organizational goals and to specify departmental objectives related to the new services which will advance these goals. Since the departmental budget must be incorporated into the total library budget, it is helpful to provide some options for different levels of support for the reference program and a description of what each level would provide. Before discussing specific aspects of the departmental budget, it may be useful to review some budgeting systems and to consider approaches to the total library budget.

BUDGETING SYSTEMS

Budgeting systems vary from institution to institution and the budget request from the library to its parent institution must follow institutional practices. It is possible, however, to incorporate elements of other systems into the internal budget planning process. Ramsey and Ramsey, in their very thorough book *Library Planning and Budgeting*,[5] identify six types of budgeting systems in use in libraries. They are (1) line-item budgeting (2) lump-sum budgeting (3) program budgeting (4) the program-planning budgeting system (PPBS) (5) zero-based budgeting (ZBB), and (6) performance budgeting.

Line-item budgets and lump-sum budgets tend to be incremental in nature and, without extensive accompanying commentary, show little evidence of planning. Line-item budgets focus on categories of cost such as salaries, benefits, materials, supplies and equipment, and travel; and, like lump-sum budgets, provide little mechanism for accountability.

Program budgets cross traditional library departmental lines to show all of the costs associated with a program or an activity. This makes it easier to state what is to be accomplished toward the library's goals and to measure progress. Program budgets are especially useful in seeking funding for new services or special projects.

The program-planning budgeting system (PPBS) which incorporates long-range planning elements, has been discussed extensively in management literature. Ramsey and Ramsey list the following steps in PPBS budget preparation:

1. Plan the goals and objectives of the library for the long and short run.
2. Develop alternative programs designed to meet these objectives.
3. Plan activities designed to carry out the proposed programs and collect cost figures for them.
4. Evaluate these alternatives on the basis of feasibility and cost/benefit analysis.
5. Select those combinations of program alternatives which provide the greatest benefit at the lowest cost.
6. Design specific quantitative measures by which program effectiveness will be evaluated.
7. Implement the selected programs.
8. Measure program performance.
9. Evaluate program effectiveness against program standards.[6]

This procedure is probably overly elaborate for annual use, but makes sense when used as part of a multi-year planning process. These steps are of particular use when changes in established operating procedures are contemplated.

Zero-based budgeting (ZBB), which requires that every budget request begin anew with justification for each element, is also most useful in connection with major operational changes. The time and cost to develop a completely new budget is hard to justify when library programs are well-established and successful, although a review of all activities on a regular basis is an important part of evaluating the effectiveness of library services.

Performance budgets emphasize quantitative measurement of

library functions and the development of standard costs. They are more likely to be incorporated with other systems than to stand alone. Librarians with budgets which are funded by formula should pay particular attention to physical output units, average cost figures, and similar statistical efficiency measurements. Performance measurement is an integral part of PPBS's evaluation of the success of programs.

THE TOTAL LIBRARY BUDGET

Budgeting is an integral part of library planning and decision-making. If sufficient funds were available to support any services and purchases considered important to the library, the budget could be a simple statement of what services are offered and at what cost. For many libraries, however, budgeting can be defined as the allocation of limited resources to meet specified objectives. As summarized by Michael D. Cooper,

> College and university libraries have had almost no net gain in financial resources since the beginning of the 1960s. As a result of inflation and increasing enrollment, the net per student expenditures for colleges and universities and college and university libraries has remained almost constant for twenty years.[7]

This period of financial austerity has also been a time of enormous increases in both the quantity and cost of library materials and of major technological innovations. In response to the former, sophisticated systems of collection development have been established. They include development of levels of collection building based on the academic strengths of the institution, resource sharing, and attention to preservation requirements. Budgetary impacts of the application of developing computer and communication technologies to library procedures and services and to the publication and dissemination of scholarly information are less well-defined, although it is now generally acknowledged that technological innovations are not reducing the level of library budgets as once predicted.

Directors of research libraries and library organizations, recognizing that libraries will never have the resources to excel in all areas, have become advocates of "strategic planning" in the 1980s. Strategic planning for libraries is defined in a SPEC kit from the Office of Management Studies of the Association of Research Libraries as:

> Strategic planning procedures are similar to other planning activities, analyzing capabilities, assessing environmental pressures and opportunities, setting objectives, examining alternative courses of action, and implementing a preferred course. However, what is different about strategic planning is the deliberate attempt to concentrate resources in those areas which can make a substantial difference in future performance and capabilities. Thus strategic planning is more a frame of reference and a way of thinking than a set of procedures. As a result, strategic planning departs from familiar incremental resource allocation and operational problem-solving patterns that are a part of university life.

> The expectation with strategic planning is that if a library can skillfully choose areas in which it has an advantage or a special opportunity and then concentrates its resources in those areas, it can achieve excellence far beyond what the size or resources of the university would apparently allow.[8]

Colleges and university administrators also find that this more active form of planning is advantageous for defining and achieving institutional goals in this period of competition for the use of limited resources, which is complicated by emerging fields of study, the increasing importance of interdisciplinary studies and changing enrollment patterns. It is essential that librarians be involved in institutional planning and be able to quantify the impact of changes in institutional goals and programs on the library. Libraries and their institutions have both suffered when librarians were not involved in the early planning for campus computer and telecommunications systems. For example, a "wired campus" provides new possibilities for access to information and may lead to major changes in traditional reference services.

Strategic planning, like the program-planning budgeting system, brings with it a requirement to develop feasibility and cost/

benefit analyses for various courses of action. Librarians and administrators of other nonprofit institutions have not always seen the importance of management information and decision support systems. Martin Cummings includes brief descriptions and references to virtually every study of library costs and effectiveness in *The Economics of Research Libraries*. He concludes that more attention must be paid to careful analysis of cost, benefits, and effectiveness of library activities and services:

> [Library directors] will need to become more aware of the usefulness of cost and performance data and management information systems for improved strategic and budgetary planning. The ultimate benefits derived from strategic planning and better management practices will be seen in improved library services that are provided at reduced costs. The technical tools and management methods to accomplish this are available; where we are lacking is in their utilization and in performance.[9]

A certain amount of skepticism exists among librarians about the link between organizational decision-making and the use of costing and performance measures. In "A View from the Trenches: Costing and Performance Measures for Academic Library Public Services,"[10] Charles R. McClure describes a pilot study which indicates that public service middle managers are distrustful of the use of cost and performance measurement data; unaware of much of the research and development done on the general topic of performance measurement; and unlikely to use such data, even if available, for library decision-making. McClure makes a number of suggestions for changing the organizational climate and reward system to foster greater acceptance and use of these methodologies.

Certainly, it is difficult for a library to make the transition from the usual incremental system of budgeting to one based on a sustained planning effort. Library-wide commitment and strong leadership are required to develop goals which support institutional policies and provide a framework for the future. The objectives to carry out the mission and goals must be achievable, measurable and linked to elements of the budget. Setting budget priorities is an important part of this planning effort. Group involvement in allocating resources to include new programs or technical developments may help to persuade middle managers of the importance of providing documentation for their funding requests. Ongoing programs must be balanced with new items, and departmental requests must be merged in a library-wide budget document which reflects long-range planning as well as serving as a guide for expenditures in the next fiscal year. Monitoring actual expenditures and progress toward achieving objectives during this period should contribute to improving the next budget cycle.

Library financial planning and budgeting cannot ignore the funding authority and library users. Cummings[11] emphasizes that close working relationships between the institution's chief academic officer, its financial manager, the computer center director, and the university librarian are essential for good program and budget planning. Their support and that of the scholarly community is vital in planning for modification of existing services and the design of new systems. A sense of excitement about expanding library services may lead to additional institutional funding, especially for the development phase, or concerted efforts to attract gift or grant support. Cooperative efforts among libraries, which have grown rapidly in the last twenty years, also require institutional understanding and approval.

THE REFERENCE SERVICE BUDGET

The course of reference service in the future is beyond the scope of this article, but the reference manager should be able to forecast the institutional reference service future as a contribution to library strategic and financial planning. Preferably, this forecast should include several scenarios for discussion, each requiring different levels of funding. For example, budget projections for elements such as staffing, on-line services, or acquisition, or for total spending could be included to show a range from what is possible with a minimal level of support to what could be done if there were no financial restraints. A tier arrangement makes it possible to indicate what improvements in service could be accomplished with relatively modest increases from one level to another. This gives library administrators flexibility in developing the overall budget request and in dealing with changing levels of institutional support. An occasional bonus for the careful planning effort occurs when unexpected additional funds must be spent quickly.

Although the commitment to strategic or long-range planning may vary from library to library, it is useful for each library department to have a sense of its mission and to develop goals and objectives. A helpful guide for this process is "Planning, Goals, and Objectives for the Reference Department,"[12] in which Charles Bunge discusses the uses of a clear statement of meaningful goals and objectives, the typical content of goals and objectives statements in reference departments, and strategies for developing them. Having these in place is a necessary step for using the more complex planning and budgeting techniques.

Some attention to the tenets of zero-based budgeting (ZBB) is useful in times of transition. An early example of the use of ZBB in reference service is in Rodney Hersberger's "Zero-Base Budgeting: A Library Example."[13] Hersberger describes a hypothetical head of reference who is considering the possibility of adding automated data base retrieval services to the library's traditional methods of providing reference services within the existing budget. Alternatives for each departmental activity are identified and evaluated and, by changing staffing patterns, a way is found to begin the new service without additional funding.

However, there will be times when this analysis leads to the realization that successfully implementing a new program requires new money. Using on-line services as an example, Marcia Pankake advises librarians to be thorough: "Construct an online services budget that will allow not only for the direct search costs (whether or not any part of these are passed on to the patron) but also for other needs: reference tools like database directories, search manuals, publicity, demonstration searches, absorbing of mistakes, training sessions and other costs."[14] Relative costs of both mediated and end user searches should also be considered. A fully developed innovative program connected to departmental, library, and institutional goals of improved access to information and including cost/benefit information is more likely to be a successful competitor for new funds.

To keep these funds, the reference manager must document and evaluate the contributions of the new program in future budget requests. For on-line services, comparisons should include CD-ROM services as well as using printed sources with attention to factors such as telecommunication charges, per-unit costs, coverage, training and support requirements and time savings for the user. The recently published *Dollars and Sense: Implications of the New Online Technology for Managing the Library*[15] should be helpful in stimulating discussion for budget planning. It takes the on-line user and manager from the basics of financial management through the effects of new technology on-line services.

Performance measures as a part of budgeting have taken on increasing importance as new programs vie with old ones for funding and as librarians look at alternative methods of carrying out basic service functions. The measures may also be mandated by state formula financing programs. Public service librarians have resisted the development of cost and performance measure methodologies, usually pleading the difficulty of establishing quality indicators. It appears that it is time for reference managers to take seriously the need to measure the costs associated with various approaches to reference services. Julie Virgo's "Costing and Pricing Information Services"[16] is a good introduction to this technique, and Ann Prentice[17] has contributed a helpful bibliography to the same issue of the *Drexel Library Quarterly*. The Association of Research Libraries has sponsored several studies on performance measurement.

The line-item budget continues to be the most common system for institutional budgeting. Budget development follows a standard format and process and can be done with little consideration of library activities. It is easy to monitor fluctuations in spending in a line over a period of time and to make spending comparisons with other institutions using a similar format, but this attention to elements tells little about the programs. As stated by Ann Prentice,

> Books, terminals, staff and space are funded rather than, say, reference service. The service must conform to the budget dollars allocated for its various ingredients. A planned program places emphasis on what is done or will be

done, and then the resources needed to carry out the plan are itemized. In the line-item format, a set of resources is identified and the task is to put them together as best one can to form a program.[18]

This obviously works best with relatively static programs where adjustment is primarily for inflation or to accommodate fluctuations in institutional funding. It is also useful in identifying the cost of replacements for equipment and furniture which are part of a capital request line-item.

CONCLUSION

Perhaps the most important point to be made about budgeting is that, whether actively or passively, it is an integral part of library and institutional planning. Decisions about how money is to be allocated influence staffing levels, purchase of materials and equipment, and continuing and new reference services programs. The reference manager who wishes to be active in the library's financial planning process needs to be aware of institutional priorities and their impact on reference services and of new developments in libraries which would contribute to local efforts before budget requests are made. Analyzing costs and benefits for print, on-line, and compact disc searching capabilities, for example, gives the library administrators helpful information for budget decision-making. Even in a library which has no formal financial planning process and adapts its programs to line-item allocations each year, proposals for innovations in reference services are strengthened by using program budgeting procedures.

NOTES

1. See, for example, Jane A. Rosenberg, "User Fees and Library Economics: A Selected, Annotated Bibliography," Appendix C in *The Economics of Research Libraries* by Martin M. Cummings (Washington, DC: Council on Library Resources, 1986), pp. 190-208.

2. Barbara J. Ford, "Reference beyond (and without) the Reference Desk," *College and Research Libraries* 47 (September 1986): 491-494.

3. "Replacing the Fast Fact Drop-In with Gourmet Information Service: A Symposium," contributions by Mary Biggs et al., *The Journal of Academic Librarianship* 11 (May 1985): 68-78.

4. Marcia Pankake, "Reaction to 'Funding Online Services from the Materials Budget,'" *College and Research Libraries* 47 (May 1986): 236.

5. Inez L. Ramsey & Jackson E. Ramsey, *Library Planning and Budgeting* (New York: Franklin Watts, 1986), pp. 18-24.

6. Ramsey & Ramsey, pp. 21-22.

7. Michael D. Cooper, "Economic Issues and Trends in Academic Libraries," Appendix A in *The Economics of Research Libraries* by Martin Cummings (Washington, DC: Council on Library Resources, 1986), pp. 166-167.

8. *Strategic Planning in ARL Libraries*, SPEC Kit No. 108 (Washington: Association of Research Libraries, 1984), p. 1.

9. Martin M. Cummings, *The Economic of Research Libraries* (Washington: Council on Library Resources, 1986), p. 140.

10. Charles R. McClure, "A View from the Trenches: Costing and Performance Measures for Academic Library Public Services," *College and Research Libraries* 47 (July 1986): 323-336.

11. Cummings, p. 138.

12. Charles A. Bunge, "Planning, Goals, and Objectives for the Reference Department," *RQ* 23 (Spring 1984): 306-315.

13. Rodney M. Hersberger, "Zero-Base Budgeting: A Library Example," *Catholic Library World* 51 (November 1979): 158-161.

14. Pankake, pp. 236-237.

15. Bernard F. Pasqualine (ed.), *Dollars and Sense: Implications of the New Online Technology for Managing the Library* (Chicago: American Library Association, 1987).

16. Julie A. C. Virgo, "Costing and Pricing Information Services," *Drexel Library Quarterly* 21 (Summer 1985): 75-98.

17. Ann E. Prentice, "Budgeting and Accounting: A Selected Bibliography," *Drexel Library Quarterly* 21 (Summer 1985): 106-112.

18. Ann E. Prentice, *Financial Planning for Libraries* (Metuchen, NJ: Scarecrow Press, 1983), pp. 94-95.

Statistical Data as a Management Tool for Reference Managers, or Roulette by the Numbers

Bruce Morton

SUMMARY. The reasons for the use, or lack of use, of statistical data as a management tool by the manager of reference services is discussed. Special attention devoted to the potential for the application of statistical information for management purposes.

INTRODUCTION

Was Disraeli correct? Are there three varieties of lies—lies, damned lies, and statistics? No, this is not a reference question. However, it is a question that each manager of reference services should be asking himself/herself. Indeed, there is an ample literature to suggest that library public service statistics should be collected. A survey of this literature makes it apparent that the profession's collective focus has been almost fully on the collection of statistics, and not on their application for management purposes. This is a matter of no small concern. We are a profession that is at once awash in numbers, and at the same time bewildered about their numerousness and skeptical as to their useful-

Bruce Morton is Head of the Reference Department, Montana State University Libraries, Bozeman, MT 59717-0022.

The author would like to express special gratitude to Thomas A. Bremer of the Montana State University Libraries Reference Department, and Shannon V. Taylor, Assistant Professor of Business Management and Administration at Montana State University, for their willingness to consider, and give advice about, the issues discussed in this essay.

ness. A less quoted, but nonetheless significant profundity in regard to lies was uttered by Pindar; paraphrased to my present intent, it goes something like this: Do not steep your speech in statistics; the test of a good manager is in action.

Unfortunately, Burns's observation of a decade and a half ago, that the compilation of statistical data on library functions is too often based on tradition or habit with unclear purpose and is used, if used at all, in a relatively unsophisticated way, is still just as valid today.[1] Most reference librarians still remain unconvinced of the worth of collecting data, and, if they do collect it, they are uncertain of the best method and of what data to collect. The main incentive to collect data still comes from administrators' pressure for some sort of quantitative measure.[2]

Paul Dressel has observed that in the field of higher education much has been made of the distinction between administration and management. Whereas the administrator conducts affairs for the benefit of others, the manager controls, directs, or conducts affairs with efficiency and frugality. The implication is that purposes or objectives are reached, or not reached, because of decisions made, or not made, by the manager. Related to the word ménage, management has overtones of training and maintaining a collection of wild animals (or, in this case, providing access to a collection of information) — the infomenagerie.[3] The problem is that librarians have become acculturated to doing without. They have managed so long, sometimes effectively, without an empirical sense of what is being done. Intuition does not suffice. Indeed, intuition has not sufficed, and that we delude ourselves that it has is one reason why most reference departments are ill-managed. This is not to say that they operate poorly or function badly, or that they provide bad service. Managing, in the daily patois of the library is as any ordinary dictionary would suggest, "to bring about, succeed in accomplishing, to take charge or care of, to contrive to get along, to conduct affairs" — in other words, *coping*.

To provide good service under such conditions of *management* more often than not it is necessary merely to react to perceptions of patron or client demand. However, if one looks to a business dictionary the definition has an edge, a cold clarity, that bespeaks a frame of reference to which statistical data might usefully be applied: ". . . planning, organizing, and controlling any enterprise . . . planning the work, staffing with competent personnel, directing the activities of subordinates and representing their views to superiors, coordinating various activities in order to meet overall goals."

OF NUMERPHOBES AND NUMERPHRENES

The integrity of any statistical data is only as good as the integrity of those collecting it; put more vernacularly—garbage in, garbage out. Data are not created in a blessed state. They are not inherently good or right—or, for that matter, bad or wrong. The usefulness of any statistical data is dependent on the person using them; numbers of and in themselves tell us nothing. The informative value of statistical data is based on several factors: (1) the clarity with which they are presented, i.e., reported; (2) the ingenuity with which they are interpreted; and (3) the purpose with which they are applied. The bottom line—an important concept when dealing with numbers—is *CAVEAT COUNTER*. Without careful planning and application, there is no guarantee that even quality data input will equal quality information output.

White is quite correct in the assertion that, "if librarians go to the trouble of keeping statistics, they ought to get something out of them locally, in their own management information systems."[4] The problem however is that too often—far too often—there are no local management *systems*. Library managers will take whatever numbers that are available and see what can be made of them. For management purposes this is statistical roulette. Not using the potential management information that can be gained from the proper application of statistical data is a regrettable situation worthy of remediation. However, the incorrect application of such data is even more egregious because instead of not addressing issues and not making decisions, the wrong issues may be addressed and the wrong decisions made, all without any apprehension on the part of the righteous statistician; passive ignorance is preferable to active ignorance.

Howard D. White is perceptive when he notes the existence of an anti-statistical bias among reference librarians: "Probably no one likes doing something while at the same time trying to record what is being done, particularly when customer pressure is high."[5] In all types of libraries and in all aspects of reference service, investigation has seldom gone beyond the first stage of measurement, i.e., description in quantitative terms.[6] The managerial question that is begged after quantification and description is, so what—what now? a light but cold-hearted assessment groups librarians who resist the use of statistical data as a management tool into several categories of resistance:

- Statistical myopia: Collect only what asked to collect with no idea of what to do with the data after collected except pass it on to some higher up.
- Statistical lacadasia: There is a resistance to collecting statistics because no one will do anything with them. A subset of this is the "halo effect," which holds that statistics are in and of themselves good, but . . .
- Statistical megalomania: There is a desire to collect every statistic possible, to want to know more than is needed to know, and no idea of what to do with the mass of data that has been collected.
- Statistical dementia: There is no idea of what one wants to know and no idea of how to collect the data to find out.
- Statistical overload: Holds that the collection of statistical data is a counter-productive process because it is too labor-intensive and will detract from the provision of service.

REASONS FOR COLLECTING STATISTICAL DATA

As a management tool statistical data can be applied to provide insight into demand based on volume of traffic. Trends can be noted and monitored. Relationships can be established between various service elements if comparable methods of collection are used—i.e., same data sets vis-à-vis time periods reported. Comparability of data is extremely important to establish internal correlations between, say, on-line searches, interlibrary loan service, and reference service. Relationships also may be internal/external, in that an empirically measurable external factor such as enrollment or number of course offerings may affect (or not) demands for services and, concomitantly, bear on staff and budget resources needed to meet demand. It is quite feasible, for instance, that although annual gross reference transactions as reported have decreased as has enrollment, but it will able to be shown that actual traffic on a per capita basis has increased.

The response of 37 groups of American Library Association (ALA) members considering the needs or reasons for collecting statistical information listed the following in priority of importance:[7]

1. Staffing patterns/traffic levels
2. Budget justification and allocation
3. Patron needs
4. Collection development & weeding
5. Evaluation of service
6. Kinds of service & use; pattern and kind of patron contact
7. Staff training, development, and efficiency
8. Objectives, priorities, and planning
9. National statistics on reference service
10. Patron affiliation, occupation, or residence

Consider the above data with the following five major reference service data needs suggested by Robert S. Runyon that library administrators, university officials, and others have:[8]

1. Measures that reflect the effects of policy, procedure, and organization.
2. Supporting data for budget requests and allocation of funds.
3. Feedback data on patron behavior.
4. Historical data for analysis of change over time, and/or for comparison with other libraries.
5. Internal data communication between department head and library administration.

Each reference manager must determine for himself/herself, based on local need, what is to be counted and how. There are guides that will prove useful[9] in engendering and focusing thought and discussion on this issue, although none should be adopted as a way to abrogate the responsibility for determination by local management of their own needs. In addition to the outline offered by Runyon and Lynch I offer a simplified alternative, not as a prescription or panacea, but as another point of embarkation.

Reference Services

What: Desk traffic: A count of pure volume of reference desk transactions. This is a simple count with no distinction made as to kind of question or degree of difficulty. Such subdata can be accomplished by means of sampling as will be discussed later in this essay.

How reported: By time of day in hourly or half-hourly increments, by week of the term, term of academic year, and by academic year.

Why: Need to show demand for service, need to show patterns of demand chronologically in order to respond with allocation of staff, want to discover any correlation with other service elements.

On-Line Services

What: Number of searches (volume); vendor used to gain access to data base; kind of search (billed or quick ref); status of patron; department affiliation of patron; costs; searcher; data base.

How reported: By week of the term, term of academic year, and by academic year.

Why: Number of searches (volume) will demonstrate demand; vendor used to gain access to data base will help make decisions in regard to anticipated usage when considering cost levels of subscription contracts; kind of search (billed or quick ref) will allow the manager to determine budget request for quick ref search support while billed search data will permit the estimation of income via search surcharges when cross-tabulated with cost data; status of patron allows insight into what levels of the curriculum are relying on on-line services; or to what degree on-line service support students at various levels; department affiliation of patron likewise gives insight into the degree to which on-line service support the work of students and faculty in the various departments of the university; the monitoring costs will permit the cross-tabulation with other data elements; searcher information provides insight into amount of searching and patterns of data base use by individual searchers, thereby providing a basis for personnel evaluation and assessment of patterns of data base use that can be applied to staff development decisions; and data base information can provide information that will be useful in decisions that relate to training staff as well as decisions in regard to the cost-benefits of purchasing alternative data base access, such as contracting with a data base producer (e.g., deal directly with Chemical Abstracts Service rather than using DIALOG) or one of the new CD-ROM products.

Instructional Services

What: Volume/demand; kind of instruction; department; course/subject; librarian; and number of students (impact/volume).

How Reported: By week of the term, term of academic year, and by academic year.

Why: The number of instructional sessions needs to be monitored in order to establish the demand for library support; the kind of instruction, orientation or class-related, is important in its proportion as characterizing the nature of the instruction program; the department for which instruction is done is useful in terms of possible correlations with increases in on-line services, reference desk, or ILL traffic as well as in showing library support for particular elements of the curriculum, which might have collection development implications; data as to the course and subject for which instruction was provided can also be used to correlate with on-line services, reference desk, or ILL data; data about the participation of librarians in the program is useful for purposes of evaluation and designing staff development efforts; and finally, the number of students reached through instruction is useful as a gauge of program impact as well as an interesting correlate in trying to interpret all other public service data.

Interlibrary Services

What: Data that is contained within the requirement of the national standard ILL form. The total volume of ILL traffic for both borrowing and lending functions; borrower patron characteristics; lender institution characteristics; borrowing institution characteristics; and success rates.

How reported: By week of the term, term of academic year, and by academic year.

Why: The total volume of ILL traffic for both borrowing and lending functions is essential in order to demonstrate demand for the service, the need for budget and staff support, to document the role of the collection in networking, and to monitor trends in both borrowing and lending; characteristics of patrons borrowing books are important in that it can provide valuable insight into deficiencies in the collection and consequently be used as a collection development tool, and, of course, department/course affiliation is important to profile the support role of the ILL operation; the data about lender institution characteristics provides insight as to what libraries are relied upon for support and the degree of reliance, which might be significant in considering agreement of reciprocity; data about libraries borrowing materials likewise is useful in decisions of reciprocity or in the assessment of fees; and success rate in filing requests is important in evaluating effectiveness of the ILL operation.

Microform Services

What: Material category (refiling); prints (copy or coin counts); head counts (entry); reliability of machines (refunds); time of day.

How reported: By time of day in hourly or half-hourly increments, by week of the term, term of academic year, and by academic year.

Why: The most reliable revelation of the importance of microforms is an exact count of materials refiled (this can be done within designated categories for additional information, e.g., ERIC fiche, college catalog fiche, other fiche, newspaper film, other film, etc., which gives a sense of how much the collection is used and the proportionate use); prints made with reader/

printers are tabulated by means of counters in the machines or by coin counts in order to document use levels of, and reliance on, the machines, which may influence decisions to purchase additional machines, to enter into service contracts, and estimate need for paper and toner; if the microform facility is monitored by library personnel, head counts of persons entering the microform area give an indication of traffic and demand on a per capita basis; reliability of machines can be monitored by noting refunds made per machine in order to help make decisions as to the need for repair, service contracts, or upgrading to newer equipment; and, in addition to the obvious relevance for anticipating staffing needs, time of day can be correlated with all of the above categories, and, in turn, be correlated with other public service operations.

This is by no means intended to be comprehensive. To repeat, local *need* should prevail. However, in any case, each element should be reported uniformly in the compatible time frames (note "how reported" above), thereby assuring the possibility for meaningful chronological correlations (see Figure 1).

Once a decision is made as to what statistics to collect, careful consideration should be given to the method of data collection. Collection forms should be constructed so that three criteria are met:

1. That registering data will not be onerous for the librarians staffing the service point. When data collection detracts from the ability to provide service, data collection at that point becomes counterproductive.
2. That the data processor's job is made as efficient as possible. Although data processors are usually clerical staff, it is a good idea to consult with them as one sets up the data collection and report programs. The idea behind collecting statistics is that their application will eventually contribute to more efficient operation. If clerical staff get bogged down processing data, efficiency at this level might be sacrificed. The transfer of raw data from tally sheets should be as easy and routine as possible.
3. That prior consultation with all staff levels from the clerical to the highest administrative level should be undertaken.

Statistics can be helpful to all elements of the service operation and each level should have the opportunity to suggest
data and reporting format that might be useful to them in
gaining insight into operations from their own unique perspective.

Once a commitment is made to the collection of statistics, a
careful assessment of what management information is desired
must be made. It is important that the need to know be balanced

		Management Posture	
		OFFENSIVE	DEFENSIVE
Level of Accountability	STAFF	Gauge performance Show productivity Show efficiency	Prove efficiency Demonstrate need Defend efficiency
	SELF	Assess program Assess productivity Assess efficiency Plan for future	Defend program Prove management Defend staff need Influence plans
	SUPERIORS	Correlate operations Show demand for service Show accomplishment Formulate plan	Correlate external factors Stave off budget cuts Defend program Argue for plan

Figure 1: Accountability/Posture Matrix

In each of the above instances statistical information may be invoked for
management purposes. There is a tendency in the offensive mode to apply
statistics inductively, while the defensive mode invites deductive
application. The Reference manager needs to ask in each case, what data
is required--to collect and to report?

against ability to collect and process data and output information. If there is not a need, or reasonably anticipated need to know, do not count it — if there is, do. Of course, the cumbersomeness of manually doing this has been the biggest deterrent to effective collection and use of numerical data for management purposes. In addition to the consideration of what to count, thought must be given to *how* to count it — in what detail, in what time frame, etc. For instance, I have encountered situations where a reference department was reporting its transactions on a weekly basis within the context of the academic term, while the circulation department was reporting its transactions and gate traffic on a monthly basis. Now, any library manager knows that there may be a likely correlation between the ebb and flow of both traffic into the library and books checked out of the library with the business done at the reference desk. However, the lack of effective managerial planning for data collection and effective reporting made any meaningful correlation impossible. Because of this oversight, potential application of correlative data was eliminated from the manager's options. This is only an isolated example; similar ones may be found in almost any library.

In terms of the data that has been traditionally collected by reference managers, there seems to be a curiously abiding fixation with the issue of professional versus nonprofessional service at the reference desk. It is certain that there are going to be x percent directional questions, which ideally might be handled by nonprofessional staff. However, there is an unpredictability to their occurrence, and if it cannot be reasonably predicted when such directional or nonsubstantive questions will occur a manager must decide whether service goals are better met by having a librarian on duty to field the most difficult question that may be presented at any given time, or to have a nonprofessional on duty with the capability of calling for librarian assistance should the nondirectional question be presented.

Reference desk data indicating a frequency distribution by category of question based on reference desk schedule could be most useful in first determining whether frequency (or infrequency) of certain types of questions would support the use of nonprofessional staff with minimal negative impact. Secondly, it would be possible to determine whether there were certain time periods within the reference schedule, based on experience, when a high proportion of directional questions could be anticipated. However, as Lopez has noted, there is difficulty that is inherent in trying to define sharply and unambiguously "the reference question." Perceptions as to type of question and measurement of response are too dependent on variables such as competence and experience of the reference librarian; the scope, arrangement, and quality of the reference collection itself; and the proximity and adequacy of the library's main catalog.[10] Yet, the fixation on this particular statistic can be traced to the so-called standardization of library statistical data.

Because reference librarians have refused, ignored, or failed their responsibility for the adaption, implementation, and interpretation of the statistical techniques, criteria, and standards for analysis of local reference service, inadequate and/or inappropriate techniques and performance indexes have been imposed.[11] Witness the several national surveys to which most academic libraries annually respond. The bifurcation of reference activity into the "reference transaction" and "directional transaction" is now legitimized in the profession's statistical catechism, the *Library Data Collection Handbook*.[12]

NATIONAL SURVEYS: THE TAILS THAT WAG REFERENCE MANAGERS

To no small degree, librarians have made their own contribution to the dilemma. As government, business, and industry have developed various techniques such as cost-benefit accounting and analysis, programmed formula budgeting, etc., for evaluation, measurement, planning, and decision-making, libraries have continued to collect statistical data in the time-worn manner of book acquired and processed, user attendance, and reference questions. Such figures are not significant of and in themselves, nor have they generally been interpreted in a meaningful manner.[13]

Indeed, in 1974 the sense of the ALA's Library Administration Division's Library Organization and Management Section's

Committee on Statistics for Reference Service was that a major problem in the consideration of reference measurement has been its orientation toward techniques rather than needs, with the result being that reference statistics have been collected but not used intelligently.[14] The 1976 Library and General Information Survey (LIBGIS) administered under the aegis of the National Center for Education Statistics was the first instance that libraries on a national scale were asked to report tallies of reference transactions. The 20th Higher Education General Information Survey (HEGIS, the successor to LIBGIS) administered in Autumn 1985 keys eight responses (lines 45-52) to questions of public service: question 48 inquires as to reference transactions in a typical week (defined as those contacts requiring the use of information resources) and question 49, on the other hand, asks for directional transactions per typical week (defined as contacts not requiring the use of information resources). The ACRL Academic Library Statistics Survey asks for public service hours (line 43), reference transactions (line 45), number of presentations to groups (line 46), number of persons served in presentations (line 47), and on-line data base services (line 48).[15]

Both of these statistical vehicles serve as a motivation for academic libraries to collect certain statistics. The HEGIS survey has been administered ten years longer than the ACRL, therefore most academic libraries have been conditioned by its demands and definitions of statistical categories. Now there exists in draft form a two-page survey from the ALA LAMA Statistics Committee that once again requires response in terms of "number of reference transactions during typical week" and "number of directional questions during typical week." The LAMA survey also solicits data as to person hours during each hour (based on on-the-hour increments, e.g., 8-9, etc.) and how many of those hours were nonprofessional. Yet, for all of this standardization of collection and reporting, the very real problems that were perceived in 1974 by the ALA Library Administration Division's Library Organization and Management Section's Committee on Statistics for Reference Service essentially still exist. This is still an orientation toward techniques rather than needs, with the result being that reference statistics have been collected but not used intelligently.

Indeed, the legacy of the emphasis on statistics collection and reporting for national surveys is what has been described as the profession's limited and narrow thinking in terms of how to define and report several limited categories of measurement.[16] As the momentum for standardized reporting grew at the national level, librarians overlooked obvious local in-house needs for data; the macro diverted attention from the micro. The effect of the entrenchment of such national surveys is that they have conditioned the profession to the kind of statistics it collects and its expectations of what will be done with them. Academic libraries are motivated to respond to the HEGIS survey because not to do so risks the loss of federal support. They respond to the ACRL survey out of professional conscience, since most academic libraries are institutional members of ACRL, or their administrators are personal members. It remains to be seen what the incentive to fill out the LAMA survey will be. The kind of gross public service statistics that are reported in such surveys have very limited use.

Primarily, they provide a measure for comparison among institutions. One can choose an institution that is deemed similar and compare volume of reference service or entering traffic. However, there are so many variables at each institution that the reliability of any conclusions drawn from such comparisons are suspect. Or, perhaps from this mass data a profile of the average academic library can be distilled? Good luck. I have been in many libraries and have yet to recognize the *average* library, if indeed, I or anyone else has ever seen it.

The Management Information System

White's recognition of SPSS® as a means of creating a management information data base that could do sophisticated cross-tabulations of data in order to gain insight into what was being done is an important contribution.[17] However, technology and software have advanced in the last five years so that more useful and inviting (user-friendly) alternatives are available to the reference manager. Smith and Hutton, reference librarians at Purdue University, created a simple statistics package for reference statistics compatible with Apple II + ™ and IIe™ microcomputers.

The program will run cross tabulations on any two designated fields from among (1) day of week, (2) month, (3) hour, (4) minute, (5) answerer, (6) type of question, (7) duration in minutes, (8) duration in seconds, (9) in person or phone, (10) patron type, (11) source, and (12) subject.[18] The work of White and Smith and Hutton is noteworthy because it reflects the recognition of need. These efforts, and others like them, represent the beginning stages of the quest for a management information system that will meet the needs of the reference manager.

In order to avail oneself of the benefits of management potential of statistics, one need not necessarily know how to execute such sophisticated statistical operations as Bayesian, Chi-square, regression, time-series, correlation, or factor analysis, analysis of variance, the T test, and nonparametric tests. If applied to public service operations such statistical operations can give valuable managerial insights into what is happening at the reference desk or other service points. Unfortunately, for the most part, librarians have not been and are not being trained in library schools in the managerial art of the application of statistics. Library educators need to recognize the need to augment library management courses to assure the development of an appreciation for the utility of statistical data as a management tool. They also need to take broad positive steps to remediate oversights of the past and undertake extended education programs, similar to the efforts of Terry Brooks of the University of Washington and George D'Elia of the University of Minnesota, who are doing on-the-road workshops to raise the statistical aptitude of librarians. One hopes that this education oversight will now change in all library schools parallel with the advent of preprogrammed software packages available for mainframe, mini, and micro computers, e.g., SPSS®, Lotus 1-2-3®, JAZZ®, dBase III®, Microsoft™ Chart® (see figures in Appendix A for sample input/output). These and many others that are presently available, as well as the many that will continue to enter the marketplace to offer even more sophistication, have the ability to manage records, process, format, and report data, and interface with graphic output capabilities for graphing and charting. Librarians do not need to become mathematicians or statisticians, but rather, in the next decade need to become statistics literate just as they have had to become computer literate during the past decade. Indeed, it is the ubiquity of the computer that has made possible the relatively easy and universal invocation of statistics as a management tool.

Standard deviation provides a measurement of dispersion from the average. How dispersed are values around some measurement of central tendency? In order to determine a standard deviation it is necessary to make complete counts for the same period of time that one might eventually wish to predict based on sampling. If one wants to know if there is a significant difference between two groups, the standard deviation of the end groups must be known. In order to effectively use already collected data to predict future phenomena by sampling, thereby reducing the labor intensity of data collection, a standard deviation is necessary.[19]

Then there is the question of centralized versus decentralized information systems. Runyon in his important essay on the need for management information systems in libraries delineates the need and the potential impact.[20] However, at the time Runyon wrote his excellent article he did not have the insight provided by the experience of the rapid proliferation of library automation during the 1980s. Usually the integrated automated system available in libraries in the more advanced stages of automation is a centralized system that will collect and generate data about the circulation function, use of the catalog, cataloging, monitor acquisitions, orders, and expenditures. However, the other public service operations such as reference, on-line searching, interlibrary services, and microform services, will still need to rely on a decentralized information system because data is not electronically captured as part of the transaction itself, but rather manually noted and later entered into an automated system. Although, with the advent of ILL subsystems on the major bibliographic utilities, much ILL data about a library's use of the subsystem is made available automatically. However, the data is not tailored to individual needs nor are all of any library's ILL transactions likely to be conducted using the ILL subsystem.

All managers in the library, not the least of whom is the manager of reference services, need to assess their relationship to, and with, extant information management capabilities. The question to ask is whether an existing system will adapt to reference needs, or whether a separate satellite management information system should be developed. The first level of access required is on a transactional basis. There is a need for a data base that records reference transactions, on-line searches, microform usage, instructional sessions or other relevant occurrences. Next, there must be the means to plot the data. One must be able to look at the numbers so that the initial engagement of the data provides an opportunity for inductive suggestion — do the data suggest hypotheses? At this point statistical analyses can be brought to bear on the data in order to prove hypotheses null or positive.

The management information system to which we aspire also should have a structured decision support system that will address decisions that must be made on a relatively regular basis. What data are needed to make those decisions? Such matters as staff evaluation, budget requests, schedules, etc. are predictable in their occurrence and in the kinds of data that will be useful in providing insight into performance or need.

Another element of the decision support system that is required for reference management is the capacity to respond to ad hoc inquiries. Such a system would permit one to think of a unique problem or question, ask what if . . . , call up the appropriate data on a CRT screen or print it out in any one of several charted, graphed, or numerical formats so that this information may be interpreted and then applied for purposes of management.

CONCLUSION

Like the search for the unicorn, reference librarians' search for an empirical measure for user satisfaction and quality of reference service remains at this time mythically elusive. Calabretta and Ross recognized this and dropped collection of data that tracked whether question was answered or not because almost all staff members perceived themselves as answering the question and it was impossible to go back and analyze queries.[21] With the ability to superimpose, cross-tabulate, analyze statistically, and graphically present data in ways that until now had been out of reach of the mortal reference manager, perhaps it will not be long until we will be able to have data from which we shall be able to accurately and dependably infer matters of quality and satisfaction.

At some point in the future there will be developed a set of models especially tailored for libraries into which data can be inserted, retrieved for a discrete purpose, and projected on a screen. Runyon recognized that this would not be likely to happen until the profession begins to think through decision-making needs in terms of a comprehensive management information system, over and above the need for consistent rules in counting public service transactions and other operational minutia.[22] He is correct. This is clearly demonstrable by what remains to be the present state of affairs. We need to move beyond a collection and measurement mind-set, and begin thinking in terms of application of statistical data. We must move beyond the use of data to describe what we do to where we can make valid interpretations of a wide range of data.

The resources for research and development, experience with statistical modeling, programming, and software development and marketing lie in the private sector. As has been seen time and time again, the private sector is not likely to develop such a system until a need, a market, is apparent. Such a need must be articulated by the potential users — the managers. This is the first step. We must now begin to reeducate ourselves in terms of what statistical data can do for the manager. We cannot afford the luxury of waiting until the technology and applications are invented, for the technology and applications are already in use in the business world. Whether such systems are developed to be part of the centralized integrated library system, or to be adjunct stand-alone satellite systems to be mounted on microcomputers is irrelevant. What is most important is that the modeling capability be pursued, so that *local* statistcs can be applied to the operational model. This would be a quantum leap from the relatively unsophisticated data base-management and graphic-presentation packages that are now available (see Appendix A for sample). Library educators, the professional associations, and practicing librarians must in concert begin working on an agenda that will finally give us the management tools necessary to do the complex job of managing a library. The question is, can we count on it?

NOTES

1. Robert W. Burns, Jr., "An Empirical Rationale for the Accumulation of Statistical Information," *Library Resources & Technical Services* 18 (Summer 1974): 254-58.

2. Samuel Rothstein, "The Measurement of Reference Service," *Library Trends* 12 (January 1964): 456.

3. Paul L. Dressel, "Mission, Organization, and Leadership," *Journal of Higher Education* 58 (January/February 1987): 101.

4. Howard D. White, "Measurement at the Reference Desk," *Drexel Library Quarterly* 17 (Winter 1981): 3.

5. *Ibid*: 28.

6. Rothstein: 457.

7. Katherine Emerson, "Symposium on Measurement of Reference," *RQ* 14 (Fall 1974): 8.

8. Robert S. Runyon, "The Library Administrator's Need for Measures of Reference," *RQ* 14 (Fall 1974): 10-11.

9. See Robert S. Runyon, "Towards the Development of a Library Information System," *College and Research Libraries* 42 (November 1981): 546-48 for a descriptive outline of a decision support system summary report; and see Mary Jo Lynch (ed.), *Library Data Collection Handbook* (Chicago: American Library Association, 1981), 37-92 for a classification scheme for recording and reporting information about libraries.

10. Manuel D. Lopez, "Academic Reference Service," *RQ* 12 (Spring 1973): 235-36.

11. *Ibid*: 240-41.

12. Mary Jo Lynch (ed.), see especially pp. 142 and 190. This report was prepared for the National Center for Education Statistics and distributed by the Office of Research of the American Library Association.

13. Lopez: 234.

14. Emerson: 7.

15. See *Higher Education General Information Survey (HEGIS XX)*, ED (NCES) Form 2300-5-85, "Part VI-Library Service per Typical Week, Fall 1985," 5-6; and see also *ACRL Academic Library Statistics Survey, 1986* (Chicago, IL: Association of College and Research Libraries, 1986), 4.

16. Runyon, "Towards the Development of a Library Management Information System": 540.

17. See White: 3-35.

18. Dana E. Smith, "Create: Customized Reference Statistics Programs," *American Libraries* 15 (March 1984): 179.

19. See Michael Halperin, "Reference Sampling," *RQ* 14 (Fall 1974): 20-23 for

detailed discussion and formulas for sampling reference traffic that emphasizes the need for determination of the standard deviation.

20. Runyon: 539-47.

21. Nancy Calabretta & Rosalinda Ross, "Analysis of Reference Transactions Using Packaged Computer Programs," *Medical Reference Services Quarterly* 3 (Fall 1984): 39.

22. Runyon: 541.

APPENDIX A

Sample input/output Microsoft™ Chart®

PLOT FALL '86

A1. INPUT: From this data
grid all other charts
and graphs in Appendix
A are generated.

week	RQs
1	1278
2	1622
3	2662
4	1854
5	2080
6	2330
7	1823
8	1854
9	1522
10	1230
11	1452
12	870

A2. OUTPUT: List by week
Reference desk traffic.

Fall '86

week	RQs
1	1278
2	1622
3	2662
4	1854
5	2080
6	2330
7	1823
8	1854
9	1522
10	1230
11	1452
12	870

APPENDIX A, continued

A.3 OUTPUT: By week the
     percentage of Reference
     desk traffic.

Percentages of Fall '86

week	RQs
1	6%
2	8%
3	13%
4	9%
5	10%
6	11%
7	9%
8	9%
9	7%
10	6%
11	7%
12	4%

4. OUTPUT: Cumulative sum of Reference Desk traffic by week.
   Figures A4, A4.1, and A4.2 all are generated from the original
   plot.

Cumulative sum of Fall '86

week	RQs
1	1278
2	2900
3	5562
4	7416
5	9496
6	11826
7	13649
8	15503
9	17025
10	18255
11	19707
12	20577

APPENDIX A, continued

A4.1 OUTPUT:
Cumulative sum of Reference desk transactions by week graphed against
weekly Reference desk transactions. Bar chart.

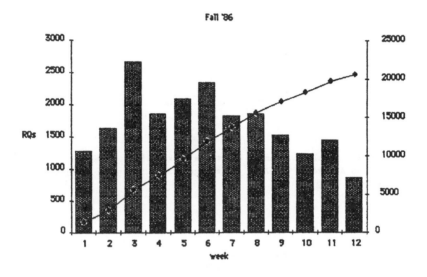

A4.2: OUTPUT:
Cumulative sum of Reference desk transactions by week graphed against
weekly Reference desk transactions. Area chart.

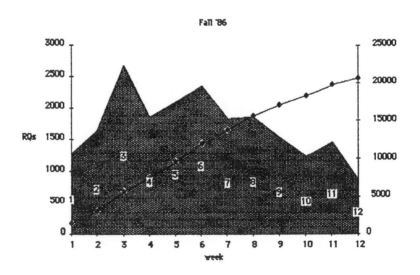

APPENDIX A, continued

A5. OUTPUT
Statistical values for the Fall '86 Reference desk data that
was plotted in Figure A1.

Statistics on Fall '86

X	Y
# of points	12
Maximum	2662
Minimum	870
Average	1714.75
Median	1823
Std. Deviation	496.70278748
Corr. Coeff.	-0.479371297

A 5.1 OUTPUT:
Statistical values for Fall '86 Reference desk traffic graphically presented.

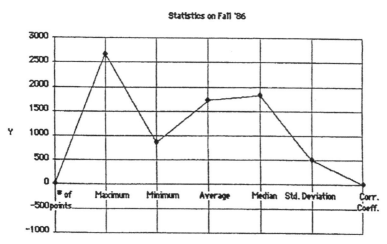

Statistics on Fall '86

Budgeting and Financing Reference Services: Managing the Unexpected and Unpredictable

Gerard B. McCabe
Constance E. Gamaluddin

SUMMARY. Reference librarians and administrators who hope to master the possibilities of reference and information services must build flexibility into planning and implementation of the reference budget. This paper emphasizes the importance of shared fiscal responsibility with a high degree of budget management delegated to the department.

Effective interpolation of departmental objectives, changing user demands, rapid developments in library technology, and the plethora of available reference materials amid prevailing fiscal exigencies presents a challenge to the most experienced professional. Cost control through ongoing evaluation of collection and services, deselection of outmoded or little used resources, careful use of staff time, and careful review of new materials is essential. Margin for change is also critical. Flexibility in the reference budget can make planning for the unexpected and the unpredictable possible and insure that the reference unit has an opportunity to innovate rather than stagnate.

INTRODUCTION

This paper expresses both an administrative and operational view of reference services, with concern for quality of services,

Gerard B. McCabe is Director of Libraries and Constance E. Gamaluddin is Head of Reference and Information Services at Carlson Library, Clarion University of Pennsylvania, Clarion, PA 16214-1232.

for costs and cost control, reductions in budget support when required, and optimum use of increases when made available.

ADMINISTRATIVE BUDGET DEVELOPMENT

In this time of rapidly changing technology, tight funding, and high community use, finding the best way to budget library departments requires careful thinking, creativity, and breaking away from traditional approaches. Our times require high operational flexibility. A not overly generous budget requires cautious management, so how can a department have budgetary leeway? Is budget decentralization a reasonable solution? The authors discuss these ideas and propose not abandonment of administrative responsibility but recognition that flexibility is a key to success in a rapidly changing environment. What is proposed is the transfer of the decision making responsibility thereby permitting a department to shift supporting funds among types of expenditure as part of its operating plan.

Achieving this comes through a thorough planning process identifying a set of departmental objectives for longer than one year (White 1984:170) subsequently funded after joint review by managers and librarians. Emphasis is on the pursuit of objectives in keeping with the library's goals for its services (Martin 1978:97-7).

Good reference service involves more than a reference librarian knowing how and where to find information timely and effectively. Before even basic questions are answered, important decisions are reached. Who is assisted? At what level? What staffing is necessary? What type and size of collection will support desired service? At some point, library mission and goals have been considered, if only in the broad sense that "we serve everyone" or "we serve only the university community." Along those lines, "we will meet basic information needs . . . or will or will not build the collection to meet specialized research needs." Somewhere in these ruminations, an experienced reference librarian will develop some feel for whether the optimum has been reached or if a concerted effort is needed to upgrade collection and services.

With staff participation in the planning process and setting of objectives, frequent consultation between and among departmental librarians and library managers assists in assuring understanding by all of what is to be done or achieved. Management places decision making at the operational level by providing authority for fund shifting, control, and planning over a longer time period. Librarians and managers center their attention not on what to do this coming year but rather on what is proposed for achievement over the longer period of time. The time length is whatever appears most practical to the people involved. With a plan formulated and funding secured for the time period, budget movement from expenditure code or allocation code is initiated at the operating level with management providing only technical support and control through a budget officer (Martin 1978:21).

A heavy load of professional responsibilities may preclude more than a cursory survey of current status and future plans for reference and information services. Yet it can be argued that only through careful analysis can an appropriate range of goals and objectives be developed. Typically, needs assessments are made at the operating level in libraries. The reference staff must address some serious questions: Is our collection adequate to meet all, most, or some of user requests? Is our staffing adequate in expertise, numbers, and experience? Are paraprofessionals used when professionals should be, or the reverse? What role should innovation have in our future reference service? How can the fiscal needs of expanding reference service be best addressed? What changes in reference service may be necessitated by an evolving academic clientele? Are greater numbers of returning adults and changing attitudes about education likely to create more stringent demands (Ordovensky 1986:1)?

After conferences of librarians and managers, perceived needs are translated into a budget request to the institutional administration (Martin 1978:94-97). By decentralizing the budget and its control some steps toward alleviating or addressing known needs are reduced.

What about priorities? With librarians reviewing and setting them and management concurring, the decision then is to organize priorities from among the objectives and plan for achievement within the agreed time period. With budget allocations reflecting commitment, everything is set for a beginning; now to make it work. First the two budgets, operating and collections, are separated, the former supplying the basic fuel running the department, and the latter the bread and butter of creative opportunity sought by the librarians. With this budget the collection is built, managed and changed as needs and judgment require. These two budgets are more fully identified in the following sections.

Building the Reference Operating Budget

For any operating library department, the administrative support costs include salaries, telephone, supplies, photocopying, printing, and training; costs common to all departments of a library often are stated in a general budget and not distributed. Costs originating with services: on-line searching, interlibrary loans, and bibliographic instruction, can be stated separately. All of these together are the reference department's operating budget.

Preferring staff built budgets, the authors advocate library administration and departments working together to build each departmental budget, simplified by an on-line financial record system using object codes for expense categories (White 1974:172). With on-line support absent the budget can be organized on a microcomputer or manually at the cost of additional labor. The objective, each department managing its own budget, in the case of reference service is clearly beneficial. No change in the department's role occurs but it better enables the department to exercise control over its own destiny, plan services, and execute changes, while retaining its established service objectives. The latter an important point for if the department offers on-line searching to users, it is a service objective, something not subject to arbitrary change, and supported. In rising cost situations, the department has the opportunity to shift funding from other costs to sustain the service. Also, the option exists for modification of on-line searching services by restricting quantities, limiting off-line printing, and other means to stay within the budget.

The authors are not concerned with relating cost and performance but with funding the department and managing its budget. Service cuts on the basis of cost alone are undesirable. This point is well explained by McClure's paper reporting the deletion of a service from a reference department because of high cost (McClure 1986:327).

> Because cost data tend not to be related to the quality of a service, decision making becomes cost driven rather than program or service driven. They provided a number of examples. In one instance, a bibliographic instruction program was eliminated after the department head conducted a study of the program's costs. Although it was highly regarded by faculty and was assessed as very effective, the costs were seen as excessive and thus, it was eliminated. When departments lack clear service objectives (as most apparently did), the cost data are viewed in isolation and decisions, apparently were made solely on a cost basis. The interviewees objected strongly to such uses of cost data.

The printing code offers a simple example of budget control. Every so often reference prints a library handbook, a decision requiring planning and cost projection. Usually a plan is developed and a request presented to administration. If funds are provided, the handbook is published. If not the handbook ages another year or goes out of print. Allocating a sum for this expense as part of the department budget, subject to shifting from year to year provides funds for audiovisual production of instructional media, tapes or video cassettes, or other uses, returning to printing when the need for a new handbook returns. Long-range planning is necessary, and the department remains in control of its operating budget with funding assured each year for changes required by the objectives.

Staff training is another example. When services require staff skills updated, new manuals may suffice or staff must travel to a training site, either way this ongoing cost is covered and the funds shifted to provide what is needed.

Building this budget requires long-range planning as implied by both examples. Experience might show that the handbook is outdated typically every three years, so the replacement effort must start early in the third year culminating in a new edition. Rather than go through the budget building cycle every third year, through planning two other objectives are scheduled for the first and second years. The same budget does this. Funding is always available, is flexible, being shifted from one noncontinuing expense to another.

Ongoing expenses require another method of control; with a budget committed to the objective every year, how is this managed? On-line searching, beneficial to students, faculty and to community users, enjoys moderate increases every year. What are the approaches to controlling its expenditure rate while providing the highest quality service possible? Among the obvious are regular upgrading of staff skills, an expense related to staff training funds, control of users access by requiring use of other means for quick and easy information such as printed resources, compacting search questions through microcomputer software, training an hourly assistant to load precompressed disks and send queries at off peak load times; this possibly at the inconvenience of users but justifiable when funds are limited. Another new alternative uses laser disk storage for certain large databases and these are searched in-house off-line on a monitor connected to a disk reader; the ERIC database on CD-ROM from Silver Platter, Inc. is an example.

Now with the nuts and bolts operating budget driving the department, the funding that provides the major resources, especially the collection and the opportunity for innovation, requires examination. Here the situation changes, this is where great flexibility can achieve positive results. The following sections will explore the collection budget.

Collection Costs

In trying to examine reference collection costs in a scientific manner, it would be interesting to try the consumer price approach—variations in the cost of a library "market basket" since 1967. Very likely, there would be considerable difficulty in making parallel comparisons. Book prices would provide one viable unit of price comparison. But that comparison would not show the increased numbers of reference materials now available and those necessary to meet the more sophisticated needs of a user group accustomed to the wonders of the information age. A review of the specialized titles issued by a typical reference publisher alone (Gale, Oryx) boggles the mind.

Staffing also may provide an element of consistency, yet that does not permit adequate comparison of salary changes accommodating requirements for subject specialization, or technical expertise of some kind. Not prevalent in the 1967 market basket would be microfiche collections of the magnitude of Newsbank, ASI, SRI, College Catalog Collection on Microfiche, or services comparable to InfoTrac, Business Collection or similar. Computerized literature searching was just a twinkle in the eyes of information scientists, something akin to Star Trek for most librarians.

Note that staff members can influence the size of the operating budget, a larger staff requiring more supplies, generating more on-line searches, using telephones more. Allowing for possible inflation, a staff reduction can reduce pressure on the operating budget. Staff size, though, does not influence collection size. The reference staff may acquire many self-contained reference materials but limit the acquisition of titles requiring frequent supplementing for the simple reason of limited available labor.

In the last decade the scope of possibilities for a reference collection has increased in vast leaps while fiscal support has become correspondingly limited.

Collection Management

Reference collections are expensive concentrations of material with strong portions of the expense attributable to the serial nature of some of the materials. The expectation for this collection is a return in usefulness proportional to the cost. Often this is determined only subjectively by reference librarians perceiving through their daily experience just how well it meets user expectations. If reference librarians believe that particular titles or services are not helping their users, they need to find others that will.

Evaluation of competitive titles is a responsibility that reference librarians must observe for the good of their service. From the managers viewpoint, cost requires this ongoing evaluation and the time expended is a budget cost. Librarians must have the time, away from service, to do this. Staff size may be a factor in providing this time and the salaries budget is affected. If this is not possible then service time requires alteration so there is non-service time available.

Space is a controlling factor of size of a reference collection and its cost. Currently, the introduction of high concentration computer-based bibliographic data can create a need to adjust space allocations. The librarians must evaluate printed sources versus the machine records and determine if space for the new can be created by cancellation of the older sources. Recovering their costs can create funding for the new service, possibly not all of the cost. Space is costly and the budget allocation decisions must reflect that and not allow space to be consumed by collections to the detriment of other needs.

ADDING INFORMATION TECHNOLOGY

In the past few years, the reference service professional literature has devoted much space to articles on various types of technology, microcomputers, CD ROM, on-line catalogs, satellite television programming, and even robots at the reference desk (Smith 1986). Librarians are becoming ever more convinced that technology is the powerhouse behind good library service.

In addition to considerable sorting through the best, the worst, and the worthless among all of the innovations, evaluating implications for current and future service, the library very likely will face considerable fiscal exigencies. "The new environment is going to be an incredibly expensive one by any standard of the past or present. How do we maintain economy and still provide maximum service" (Snyder 1986:565)?

An unexpected budget expense in reference used to mean a few hundred dollars for a new encyclopedia. Now the damage is counted in thousands and often generates costs for staff training. The essentially static collection budget with a built-in inflation factor is no longer functional.

The rapidly changing kaleidoscope of information technology with its potential significance for reference services is of undisputed importance for the librarian and those responsible for the departmental collection budget. A new product like Information

Access' InfoTrac can easily consume a year's budget all of itself. Van Arsdale provides some perspective on this by noting its annual cost for a four-station system compared to the cost of the entire set of Wilson indexes (Van Arsdale 1986:515). Working even one year ahead on the reference budget can make accommodating innovative technology difficult; working in a multiyear time frame makes intelligent planning almost impossible at least without some reform in personal perspective. No doubt the times are changing and so must our method of planning for service and fiscal management.

Planning for technological innovation must receive increased emphasis in the budget process. Librarians must join their contemporaries in business and industry in implementing procedures for accurately predicting the unpredictable as well as building a corresponding flexibility into the budget. Opportunities for improved service should not be stifled automatically by a static collection budget. Somehow we must achieve the enviable balance between desirable ends and available means.

As Alvin Toffler stated in *Future Shock*,

> Today we need far more sophisticated criteria for choosing among technologies. We need such policy criteria not only to stave off avoidable disasters but to help us discover tomorrow's opportunities. Faced for the first time with technological overchoice, the society must now select its machines, processes, techniques and systems in groups and clusters, instead of one at a time (Toffler 1970:372).

Only within the past two decades have librarians had much incentive to develop strategies for innovational technological forecasting. Much of librarianship has been based on the anchor of tradition rather than the arrow of innovation. The impact of computer technology in all phases of librarianship and need for control in the information age have made significant inroads on the attitude of librarians. Librarians involved in bringing technology and other types of change to their libraries would likely concur that without planning, controlling innovation is akin to directing a team of runaway horses.

Corporate executives experienced in the intricacies of innovational planning suggest that for purposes of technological fore-casting it is not necessary to predict the actual form that the tech-nology will take (Morgan 1972:78). As in other types of forecasts, the goal is evaluation of the probability and signifi-cance of various possible developments. In recent years, it seems that new developments in the field have materialized like a genie out of a bottle with little advanced warning. In the rush of daily responsibilities we may have merely overlooked the signals of coming change. Preparing and budgeting for innovation may be a matter of becoming better attuned to the climate around us. It is important that the environment be monitored for signals that sug-gest what may be forerunners of technological change and iden-tify possible consequences for reference services and our li-braries. Radical new technological change rarely comes into common usage without some written clue of its impending ap-pearance. The literature, professional conferences, and aware-ness of changes in the world around us (e.g., the advent of the microchip, the laser disks) can all be helpful in this process of innovation.

Once the new information technology is identified, the librari-ans and managers must try to forecast the specific impact of that technology or new type of service on the local institution. The object will be to plan how to maximize the positive and minimize negative impacts of implementation/nonimplementation.

In *Managing Change*, four ingredients for successful manage-ment of change are cited including courage, information, real-ism, and simplification (Morgan 1972). The courage to accept and even seek out that beyond the status quo seems obvious. Information too should be a natural for those of us in the informa-tion business. Yet this may be one of our weakest areas in this brave new world of innovation. When the project at hand falls outside our normal scope of expertise, we tend to believe what someone tells us. If the computer analyst advises that brand X computer is the best the market has to offer, the novice innovator may feel uncomfortable in challenging his expertise, however, more information should be garnered before a decision is made. Asking questions of the technologist is also a good way to get needed information. Colleagues in the field can offer valuable input. And then there is always READING. The administrator must keep in mind that although the technologist or the salesperson, and the colleague all know the product, they will lack other important information about library goals, personnel capabilities, user needs, budget, and departmental objectives. It is up to the librarian or administrator to integrate all of the information and make an informed decision.

Realism is also important. No matter how fantastic that specialized $4000 per year database may be, chances are that it is not going to be practical in the schema of a collection budget totalling $20,000; nor is it likely that any small academic library is going to be on the cutting edge of technological change. On the other hand (realistically speaking) to survive and to meet the anticipated user needs, the library must be aware of what is available and interpolate technology and services to the level of service and fiscal resources available.

Simplification is the final element on the list. This step might be equated with taking the terror out of technology . . . or getting down to brass tacks. What is the technology/innovation? What can it do for the library? What are the benefits? What are the costs? What are the potential problems? What is the long-term prognosis for use and effect on the budget? Can the regular budget accommodate the change? If not, is there another source of funding? In short, we need to cut through the awe and confusion that sometimes surrounds innovative ideas and think through real long-term effects on us and the organizations we serve.

Coping with new information technology is a challenge for the reference department. On-line databases, the laser disk and microcomputer, the satellite dish, all offer great opportunities for expanding access to information and improving service. The on-line database, with us for some time now, is well-established, but the others require evaluation of their usefulness in a library situation. The laser disk coupled with a microcomputer offers rapid retrieval and so libraries with them report high user acceptance.

Turning to the review and evaluation process and attempting answers to the budget questions cost displacements and trade-offs are the first consideration. For example, an index on a laser disk displaces a printed guide freeing its costs for the disk costs.

If they are not equal another decision must be made to pay the cost or reassign the savings. The latter is easy, but the former may require reductions in other costs. Before an enterprise of such magnitude is undertaken these matters should be resolved. Another example is the periodical database on a disk. Paper-based index subscription cancellations may equal the cost, or possibly a staff vacancy is left unfilled, difficult questions but ones that must be raised.

Evaluating the new tool may require more than a vendor's demonstration. A trial period at the vendor's risk may be the solution; if it is of a reasonable length the questions of displacement of alternatives can be resolved, and the matter of the displacement costs the librarians can live with is ascertained as well. In this process, librarians consider also the cost of space as a factor; if this new system moves people along and they have satisfactory results from their queries, then a space savings has occurred and this is worthwhile. If users tending to form queues at the card catalog now move along faster after finding the information they were seeking, a substantial saving has occurred in space alone; that is a factor to note when negotiating with institutional managers. The same applies to space saved when paper materials are displaced, a building need not be expanded. The last item is the savings in librarians' time, if that is measured and reflects a savings then a strong case has indeed been made. Potentially, staff growth may reduce or decrease, but a corresponding increase in efficiency and productivity occurs as job assignments change.

A combination of new funds and displacement funds generates a budget for the new information technology. Careful analysis and review of all factors justifies a purchase. But what if funds fall short, what other inducements are there for the persuasion of institutional administrators? What is needed now is evidence directly supporting increases in staff efficiency, possibly even curtailment of staff increases (otherwise thought essential if the population served is increasing or academic programs are turning to library intensive areas) or some demonstrable evidence of a future savings, e.g., reduction or curtailment of collection space growth due to some high density storage medium.

Some of the new products will capture the library public's

imagination quickly because they eliminate tedious work, e.g., looking up sources in printed materials, and have a "razzle dazzle" quality. Is the price worth paying for a crowd pleaser which offers nothing more than a savings in time? Here is a difficult choice to make. To please the audience, sacrificing printed sources is essential thereby generating some savings but perhaps not enough. If the reference collection can't stand up to crowd pressure without duplication or redundant sources, buy the crowd pleaser. If the collection can, then look for more substance, greater innovation, and buy. The sacrifices made will bear greater productivity and so create savings.

COPING WITH BUDGET REDUCTIONS

With many libraries operating under very tight budgets, the reality is that budgets can get tighter, sudden reductions may be required. An affluent society, for example, oil rich Texas in 1986 suddenly experiencing a severe downturn in oil prices, directs fast budget reductions for its public agencies. White discusses several strategies for coping with reductions (White 1984:177-9).

Does decentralized budgeting offer any advantages over the more common centralized process especially when a percentage reduction can be made in the latter? Here goals and objectives can be used as controls with the reference librarians determining cancellations, postponements or alternatives, directly deciding the fate of other services. Surely this will be more effective than a quick across the board reduction with services modified according to actual need. Subjective judgments are made, true, but the librarians evaluating the effectiveness of their program are in the best position to determine what is cut and what stays.

The operating budget tied to its objectives is modified by revising the objectives. New handbooks are delayed, supplies reduced. The staff remains in control of the department's destiny. The collection budget, with no routine increase, can lose its viability for innovation. Some alternatives such as delays in replacement policies (annuals, encyclopedias, etc.) may forestall moribundity, but all need not be lost. In severe cases, competitive titles, especially those of a continuation type, can be reduced. Updating can be delayed. Unfortunately, some pressures can transfer to other library areas. Budget reductions do not reduce user demand and nonpublic service areas suffer as a consequence. Fallback measures, however, should not be built around some modicum of status quo. The information world is not standing still and cutbacks or not, the user pressures will not abate. If objectives call for advancement of information services, then while cuts and delays are going into effect, the review and evaluation process continues; if a new information source comes along and proves meritorious, then the further cuts that will make its acquisition possible are made.

In the best of planning environments, goals and objectives have built into them statements of value, longevity, and removability. With realistic foresighted planning, reductions can be made with less shock and reaction than otherwise might be expected, and progress still proceed.

REFERENCES

Martin, Murray S., *Budgetary Control in Academic Libraries*. Greenwich: JAI Press, 1978.

McClure, Charles R., "A View From the Trenches: Costing and Performance Measures for Academic Library Public Services." *College and Research Libraries* 47, no. 4, (July 1986): 323-336.

Morgan, John Smith, *Managing Change: The Strategies of Making Change Work for You*. NY: McGraw Hill, 1972.

Ordovensky, Pat, "Women Lead Surge at College." *USA Today* (December 22, 1986): p. 1.

Smith, Karen F., "Robot at the Reference Desk?" *College and Research Libraries* 47, no. 5, (September 1986): 486-489.

Snyder, Henry, "Quiescence, Query, Quandary, Quietus: Public Services in the Library of the Future." *College and Research Libraries* 47, no. 6. (November 1986).

Toffler, Alvin, *Future Shock*. New York: Random House, 1970.

Van Arsdale, William O. & Anne T. Ostrye, "Info Trac: A Second Opinion." *American Libraries* 17, no. 7 (July-August 1986): 514-515.

White, Robert L., "A Library Budget Process: Incorporating Austerity Management." *Journal of Educational Media and Library Sciences* 21, (Winter 1984): 169-179.

SOME SPECIFIC SITUATIONS INCLUDING REVENUE GENERATION

To Charge or Not to Charge: No Longer a Question?

Sally F. Williams

SUMMARY. In the last ten years, charging fees for Library Services has become a widespread practice. The trend to charge for library services will continue because libraries face escalating costs with limited resources. Many libraries have added fees without reviewing existing fees for consistency and appropriateness. Reference librarians and financial administrators should review financial policies of public services with the goal of establishing fee structures to provide optimal funding for services that are changing rapidly. This article suggests a framework and philosophy for doing so.

It is ten years since American Library Association (ALA) stated in its ALA Policy Manual, Positions and Public Policy Statements, paragraph 50.4 "that the charging of fees and levies for information services, including those services utilizing the

Sally F. Williams is Associate Librarian for Financial Affairs, Harvard College Library, Cambridge, MA 02138.

latest information technology is discriminatory in publicly supported institutions providing library and information service.''

The issue hotly debated in the early years of this decade centered largely on whether or not libraries should charge for library services. Charging fees was a particularly sensitive issue for publicly supported institutions, less so for privately supported libraries. Although libraries impose a variety of charges to users, the service most frequently contested as a legitimate candidate for fees was computer-based literature searching. In the latter part of this decade, however, the attention of the published literature has been focused less on the theory of whether or not to charge for services, and more on management of fees issues such as the scope of services eligible for fees and the mechanics of fee-based services. Charging fees is a commonly accepted practice today. Lynch[1] found that while 72% of all types of libraries surveyed charged fees for services, 86% of academic libraries did so. Mckinney and Mosby[2] found 84% of academic libraries that offered on-line database searching as a service charged a fee. Watson[3] reported only one research library not charging for database searching.

There are several reasons for this change in attitude and practice. The most obvious factor is financial. Libraries experienced significant cost increases. Prices for goods that traditional libraries purchase, particularly books and serials, increased at a much higher rate than general consumer goods. Programs that libraries have undertaken, particularly automation, have required large expenditures. At the same time, however, library budgets were shrinking or, at best, not increasing at a rate commensurate with program needs. More and more libraries seemed to have decided that charging fees was the easiest if not the only option for maintaining existing services or introducing new services that were expected to be used by relatively few of the potential library users without unduly compromising the support of traditional library services used by the majority.

The second factor was technology. New technology brought new library services and user needs and it also made it easier to identify some of the costs so that these could be charged back to users. A third factor was increasing demand. Receiving information is increasingly important to users but getting it is increasingly difficult. More and more users seemed willing to pay for the services of an intermediary expert at retrieving quickly the right information.

Will this trend continue? Yes. Has the controversy ended? No. Most libraries will continue to face the prospect of increasing costs and limited resources. The financial need to develop alternatives to traditional sources of funding will encourage the trend to charge for services. Simultaneously advances in technology will likely require radical changes to the services demanded, the type and number of users and the existing mechanisms for charging. For example the trend toward increasing use of microcomputers for remote access to databases, hastened by advances in local area networking, direct access to data, CD ROM possibilities and relatively inexpensive hardware/software will force a change in database searching services needed and the type of clients demanding new services. As more vendors produce user-friendly interfaces, more users will become end users who may need to rely on librarians less for actual searching and more for advice on which database is best searched and how. Librarians will probably be spending more time with each user, but unless fee structures are changed, income is likely to decline. Should users continue to be charged in the same old manner? Should the library extend services? As technology evolves, existing services become inappropriate, clientele changes, present methods of charging fees no longer serve well the original purpose. In short the perennial question of who should pay and for what will not go away and is likely to return with renewed emotion and challenge as libraries make the transition from emphasizing ownership of materials toward emphasizing access to information.

While librarians urge the issues to be addressed at higher and higher levels, library life goes on. Budget deadlines must be faced. Impatient patrons must be made to comprehend and sympathize with library policies that appear unfathomable.

What can reference librarians who must implement policies and convert lofty ideals into workable practice and realistic dollar amounts do? In the short-term perhaps the most useful task that practicing reference librarians can perform with financial administrators is to review the library's public services from a cost/benefit viewpoint.

Many libraries have not reviewed systematically their policy and practice of charging services. If new charges are levied but existing charges not adjusted a library may end up with a hodge-podge of fees for a variety of services to a variety of clientele at a variety of prices, possibly contradictory and no longer serving the original purpose which should be to provide adequate funding to ensure steady and reliable delivery of services. In addition to financial considerations this situation can be harmful to the library if confusion over fees leads to alienation of users or staff or administration.

Public services staff should be involved in any review of services and their financial implications. Public service staff know more about user needs, expectations and opinions of library practice than other library staff members. Reference librarians in particular develop an intimate knowledge of the library that is rarely achieved by administrators. On the other hand, public services staff members may not be aware of the costs of delivering public services or the broader economic and political environment of the library as a whole. When the two are brought together there can emerge a carefully considered financial philosophy of public service that should lead to stable funding of services even in the face of limited and erratic library resources. The mutual goal and joint responsibility is to optimize the value given as well as received.

The purpose of this article is to suggest a framework in which reference librarians and administrators can review the services provided for appropriateness of fees and the amount charged to each category of user.

Appendix A contains a list of services libraries generally offer, many of which are performed in reference departments, to aid in identifying services offered in a particular library. Appendix B is a list of services commonly charged in libraries. The library should inventory the services it offers, then evaluate using the following guidelines to decide which services might be charged and the extent of cost to recover. The next step is to classify users as primary, secondary, tertiary, etc., and determine what level of fee is appropriate to the category. It is suggested that the final product be a matrix made for each service showing each classified type of user and suggested level of fee, if any.

SERVICES ELIGIBLE FOR FEES

1. Services in which the benefits to users are private rather than collective in the economic sense. Private benefits accrue to a single individual and do not accrue to the public at large. Services with collective benefits are those which cannot be separated and withheld from those who do not pay directly. All primary members ought to receive collective benefit services since members have already paid for them in the form of taxes, student tuition, institutional budget support, membership dues, or the like. Examples of services whose benefits are clearly private are highly specialized or expedited services. Ideally, but not necessarily, the user also has a choice between using a library service which may take more time or be less complete which is offered at no extra charge or using a fee-based service for faster or more extensive service.

2. Services which will be used by few rather than many.

3. Services whose demand is elastic rather than inelastic in the economic sense so that fees will serve the function of efficient allocation of library resources. Users who pay will in theory not pay for services perceived to be unneeded or of poor quality.

4. Services for which nonpayers can easily be excluded. Fees should not be paid by those who do not use the service, and those who do not pay should not be able to use the service.

5. Services that could not be offered without diverting significant resources from services offering collective benefits.

6. Services whose expenses could easily outstrip a library's ability to pay. Unlimited free database searches is an example that comes readily to mind.

7. Services where management information can be collected and evaluated periodically in order to ensure appropriate quality and level of service. Management control is needed to ensure the success of the service by monitoring quality. People who pay for services weigh value of service delivered against cost. Since they will not purchase services that are inferior, the library will not have received good value for its capital investment (equipment, supplies, documentation, training, promotion in the case of online database searching) if the service performed is not of appropriate quality. Then, too, management control is needed to en-

sure an appropriate balance among services offered. Services offering collective benefits should not be made to suffer merely because of demands for private services from those who are willing and able to pay extra. Libraries should set up periodic formal review to evaluate existing services. Doing this quarterly is not too frequent in this era of rapidly changing technology. Libraries could also use the opportunity of this review to discover new services to offer.

8. Services whose growth could continue to be largely supported by fees independent of regular budget support. Admittedly it is difficult to predict the future but a library should not undertake on a fee basis a service that is certain to require infusions from a regular library budget that by definition is already inadequate. One of the prerequisites for a successful service is that it be reliable. Services that are withdrawn and reoffered frequently cannot be perceived as reliable by users and they will seek alternative service elsewhere.

9. Services which are especially time consuming, disruptive or otherwise difficult to perform. Examples are rush service, preparing lectures and exhibitions.

10. Services in which library responsiveness is particularly desired. Nielsen[4] found "that in the libraries where fee charging was established policy, the librarians *were* more responsive to their on-line search service clients, as measured by three of the responsiveness variables." But Nielsen also warns that "although librarians who work in situations where a fee is involved are likely to be more responsive to fee paying clients, they are actually less responsive to the totality of service demands in the workplace."

11. Services with high hidden costs and high opportunity costs. Hidden costs come to light from the ripple effect. A hidden cost of purchasing a lower priced but poor quality database is the increased staff time or other resources needed to correct errors or complete gaps in the information retrieved for users. Another example is the increased demand for purchase of library materials not owned or interlibrary borrowing that may result from increasing user access to bibliographic citations. Opportunity costs are the sacrifices made by selecting one alternative over another.

What might staff be doing if not occupied with X service for Y user? What other income is sacrificed because fees for X service are levied? Hidden costs and opportunity costs are extremely difficult to quantify but even when not precise are very important to identify in the decision making process.

GUIDELINES FOR FEES

1. Fees should be consistent with institutional and networking, e.g., cooperative agencies goals and objectives.

2. Fees should not erect undue barriers to access to service. Charges should be realistic, equitably applied to primary members, and not unduly compromise access. Subsidizing those who cannot pay might be an option provided the mechanism for identifying these is relatively simple. For example, academic libraries experiencing low use of on-line database searching by undergraduates might opt to target this group for subsidy, perhaps by charging a low fee or by including a fixed number of citations free of charge.

3. Fees should aim to discourage frivolous use of services but not impede legitimate use.

4. Fee structure must be logical and easily understood by those who pay them and by those who administer them.

5. Fee structure must be simple and inexpensive to implement relative to the amount of income received. The full cost of collecting fees is probably higher than most libraries believe.

6. Fee must be reasonably predictable in order to allow the user to make a rational decision as to the value of the particular service.

7. Fee structure should be based on actual costs of providing the service. Costs may be defined in many different ways, but there are two chief concepts, namely accounting costs and economic costs. Economic costs are opportunity vs. outlay cost, future vs. past cost, long run vs. short run and replacement vs. historical cost. Economic costs should be considered in the decision of whether or not to charge a fee, but the fee itself should be based on accounting costs. Accounting costs may be defined differently in each institution, but the terms that are most frequently

used in library literature are direct vs. indirect, fixed vs. variable, one-time or start-up vs. ongoing, incremental, and total or full cost. In the example of on-line searching the costs and financing committee of RASD/MARS[5] defines direct costs as the costs incurred by an on-line search session and identifies these as telecommunications, citation charges and searcher's time. Indirect costs are (1) acquisitions of equipment (terminal, modem, telephone, maintenance contracts) and documentation and supplies (manuals thesauri, subscriptions to professional literature, printing paper and supplies) and (2) operating expenses of personnel (including coordinator/administrator, searcher and clerical support staff), training expenses (vendor training, seminars and workshops, travel expense, professional memberships and online practice time), promotion (printing and graphics, on-line demos, complementary searches) and overhead (facility use and modification, furniture). Other expenses include labor and supplies associated with the collection of fees.

8. Total amount of the fee should equal or exceed the incremental cost of providing the service. Not all incremental costs can be accurately identified with ease, however, so trade-offs may have to be made. In the example of on-line searching, direct costs are the minimum incremental costs of providing the service. Indirect costs are also incremental. Whether or not to recover total cost or partial cost or none at all is a decision each library must make. For strictly financial considerations the direct or variable costs are the minimum costs that should be recovered. Most libraries recover direct costs but not total incremental cost and certainly not total cost in its fullest sense. Inclusion in or exclusion of specific costs from the fee structure is a decision each individual library must make for itself. (See also discussion in item 7).

There is financial risk in trying to recover total cost of a service. If estimates of activity are too high or price is too high revenue may not equal expense. There is particular financial risk in trying to recover too much of the cost of salaries. The library can become dependent on income from services that may be not stable income producers. For example, the paying customer of today's mediated database search may become the nonpaying end user of tomorrow who no longer pays for charged mediated search services but who may seek noncharged services such as advice on which database to access or technical advice on how to access. Financially this is a concern because the cost of providing the service, i.e., staff time, is the same or greater if staff is spending more time with this type of user, but income received is less. Some libraries may have the option of putting income into accounts that permit carrying funds over into the next fiscal year as a hedge against changes in the level of income.

9. Fee structure must permit periodic rate changes needed to reflect actual costs. For most libraries the minimum period to reconcile rates with costs should be one year. This is necessary only for those formulas where estimates are made. For example with on-line searching libraries charging only the actual direct costs of connect time, telecommunications and prints would not need to proceed with this exercise. Libraries which charge staff time and other expenses subject to change should revise rates periodically. Too frequent rate changes will irritate users, especially users who must budget costs into grant proposals in advance. It goes without saying that whenever rates are revised the potential clients should be given fair advanced notice of the change.

In the last decade the attention devoted to the issues of fees has diverted attention from the larger question of the cost of library operations.

In most libraries today the cost of providing collective benefit services far exceeds the cost of providing private benefit services. Charging fees actually adds to the cost of delivering the service. Even if total cost could be recovered the amount of money that can be recovered through fees is probably slight when compared to a library's total budget. This realization should lead libraries to question the cost effectiveness of their total operations, not just their rationalization for charging fees for a few public services. Libraries should not stop after reviewing their public services, but should continue their probe into the larger question of the economics of access to and delivery of information. The unit cost of technical services today is so high that to suggest charging an appropriate fee is to invite ridicule. The trend of charging fees may continue but the practice should continue to be questioned.

NOTES

1. Lynch, Mary Jo, *Financing Online Search Services in Publicly Supported Libraries: The Report of an ALA Survey*. Chicago: American Library Association, 1981.

2. McKinney, Gayle & Mosby, Anne Page, "Online in Academia: A survey of online searching in U.S. Colleges and Universities," *Online Review* v.10 no. 2, April 1986, pp 107-124.

3. Watson, Paula D., *Reference Services in Academic Research libraries*. Chicago: Reference and Adult Services Division, American Library Association, 1986.

4. Nielsen, Brian, "Do user fees affect searcher behavior?" in *Dollars and Sense; Implications of the new online technology for managing the library* by Bernard F. Pasqualini (ed.), Chicago: American Library Association, 1987.

5. "Online Reference Services: Costs and Budgets," created by the members of the Costs and Financing Committee of RASD/MARS, December 1983 and revised June 1986 in *Dollars and Sense; Implications of the New Online Technology for Managing the Library*, by Bernard F. Pasqualini (ed.), Chicago: American Library Association, 1987.

APPENDIX A

SELECTED SERVICES LIBRARIES PROVIDE TO USERS

Reading/Study/Conference space and furnishings; other space and facilities

- Smoking facilities
- Water and other refreshments
- Lavatory
- Coat/personal article check
- Change
- Typewriters, computers, other equipment and supplies

Access to materials

- Processed library materials in various formats
- Materials in process
- Interlibrary borrowing of materials not owned or located in library
- Document delivery
- Stack maintenance

- Staff search for materials
- On-demand staff retrieval of materials, i.e., paging
- Personal materials order and receipt

Exhibitions and lectures
Borrowing privileges

- Circulation of materials outside library
- Renewal of materials
- Recall of materials in circulation
- Holding material
- Reserves

Reproduction of materials: library owned and/or user owned

- Self-service reproduction, usually coin-operated
- Staff assisted reproduction

Reference

- Directory assistance
- Orientation and library user education: formal, informal; to library staff, to general users, to special users
- Telephone queries, mail queries, electronic mail queries
- Bibliographic verification
- Library holdings verification
- Reading advisory services
- Instruction in use of library catalog
- Bibliographic instruction: formal, informal
- Literature searches/database searches: manual, on-line, off-line
- Compiling bibliographies
- Indexing special collections
- In-depth subject consultations
- End user training and advice, on information retrieval: in house files, commercial data files
- Technical advice on data files

Current awareness

- Selective dissemination of information (SDI)
- New materials lists

Publications: guides, maps, bibliographics
Translations
Protection of materials

- Security
- Preservation: preventive and restorative

Access to information

- Library holdings: printed, electronic
- Other library's holdings: printed, electronic
- Indexes, abstracting services, reference material: printed, electronic
- Machine readable data files. Staff assistance in use of the above to users on-premises and off-premises, including end users.

APPENDIX B

SERVICES COMMONLY CHARGED IN LIBRARIES

- Rental of space and facilities
- Rental of equipment and materials
- Lockers, usually coin-operated
- Extended hours of service
- Use privileges including borrowing privileges
- Extended borrowing privileges
- Abuse of borrowing privileges, i.e., fines for overdue lost and damaged materials
- Permissions fees for publications
- Reproduction of materials
- Interlibrary borrowing
- Selective dissemination of information (SDI)
- Database searching
- "Information" services
- Compiling bibliographies
- Preparing translations
- Thesis deposit
- Document delivery

The Reference Department Budget in the High Tech Era: An Endangered Species?

Kathleen Coleman
Linda Muroi

SUMMARY. Machine-based information products, such as optical disc databases and microforms, compete with traditional print resources for limited budgets in today's reference departments. The authors surveyed the reference departments of 159 large academic libraries regarding their use of optical discs, and 19 libraries regarding their use of microforms. Despite the high cost of the first generation of optical disc systems, 55% of the reference departments reported using them. User response to the systems is generally very favorable. Problems noted by librarians included equipment failure, uneven database quality, and frequent need to service the systems. Respondents overwhelmingly felt that optical discs will play a significant role in the future of reference service. However, until equipment compatibility problems are resolved and system prices drop, prudent reference librarians will purchase optical discs selectively. The survey of 19 California State University libraries on their use of microforms revealed that 17 use them in the reference department and consider them an important part of the reference collection. However, because of user resistance and other problems, only one library plans to add more microforms.

One of the greatest challenges facing reference departments today is integrating new information into physical facilities and budgets which were designed for print media. In recent years, new information products such as COM (computer output mi-

---

Kathleen Coleman and Linda Muroi are Reference Librarians at San Diego State University, San Diego State University Library, San Diego, CA 92182.

137

crofilm) indexes, directories and catalogs in microfiche, and databases on optical disc have appeared in reference departments, in many cases competing with traditional print resources for a share of the materials budget. Unfortunately, this proliferation of technology-based information products comes at a time when the prices of print reference sources are rising, and reference book/serials budgets rarely keep abreast of price increases.[1] These new materials require substantial investment in equipment, and a budget for microcomputers, disc drives, reader-printers, etc. is often nonexistent in reference departments. And maintaining these new collections and the required machinery is an added burden on reference department staff.

Optical disc databases are an exciting new technology with great potential in reference work. They can store enormous amounts of information—one 4.75-inch disc holds 600,000,000 characters[2]—and, with accompanying software packages, the data is quickly accessible. An optical disc system can also include a printer, giving students a ready-made bibliography or other printout. There are two types of optical disc systems on the market today—those using 12-inch videodiscs (primarily Infotrac and the related databases produced by Information Access Corporation), and those using 4.75-inch CD ROM (compact disc-read only memory).

At San Diego State University, we have subscribed to Infotrac (four stations, at $16,000 per year). Our users' reactions have been just as favorable as those reported in the professional literature (see literature review which follows). We would very much like to purchase one or two CD ROM databases, as well. Our users would almost certainly like them, and we could save a great deal of staff time by switching some users of our mediated on-line search service to CD ROM products. (Last year, of the 1035 searches we conducted, 363 were on Medline and 354 were on ERIC; both of these databases are available on CD ROM.)

But CD ROM indexes are relatively new, and the published literature about library experiences with them is limited. *Library Literature* led us to an abundance of glowing announcements from vendors, but not many articles by librarians evaluating the products they have used. (The two we found are summarized in the literature review.) Like most reference departments, we do not have money to spend on expensive mistakes, and CD ROM is expensive. A microcomputer, printer, and compact disc drive, which in most systems serve just one user at a time, can cost $4,000 or more. And leasing a database such as ERIC for a year from Dialog On Disc costs a library nearly $3500 in addition to that.[3] Our reference book budget for 1986-87 is roughly $28,300; the equipment budget for our entire library this year is just over $34,000. Like most academic reference librarians serving large numbers of students and a broad range of academic programs, we are simultaneously tempted by and cautious about expensive products with considerable appeal and promise, but almost no track record.

An ever-expanding microforms collection, with its inherent equipment needs, adds to the squeeze on our reference department budget. Our reference microforms collection has grown rapidly in just a few years, and now includes a whole drawer of Phonefiche, several years of Statistical Reference Index microfiche, the Corporate and Industry Research Reports, plus several collections of directories, catalogs, and union lists. We currently have three microfiche readers in the department, and feel that we need a reader-printer. (Presently, users who want to make copies must take the microfiche downstairs to the principal microforms area.) Things have changed a great deal since the time, about ten years ago, when our reference librarians made a policy that no microforms should be in the reference department.

LITERATURE REVIEW

The advantages of optical disc reference products are well documented in library literature. Optical discs have great potential for information storage.[4] If a library has a high volume of on-line searching, optical discs can be cost effective. There is a fixed annual cost for use of the disc, and there are no telecommunication costs.[5]

However, the literature also reflects problems with this relatively new technology. There are high costs for startup equipment, along with the added frustration of occasional equipment malfunction.[6] Furthermore, the lack of compatibility in current hardware and access software is a common complaint. As one editorial states, ". . . what happens when a couple of dozen publishers decide to offer their own individual systems? Instant chaos!"[7]

Infotrac, the first optical disc system in widespread use, is produced by Information Access Corporation. The literature reveals mixed reactions to this system. Herschman and Maultsby report on a favorable test experience with the system at University of California, San Diego.[8] Walker and Westneat state that Infotrac is very popular with undergraduates at the University of Dayton. It is very easy to use, and requires no instruction. However, it has drawbacks. The system does not have Boolean search capability, and subject subheadings cannot be accessed directly. Also, equipment malfunction and supplies (paper and ink) are costly in both time and money.[9] Beltran describes the experience of Indiana University. Although Infotrac offers only a linear, displayed index, it does meet student needs for short papers and current materials. Beltran also notes that Infotrac is very popular with the students. She states, "If we tried to discontinue it, we might have risked a sit-in. No other reference tool has ever drawn the attention that Infotrac has."[10] Other favorable experiences with Infotrac are reported by Stephens[11] and Ernest and Monath.[12] On the other hand, Van Arsdale and Ostrye[13] found that the costs of Infotrac were too high, given the system's limitations.

Other articles describe the experiences of academic libraries with CD ROM databases. Halperin and Pagell[14] describe the University of Pennsylvania's experience with Compact Disclosure. The system is capable of using either menu or Dialog commands, and the data can be downloaded to a spreadsheet. There are no linkup problems as with on-line systems, but the information is not as current. Fries and Brown[15] describe experience with Datext at Dartmouth College. Datext includes six on-line databases; as with Compact Disclosure, information can be downloaded. The system's principal disadvantage, as with Compact Disclosure, is that information is less current than that found in on-line databases.

There is relatively little in the literature about microforms in reference departments. Saffady[16] discusses micropublishing, bibliographic control, and equipment. Hernon[17] recommends specific microform materials for the reference collection and suggests ways to motivate patrons to use them.

SURVEYS:
NEW TECHNOLOGY IN REFERENCE DEPARTMENTS

Like many other reference librarians, we have traded anecdotes and suggestions about new technologies and materials with colleagues from other institutions at professional meetings. However, we felt that a survey asking many medium-sized and large academic libraries about their decisions and practices regarding these new resources might produce a useful planning tool for reference departments.

We surveyed 159 academic libraries located throughout the United States with annual book budgets of at least $400,000 from the *American Library Directory*.[18] Considering the high prices of the first generation of optical disc databases, we decided to query only the largest libraries, assuming that those with book budgets much below $500,000 would be unable to afford optical disc products, even though they might want them. Our original intent was to send the survey to all academic libraries in the United States with book budgets of $500,000 or more. However, this yielded just 122 libraries. Since we wanted a slightly larger sample, we randomly selected 27 additional libraries with book budgets of at least $400,000. We divided the libraries into four categories, as follows:

- Category 1 Book budget below $500,000 (27 libraries)
- Category 2 Book budget $500,000 to $749,999 (48 libraries)
- Category 3 Book budget $750,000 to $999,999 (33 libraries)
- Category 4 Book budget $1,000,000 or more (52 libraries)

In a few cases, the *American Library Directory* did not indicate a library's book budget, but gave only a total operating budget. In those instances we estimated the book budget by using the Association of Research Libraries' median percentages of total library expenditures, as given in ARL's 1984-85 statistical compilation. From the ARL tables, we derived a median figure of 15% for books as a percentage of total operating expenditures, and multiplied that figure by the total budget figure given in the *American Library Directory* to get an estimated book budget.[19]

Initially, we had hoped to survey all 159 libraries about their experiences with both reference microforms and optical disc products. However, the questionnaire for such a survey would have been nine pages long, and we wanted to send out a short survey which respondents would find easy to answer. Therefore, we divided the survey in two. The first part, the questionnaire on optical disc reference products, was sent to all 159 libraries. We made the questions about microform reference products into a second survey, which we sent to the libraries of the 19-campus California State University, the system to which our library belongs. Most CSU campuses have libraries with substantial budgets, with materials expenditures ranging from approximately $558,000 at the smallest campus to $1,800,000 at the largest in 1985-86.[20]

The two surveys were mailed in November, 1986, and replies were received by the end of December, 1986. (Appendix A is the text of the optical disc survey; Appendix B is the text of the survey on reference microforms.) The response rate for the optical disc survey was so favorable (74% overall) that we did not send a follow-up mailing. Because the group of libraries receiving the microforms survey was so small, we wanted to have 100% data. Therefore, we made follow-up telephone calls to get data from the four campuses that did not answer the mail survey.

Optical Disc Survey

The high response rate for the optical disc survey confirmed what we already knew: reference librarians are keenly interested in the potential of this new medium, and are eager to share information and experiences. Table 1 gives the number and percent of libraries reporting in each budget category.

A surprising number of libraries, even in the smallest budget category, have already purchased optical disc products. Table 2 indicates the number and percentage of libraries in each of the four budget categories which currently have optical discs.

We were not surprised to find that Infotrac was the most frequently-owned optical disc product in all four budget categories. Information Access Corporation's related index to U.S. government publications and ERIC tied for second place. Next came LegalTrac, IAC's optical disc equivalent of *Current Law Index*, and Compact Disclosure. Table 3 indicates, for each budget category, the most frequently-purchased optical disc products.

We also asked librarians to indicate products they plan to buy

Table 1. Number and Percent of Libraries Reporting in Each Budget Category

	Cat. 1	Cat. 2	Cat. 3	Cat. 4	TOTAL
Number of questionnaires sent	27	48	33	52	159
Replies received	21	34	28	35	118
Percent reporting	78%	71%	85%	67%	74%

Table 2. Number and Percent of Libraries in Each Budget Category Which Have Purchased Optical Disc Products.

	Cat. 1	Cat. 2	Cat. 3	Cat. 4	TOTAL
Have purchased optical discs	12	12	16	25	65
Have not purchased optical discs	9	22	12	10	53
Percent which have purchased	57%	35%	57%	71%	55%

Table 3. Optical Disc Products by Frequency of Purchase

Optical Product Purchased	Cat.1	Cat.2	Cat.3	Cat.4	TOTAL
Infotrac	7	11	13	22	53
Government Publications	2	4	2	5	13
ERIC	1	4	1	7	13
LegalTrac	1	0	3	3	7
Compact Disclosure	0	1	1	5	7
Dissertaion Abstracts	0	2	1	3	6
PsychLit	1	1	0	3	5
ISI SCI	2	0	0	2	4
Academic American Encyc.	0	1	0	3	4
Medline	1	0	0	2	3
Aquatic Sciences & Fisheries	0	0	0	2	2
Datext	0	0	0	2	2

at some time in the future. The most frequently chosen products, by far, are ERIC and PsychLit, which are CD ROM versions of popular on-line databases. Next most popular are Books in Print, Compact Disclosure, and Dissertation Abstracts. The answers to this question are summarized in Table 4.

We next asked librarians how their users have responded to the optical disc products already purchased. Here, nearly all librarians who have tried or purchased systems replied that response was very favorable. (Given a Likert scale ranging from "very favorably" to "very unfavorably," 55 checked "very favorably," and four checked "somewhat favorably." No respondent checked "neutral" or lower.) Since most of the systems now in use are the three Information Access Corporation products Infotrac, LegalTrac, and Government Publications Index, most comments pertain to these systems. When asked to comment on user response, 23 librarians replied, "They love Infotrac." Eleven expressed concern that their users do not understand the system's limitations, but expect it to include "everything." Eight noted that students will wait in line rather than use another index, and that the printing feature is a major attraction of the system. "Definitely user-friendly" was an observation made by five librarians. Two noted that use of government publications has increased since installation of the Government Publications Index, and two other respondents stated that the printout is helpful for librarians, especially in the government publications department, where students used to make mistakes with the Superintendent of

Table 4. Optical Disc Products Respondents Plan to Purchase

Planned Optical Disc Purchases	Cat.1	Cat.2	Cat.3	Cat. 4	TOTAL
ERIC	8	12	8	12	40
PsychLit	3	13	7	14	37
Books in Print	4	5	2	7	18
Compact Disclosure	1	7	3	6	17
Dissertaion Abstracts	3	5	1	8	17
Ulrich's	4	3	0	7	14
Public Affairs Info. Serv.	3	4	1	5	13
Infotrac	2	6	1	1	10
Government Publications	0	4	2	4	10
Academic American Encyc.	0	2	3	4	6
Newsbank	1	3	1	1	6
Medline	0	3	1	1	5
Life Sciences	0	2	0	3	5
Datext	0	0	1	3	4

Documents classification numbers. One respondent from one of the largest libraries noted, "We and our patrons find the laser disc services so useful, we are watching out for more databases to buy."

A few librarians who have purchased optical disc products from vendors other than Information Access Corporation also commented on this question. While one observed, "Systems not user-friendly (major problem)," three others commented that their users were comfortable with the new systems. Two others indicated that many users gladly accepted CD ROM indexes instead of on-line searches:

> Patrons seem willing to learn to use these systems on their own. They are enthusiastic about printing capabilities and, as they learn more, they become hooked on the Boolean capabilities. Best of all, of course, is that there is no fee for use.

Problems with Optical Disc Systems

Our next question asked respondents what problems they had encountered with optical disc systems. The most commonly cited problems were equipment failure, database quality, and frequent need to repair the system. Table 5 summarizes the response to the multiple-choice section of this question.

In their comments on this section, 22 librarians singled out the printers, with problems such as paper jams, frequent need for servicing, and stolen ink cartridges. Nine respondents expressed concern about the drain on the reference department's supply budget resulting from the system's prodigious use of paper and ink. One librarian estimates that "we are spending approxi-

Table 5. Problems Encountered with Optical Disc Systems

Problem Encountered	Number of Libraries
Equipment failure	34
Database quality	27
Frequent need to service system	18
Software security	12
System not sufficiently user-friendly	8
Equipment security	3

mately $170 per month on paper and ink," and went on to point out that the vendor did not inform her of that hidden cost before installation. Fourteen librarians described other equipment problems ranging from the videodisc player overheating to a sticking "print" key which occasionally prints the same screen on an entire ream of paper. Occasionally, the system goes down for no apparent reason: "Sometimes it seems that Infotrac needs a magic wand to get all the stations going." One librarian whose reference department has purchased several CD ROM products expressed frustration that the various packages are incompatible; those from different vendors require different equipment configurations. Eight librarians, having found indexing errors in Infotrac, expressed dissatisfaction with database quality. Two wished that Infotrac would cover more scholarly or scientific material, while another was dissatisfied with the system's high cost and limited searching capabilities. Three purchasers of CD ROM systems complained of inadequate system documentation. Vendor cooperation received mixed reviews. Two described a company as "not helpful when we have difficulties," while another described the same vendor as "very helpful, willing to send replacement parts."

Other problems noted stem not from the systems themselves, but from library users. Ten librarians stated that some students refuse to use anything but Infotrac, even if it is inappropriate for their projects. Another indicated that "huge numbers of students use Infotrac for the same widely assigned or popular term paper topic. They all get the same citations, and those articles get cut out of the magazines." Document availability is a problem with Infotrac in another sense: the database includes citations to many publications not owned by even the largest academic libraries, as noted by one respondent.

System security has been a problem in a number of libraries. We at San Diego State have had floppy discs stolen from the Infotrac microcomputers, and seven survey respondents noted the same problem. One library has had users pull out the system software and use the microcomputer for their own word processing. Another library noted keyboard mutilation.

One librarian brought up a major problem with many optical disc products:

We are especially concerned about how we can make sure that the information we're leasing will be in the collection in the future. We have not bought IAC's retrospective indexing and at this point will lose data as the discs are updated. . . . We will not have coverage later on although we're certainly paying for it now.

Optical disc products, in most cases, command a price many times that of the equivalent print products, yet libraries often do not own the data after paying that price. Because the discs are not owned, but leased, librarians cannot cancel print subscriptions when they subscribe to indexes on optical disc.

Reasons for Deferring Optical Disc Purchase

The next question asked librarians who have not yet purchased optical discs why they have decided to wait. (Seven librarians who have Information Access Corporation systems answered this question, giving their reasons for not purchasing CD ROM products. To simplify reporting, their replies were added in with others.) The most common reasons for deferring purchase was, not surprisingly, "Too expensive" (58 replies). As one librarian who has not purchased any system commented:

Infotrac will be fine for undergraduates, but it's not cheap at $16,000. That's about 15% of our reference budget. We serve so many diverse programs that it's hard to find that amount of money for one resource tool.

Forty-four respondents checked "Concerned about lack of standards/compatibility in products." If optical disc materials proliferate, as they almost certainly will, reference librarians want equipment which can be used with more than one database. When a standard is finally established, and existing products eventually conform to it, libraries which have purchased nonconforming equipment will find themselves owning expensive mistakes. Lack of necessary equipment is a stumbling block for 34 of the libraries responding to the survey. Twenty-eight librarians checked, "Products too new; want to profit from experience of other libraries.'' Table 6 reports responses to all items on this question.

In their comments on this question, three librarians noted that their libraries had tested Infotrac, but decided not to buy it because the system lacks keyword and Boolean searching, and has limited subject coverage. Three other respondents added, ''We want to wait for a quality product; have heard about problems with those available now.'' Another reservation expressed by two respondents is that most systems allow only one person at a time to use the database. Two others did not purchase optical disc systems because they were concerned that students might not be willing to use anything else.

Future Importance of Optical Disc Products

The last question on the optical disc survey asked, ''Do you anticipate that optical disc products will eventually have a significant place in your reference department? Please comment.'' Almost all respondents answered ''Yes.'' Many commented on optical disc's likely impact on the future of reference service. Seven respondents described optical disc as ''the wave of the future.'' Three replied, ''They already hold a significant place considering the brief time we have had them.'' Several respondents commented that their users love optical disc services, and that these new products increase the perceived value of the library for patrons. Five librarians who have not purchased systems believe that optical disc will be widely used in the future; they would like to give their users the opportunity to become familiar with them.

Other respondents pointed out the practical advantages of opti-

Table 6. Reasons for Deferring Purchase of Optical Disc Systems

Reasons for Deferring Purchase	Cat.1	Cat.2	Cat. 3	Cat.4	TOTAL
Too expensive	10	19	15	14	58
Concerned about lack of standards/compatibility	8	14	13	9	44
Lack of necessary equipment	3	10	13	8	34
Products too new; want to profit from experience of other libraries	4	11	7	6	28
Lack of space	1	5	4	0	10
Lack of security for equipment	1	2	0	1	4
Lack of security for software	1	1	0	0	2

cal discs. Thirteen librarians believe that optical discs will re-place on-line searching for some users. As one commented:

> With the flat fee for a compact disc, the library can evaluate the costs and include them in the budget. Since the user is not financially penalized for mistakes while learning, this encourages independent use (leading to a savings in staff time).

Another respondent added, "We have tried menu-driven end-user searching and have not been satisfied with the response — very little receptivity. With CD, users are very positive and asking for more." Four respondents observed that optical disc may eventually save space by replacing large reference sets which now take up a good deal of reference department floor space. Three librarians answered that optical disc will allow better access to materials, and one noted that CD ROM materials are less likely to be mutilated than paper.

A number of respondents described their future plans for optical discs. Twelve noted, "Eventually we will purchase." Seven said that they were looking into several products to purchase in the near future. Four librarians described their reference departments' plans for an automated reference center, to include optical discs, on-line searching, on-line catalog terminals, and access to OCLC and/or RLIN. (For a description of such a center at the University of Rochester, including floorplans, see;[21] for a description of the one at University of Vermont, which includes optical discs, see.[22]) Two respondents stated that their libraries are now setting up microcomputer labs, which will include on-line searching and optical disc indexes.

Many respondents indicated that they will buy optical disc products, but only when certain practical requirements are met. These requirements include funds being available (16 respondents), prices lower (11), products standardized/compatible (8), multiple discs accessible with one machine (8), space available (6), and equipment available (6).

Several librarians expressed reservations about optical disc. Five stated that until the "one user—one station" problem is resolved, they will not invest heavily in CD ROM products. Four respondents who have purchased optical disc indicated that frequent system breakdowns have forced librarians to neglect reference service and fix the machines. As one stated it:

> I'd like to see optical discs, CD ROM's, and the like as part of a microlab staffed by personnel who can service machines properly. We find an enormous breakdown rate in our CD ROM systems that's forced us to become mechanics. My sense is that students don't need our professional expertise as much as our mechanical expertise with these systems. If that's so, let's put them someplace where people can service them properly.

Two librarians who already have several optical disc systems stated that they are unlikely to acquire any more until technological improvements give them more flexibility. They now have dedicated equipment for each product, and are running out of microcomputers, floor space, and electrical outlets. Another librarian, whose reference department has not yet purchased optical discs, expressed a concern shared by several other respondents:

> Since our budget is relatively small (and getting smaller) and our collection scope large, I believe optical disc products will have to replace printed products, not just supplement them, in order for us to justify the cost. For example, acquisition of Infotrac would not allow us to cancel either *Business Periodicals Index* or *Readers' Guide to Periodical Literature*.

Microforms

In our second survey, we asked the reference departments of all libraries in the California State University system to tell us about their use of microform materials. Of the 19 libraries, 17 maintain microform collections separate from the library's principal microform collections, while two do not. The second question asked librarians to check the titles of microform sets they either own or plan to buy. The answers to this question were very diverse, reflecting the great variety of materials which are available. We were surprised to find that only one library identified a title which they do not own, but plan to buy. Apparently, most of the reference departments are not actively seeking to augment their existing microforms collection. Table 7 lists all microform publications held in the reference departments of three or more CSU libraries.

We next asked the respondents who is responsible for such maintenance tasks as checking in microforms, filing and refiling, and searching for lost or misplaced items. Twelve librarians checked "paraprofessional staff," and 12 checked "student assistants." (Some respondents checked both.) When asked if they had microform readers and/or reader-printers, 17 answered "yes" and no one answered "no." Our question also asked the librarians how many readers or reader-printers they had in the reference department (see Table 8).

While all of the reference departments with microform collections have viewing equipment for their microforms, more than half have no reader-printers available. The sixth question asked who is responsible for servicing the reference microform equipment. Seven respondents checked "reference department staff," and seven checked "campus maintenance staff." Other replies included "microforms area staff" (6 replies) and "outside ser-

Table 7. Microform Publications in CSU Reference Departments

Title of Microform Publication	Number of Libraries Holding
California Academic Libraries List of Serials (a union list for major academic libraries)	11
CLASS California Union List of Periodicals (includes public as well as academic libraries)	10
Magazine Index	10
Business Index	10
College Catalogues on Microfiche	9
Library of Congress Subject Headings	8
National Union Catalog	8
National Newspaper Index	6
Phonefiche	6
Q File	5
Human Relations Area File	4
Corporate and Industry Research Reports	4
Area Business Data Bank	4
New York Stock Exchange Annual Reports	4
American Stock Exchange Annual Reports	3
Over the Counter Annual Reports	3
ERIC indexes	3
Newsbank	3
Statistical Reference Index Microfiche	3

Table 8. Microform Viewing and Copying Equipment in CSU Reference Departments

Number of Readers		Number of Reader-Printers	
None	0	None	9
3 or fewer	9	3 or fewer	6
4 to 6	3	4 to 6	2
7 to 9	2	7 to 9	0
10 or more	3	10 or more	0

vice firm'' (3 replies). Again, several librarians checked more than one response.

Our final question asked whether, on the whole, microforms are an asset to the reference collection. Several respondents, in answering affirmatively, commented on the value of their microform materials. Eight felt strongly that microforms have enriched their reference service, and named sets which have proved especially useful. Sets or types of materials named by two or more librarians included the Human Relations Area File, Phonefiche, corporate information, union lists, and statistical databases. As one stated, ''When students see the CIRR, job information, and SRI statistics on microfiche, they are so grateful to have the information that they don't complain about them being in microform.'' Two others indicated that all reference collections on fiche are indispensable and heavily used.

Several respondents stressed the practical advantages of microforms in their answers. Four mentioned that microforms save space, and two pointed out that reference tools on fiche are generally less expensive than paper copies. Two librarians felt that microforms are less likely to be mutilated or stolen than paper copies. Another stated that, in the case of prepackaged sets such as college catalogs and corporate annual reports, ''the microfiche subscription saves us the work of collecting and organizing the material.'' Furthermore, paper copies require much more staff time to maintain than microfiche. (Having watched student assistants spend endless amounts of time in a futile attempt to keep tattered paper phone books in order, we agree with much of the above.)

A few librarians pointed out disadvantages of microform. Two are looking forward to having some of the information presently in microform on optical disc in the future, to speed retrieval and eliminate fiche filing and handling. Another expressed frustration that "the technology to house, view, reproduce and secure microforms has not kept up with their proliferation." One respondent noted that users are frustrated by the National Union Catalog on fiche, but find other sets easier to use than the paper equivalents. Another librarian stated, "We avoid microforms if possible, but buy them if the information is not available in another format."

DISCUSSION

Machine-based reference products, of which optical discs and microforms are but two examples, are increasing in importance in reference departments. These products make demands on virtually all of a department's resources, including materials, supplies, equipment, staff time, and space. The largest libraries, our survey respondents, have invested substantially in these products already, and smaller ones will almost certainly do the same. User demand is generally strong; users of on-line catalogs, on-line searching, and bibliographic utilities are unlikely to be satisfied forever with print periodical indexes. Librarians must plan now to avoid having reference departments cluttered with incompatible machines, extension cords, and makeshift security devices in the year 2000.

Microforms have become an important part of reference collections in the past ten years. Because the microform technology has existed for a long time, formats and equipment are standardized. Microforms are valuable because they save space and money. Also, it would be uneconomical to publish some materials, such as statistical databases and large collections of information about corporations, in hard copy. Prepackaged collections, such as microfiche of college catalogs, telephone books, and annual reports, save the staff time which would otherwise be required to request and process the individual items in hard copy. Because individual fiche can be read separately, more than one user can use a large microfiche set at the same time. Microforms are less likely to be mutilated than paper copies. Despite all these advantages, most librarians will not buy microforms unless they have no other choice. The answers to our survey of California State University libraries suggest that reference microform collections have peaked. While 17 of the 19 CSU reference departments have microforms, only one plans to buy any more. Microforms must save a substantial amount of money or space over hard copy because of user resistance. Users dislike manually paging through fiche and film, and image quality is not always satisfactory. Making copies from microform yields varying results. While some reader-printers give good copies, all too many produce blurred copies in *New York Times* gray, with a disagreeable odor.

User reluctance is definitely not a problem with optical discs. They share the mystique of the computers used to access them, and library users love them. They provide even more compact storage than microforms. Paper copies are produced by a computer printer, and are cleaner and easier to read than many copies made from microforms. They can replace large reference sets, such as *Dissertation Abstracts*; optical disk versions of indexes can replace many routine mediated on-line searches.

However, the cost of optical discs, along with the problems inherent in any new, complex product, should make even the largest libraries proceed with caution. The reasons for being cautious were effectively stated by our respondents. First, prices of this first generation of optical disc products are too high. By a 1985 estimate, mastering a CD ROM disc costs approximately $10,000.[23] Individual discs can be produced for approximately $10 each excluding mastering and information rights.[24] It seems to us that producers of CD ROM databases are trying to recover their development costs rapidly with their current prices of $5,000, $10,000 and more.

Second, reference librarians are wise to question products which the library does not own, but leases; this is the case with most of the optical disc products now offered. The manufacturers and vendors of many optical disc products are creators and distributors of on-line databases. They are accustomed to selling a service. But librarians, while they offer those services to library users, are also interested in building a reference collection. In the past, the on-line database was a service; the print version became a permanent part of the reference collection. Now, optical disc vendors expect librarians to pay a premium for a product which cannot entirely replace on-line searching because updates are usually only quarterly, and which cannot replace the print version because the optical disc ultimately belongs to the vendor, not the library.

Librarians need to make long-range plans, to visualize their reference departments in 10 to 20 years. Microcomputers and terminals of various kinds are almost certain to have a prominent place in our facilities. Before systems and products are added one at a time, reference librarians should have a direction in mind. We believe that CD ROM products should be offered in a configuration which gives us and our users flexibility. There should not be an ERIC machine, a PsychLit machine, etc., but a number of terminals connected to disc drives in such a way that a user at any terminal could select from any of the optical disc databases available in the library.

A security system also needs to be built into the reference department which plans to invest substantially in machine-based systems. Terminals, printers, disc drivers, and even discs and software must be protected against theft and vandalism. Budgeting for the new technology should also include provisions for alarms, surveillance, or other security systems.

Servicing and maintenance must also be included in the budget, no matter how much vendors claim that their products are trouble-free. There should be someone available other than the reference librarian on duty to fix paper jams, replace empty ink cartridges, get a stalled system functioning again, etc. Speaking of paper and ink, their cost is substantial, and also needs to be included in the budget.

Although optical discs may be the wave of the future, the only reason to purchase them now is because they make sense in today's reference program. Equipment specifications and configurations will eventually be standardized; also, as the large librarians become saturated and vendors look to smaller institutions for a market, prices will drop. For now, selective purchasing is in order. Optical discs for databases the librarians or end users search heavily are probably worth buying. Should your reference department get Infotrac? At a large public university, Infotrac lures many undergraduates into using periodicals for the first time. Many would not have come to the library at all if someone in their fraternity had not suggested that they "get some references off the computer." In another college or university where students are highly motivated and already library-oriented, Infotrac might be an unnecessary distraction from more scholarly literature.

While high tech products challenge reference librarians who must work within finite budgets, they can definitely enhance reference service. Most of our respondents were optimistic when describing their reference department's current uses of and future plans for machine-based information products. As a reference librarian from Tennessee expressed it:

> Optical disc products are here to stay; users, once they become familiar with capabilities, will demand them, similarly to the way they created a demand for on-line services. The cost is a significant factor, as are equipment security, compatibility, and all the other factors which become apparent to you as you explore this topic. However, librarians are resourceful persons, and given the success they have had at learning to afford and manage microforms, and the concurrent success at finding funding for millions of dollars' worth of on-line catalog development, I feel confident that in the not too distant future we will look at optical technology and wonder how we could have lived without it in the past.

NOTES

1. Nancy R. Posel, "'Pricing Us Out of the Market': Are Publishers Biting the Hand That Feeds Them?" *American Libraries* 16:506-7 (July, 1985).

2. Carol Tenopir, "Databases on CD ROM," *Library Journal* 111:68-69 (March 1, 1986).

3. "Dialog Launches CD ROM Product Line," *Information Intelligence Online Newsletter* 7:1-2 (December, 1986).

4. Carol H. Fenichel, "For Optical Discs and Information Retrieval the Time is Now: A Librarian's View from the NFAIS Meeting," *Database* 9:6-8 (June, 1986).

5. Tenopir, "Databases on CD ROM."

6. Carol Tenopir, "CD ROM Database Update," *Library Journal* 111:70-71 (December, 1986).

7. "Videodiscs and the Impending Demise of the Index Table," *Technicalities* 6:1 (June, 1986).

8. Judith Herschman & Kristin Maultsby, "Sidebar 1: Infotrac: Impressions from a Beta Site," *Library Hi Tech* 3:93-94 (Issue 2, 1985).

9. Mary Ann Walker & Helen Westneat, "Using Infotrac in an Academic Library," *RSR* 13:17-22 (Winter, 1985).

10. Ann B. Beltran, "Use of Infotrac in a University Library," *Database* 9:63-66 (June, 1986).

11. Kent Stephens, "Laserdisc Technology Enters Mainstream: Easy-to-Use Periodical Index Gets Heavy Use at California University," *American Libraries* 17:252 (April, 1986).

12. Douglas J. Ernest & Jennifer Monath. "User Reaction to a Computerized Periodical Index," *College & Research Libraries News* 47:315-18 (May, 1986).

13. William Van Arsdale & Anne Ostrye, "Infotrac: A Second Opinion," *American Libraries* 17:514-15 (July, 1986).

14. Michael Halperin & Ruth A. Pagell, "Compact Disclosure: Realizing CD Rom's Potential," *Online* 10:69-73 (November, 1986).

15. James R. Fries & Jonathan R. Brown, "Datext—Using Business Information on CD ROM," *Online* 10:28-40 (September, 1986).

16. William Saffady, "Micrographics and the Reference Librarian," *Reference Librarian* no. 5-6:23-31 (Fall-Winter, 1982).

17. Peter Hernon, "The Use of Microforms in Academic Reference Collections and Services," *Microform Review* 6:15-18 (January, 1977).

18. *American Library Directory*, 39th ed., ed. Jacques Cattell Press (New York: Bowker, 1986).

19. Association of Research Libraries, *ARL Statistics 1984-85; a Compilation of Statistics from the 118 Members* (Washington: The Association, 1986). The "Analysis of Selected Variables of University Libraries" (p. 18) gives 32% as the median for materials expenditures as percent of total operating expenditures. The median for serials as percent of materials expenditures is 53%, leaving 47% for books and other nonserials. Since 47% of 32% is approximately 15%, we multiplied our respondents' total budgets by 15% to obtain an estimated book budget.

20. California State University, *1985-86 Library Statistics* (Long Beach, CA: Office of the Chancellor, 1986), p. 16.

21. Margaret Becket & Henry B. Smith, "Designing a Reference Station for the Information Age," *Library Journal* 111:42-46 (April 15, 1986).

22. "Issues in Implementing Optical/Online End-User Reference Center Discussed," *Advanced Technology Libraries* 15:4-6 (December, 1986).

23. Frank A. Pezzanite, "The LC MARC Database on Video Laserdisc: The MINI MARC System," *Library Hi Tech* 3:59-60 (Issue 1, 1985).

24. David C. Miller, "Finally It Works—Now it Must 'Play in Peoria'," in Steve Lambert & Suzanne Ropiequet, *CD ROM: The New Papyrus* (Redmond, WA: Microsoft, 1986), p. 21-35.

APPENDIX A
Questionnaire: Optical Disc Information Products in the Academic
Library Reference Department

1. Has your library acquired any optical disc information products
(either videodisc, such as Infotrac, or CD/ROM, such as the SilverPlatter
indexes)?

```
_____Yes              _____No
```

2. Which of the following optical disc products have you either
obtained already or plan to buy?

```
                                                          Plan
     Title of Product/Price                    Have    to buy
(A list of 20 optical disc products followed)
```

Other:

Note: Price information based on the four-part "Laserdisk Direc
tory" by Bruce Connolly which appeared in the June and August
1986 issues of Database and the July and September 1986 issues of
Online.

3. If you have optical disc products in your reference department
already, how, on the whole, have your users responded to them?

Very favorably	Somewhat favorably	Neutral	Somewhat unfavorably	Very unfavorably
_____	_____	_____	_____	_____

Comments:

4. If you have optical disc products, what problems have you
encountered with them? (please check all that apply.)

```
          _____Equipment failure

          _____Equipment security

          _____Software security

          _____Frequent need to service system

          _____System not sufficiently user-friendly

          _____Database quality
```

Other (Please specify):

APPENDIX A (continued)

5. If you do not yet have optical disc products, why have you decided to defer acquiring them? (Please check all that apply):

_____Too expensive

_____Lack of necessary equipment

_____Lack of security for equipment

_____Lack of security for software

_____Products too new; want to profit from experiences
        of other libraries

_____Lack of space

_____Concerned about lack of standards/compatibility
        in products

Other (Please specify):

6. Do you anticipate that optical disc products will eventually have a significant place in your reference department? Please comment.

APPENDIX B
Questionnaire: Impact of Microform Information Products on Reference Service Administration in CSU Libraries

While microforms are not new in academic libraries, substantial microform collections (National Union Catalog supplements, phonefiche, etc.) have been leaving their traditional home in microforms areas and developing in reference departments in the past few years. Has this phenomenon affected your reference department? Please tell us by answering the following questions:

NAME OF CSU LIBRARY:_____

1. Do you maintain a collection of microforms in the reference department (separated from the library's principal microform col lections)?

_____Yes   _____No

If you answered "No" to question #1, please skip to question #8.

2. Here is a list of some microform sets often held in reference collections. Which of these sets do you own or plan to buy? Please check the appropriate space opposite each title.

Title of Microform Set/Price	Own	Plan to Buy

(A list of 35 microform products followed)

Are there other microform sets which you now have in the reference department or plan to purchase for your reference collection?

APPENDIX B (continued)

3. Who is responsible for maintaining your reference microform collection? (Maintenance includes check-in, filing and refiling, searching for lost or misplaced items, etc.)

_____Paraprofessional staff

_____Student assistants

_____Other (Please specify)

4. Approximately how much staff time is required each week to process and maintain your reference microform collection?

_____Less than 2 hours per week   _____8-9 hours per week

_____2-4 hours per week   _____10 or more hours
                                                per week

_____5-7 hours per week

5. Do you have microform readers and/or reader/printers avail able in the reference department?

_____Yes   _____No

If you have microform viewing equipment in the reference department:

_____Number of readers   _____Number of reader/printers

6. If your answer to question #5 was "Yes," who services your readers and/or reader/printers?

_____Reference department staff

_____Microforms area staff

_____Campus maintenance staff

_____Outside service firm

_____Other (Please specify)

7. Do you find that, on the whole, microforms are an asset to your reference collection? Please comment.

Integrating Electronic Information Systems into the Reference Services Budget

Nancy L. Eaton
Nancy B. Crane

SUMMARY. This paper describes the Automated Reference Center, a new unit within the Reference Department of the Bailey/Howe Memorial Library. It analyzes initial start-up and ongoing costs; and it compares the average per search cost of end-user optical disc databases, end-user on-line services, and mediated searches. It reviews costs associated with end-user training and changes in support required for traditional services such as reference service, interlibrary loan, and microforms, due to increased demand emanating from end-user database searching.

INTRODUCTION

Based on recommendations in its 1983 long-range plan, the University of Vermont (UVM) Libraries have begun to treat electronic information systems as standard information resources equal in importance to the monograph, periodical, and nonprint collections.[1] Costs associated with access to these databases are being integrated into the library's "Materials and Access" budget, and most services are provided without charge to university faculty, staff, and students. (Approximately 40% of the main library's mediated searches and all medical mediated searches

Nancy L. Eaton is Director of Libraries, University of Vermont, Burlington, VT 05405; Nancy B. Crane is Head of Reference, Bailey/Howe Memorial Library, University of Vermont Libraries.

161

still have charges associated.) Search logic and search techniques are being integrated into the bibliographic instruction program. This approach to integrating electronic information systems into standard services has had a major impact upon the organization of and budgeting for reference services. While this approach is common to both the Bailey/Howe Memorial Library (the main library) and the Dana Medical Library, only the costs associated with services in Bailey/Howe Library are described here.

THE AUTOMATED REFERENCE CENTER

The reference department of the Bailey/Howe Library was asked by the Director of Libraries in May, 1986, to prepare a plan for integrating end-user electronic information systems into its basic service plan and to prepare a budget analysis for implementing these systems. The outcome of that plan was the inauguration of the Automated Reference Center (ARC), which began full service in September, 1986, and serves a university community of 11,096 students, 1,043 faculty members, and 4,883 staff members. The ARC is aimed at the end-user and provides an assortment of laser-disc and on-line systems for direct patron searching. At present, the ARC provides access to INFOTRAC (including Government Publications Index) on digital videodisc, SilverPlatter's ERIC and PsycLit on CD-ROM, and on-line end-user access to WILSEARCH, BRS/After Dark, and Knowledge Index. Additional CD-ROM databases will be added in the future. Selection of these services is now part of the library's collection development policy.

Physically, the ARC is in a room immediately adjacent to the main reference desk. The room is monitored at all times by a student assistant who aids users in the use of the systems, checks discs in and out, and gives out the self-paced CAI instruction package required of first-time users of the ARC. Professional reference assistance is available at the main reference desk for constructing search strategies or assistance with content of the databases which exceed the knowledge of the student assistant.

COST ANALYSIS

Start-up and Continuing Costs

Costs associated with the ARC break down into one-time facilities and hardware costs and ongoing costs. Tables 1 and 2 summarize the initial investment for electrical work, furniture, telephone lines, and workstations, and the annual subscription fees for INFOTRAC, ERIC, and PsycLit. Annual costs for the end-user on-line services were calculated by estimating the number of searches which could be scheduled at each workstation per week and budgeted at the maximum projected usage. Users must schedule time on each database (except for INFOTRAC), and the

Table 1

Start-up Costs

Station Description	No. of Stations	Hardware Costs/ Station	Furniture Costs/ Station	Total Costs
Search Lab				
INFOTRAC	3	$1,700[1]	$500	$6,600
ERIC	1	$2,500[2]	$500	$3,000
PsycLit	1	$2,500[3]	$500	$3,000
Dial-out Knowledge Index BRS/After Dark Wilsearch	2	$3,050[4]	$500	$7,100
Classroom				
CAI/dial-out	5	$1,650[5]	$500	$10,750
Kodak Data Show Micro Projector	1	$1,200		$ 1,200
COMPAQ Plus/modem	1	$3,085		$ 3,085
Electrical work				$ 2,990
TELCO phone line installation				$ 3,665

[1] IBM PC's, controller cards, printers (HP Thinkjets)
[2] AT&T 6300, Hitachi CD-player, printer
[3] AT&T 6300, HItachi CD-player, printer
[4] IBM PC's with 20MG hard disk, security boards, modems, printers
[5] AT&T 6300's, printers, modems

cost of the services are therefore limited by the number of work-stations and scheduled hours available.

Preference is for optical systems, since subscription costs can be predicted and unit costs per search decrease with increased usage. Thus, as the end-user on-line systems bring out back files on CD-ROM, with workstation gateways to the on-line databases for current information (such as WILSEARCH has announced), the ARC will convert to those systems.

Table 3 provides a comparison of end-user searches and librarian mediated searches for fall semester, 1986, versus fall semester, 1985. Five hundred fifty seven students and faculty have

Table 2

Annual Database Costs

INFOTRAC[1]	$ 14,000
ERIC (SilverPlatter)[2]	$ 4,000
PsycLit (SilverPlatter)[2]	$ 5,000
WILSEARCH, Knowledge Index, BRS After Dark[3]	$ 28,000

[1]Includes INFOTRAC and Government Publications Index subscriptions and digital videodisc players. IBM PC's and controller cards are provided by the library.
[2]Includes current and archival CD-ROM discs
[3]Figured on maximum usage - hours the systems are available and that the search center is open.

Table 3

Total Number of Searches:
Automated Reference Center versus Librarian-Mediated Services

Month	End-User Services Fall, 1986	Librarian-Mediated Service Fall, 1985	Fall, 1986	% change in Mediated Service Fall, 1986
September	101	40	37	-7.5%
October	594	116	76	-35.0%
November	378	80	63	-21.0%
December	122	53	44	-17.0%
TOTALS	1,195	289	220	-24.0%

taken the CAI tutorial or workshop and are now doing their own searching. As Table 3 indicates, mediated searching has decreased by 24%, but overall searching has increased by 413% in three months. In addition, as Tables 4 and 5 show, the unit cost for database searching on optical media is dramatically lower than on-line searching.

On-Line versus Optical Costs for Information

"The most common method of determining the cost of an online search is to include charges for computer connect time, communications, and off-line prints."[2] This corresponds to what

Table 4

Average Costs of Searching, by Month (Fall 1986)

Date	End-User Service CD-ROM[1]	Dial-Out[2]	Librarian-Mediated Service Dial-Out[3]
9/86	$ 6.24[4] (9/22->)	$ 2.98[5] (9/22->)	$ 19.95
10/86	1.61	9.28	22.14
11/86	3.06	6.14	15.75
12/86	13.26	2.39[5]	14.54

[1]SilverPlatter's ERIC and PsycLit
[2]BRS/After Dark, Knowledge Index, WILSEARCH
[3]BRS, DIALOG, WILSONLINE, and VUTEXT
[4]ERIC only
[5]Heavily weighted by WILSEARCH use

Table 5

Average Costs of Searching by Type of Service, Fall 1986

COSTS	End-User Service CD-ROM	Dial-Out	Librarian-Mediated Service Dial-Out
Total costs:	$2498.75	$2881.85	$4053.17
# of searches:	790	405	220
Fall '86 av.cost:	$3.16	$7.12	$ 18.40

Koch calls production costs in her review of costs of on-line searching.[3] She also identifies support costs (hardware, supplies, etc.)[4] and overhead costs (costs associated with planning and administering the service).[5] For ease of transfer of information to other institutional settings, this paper looks at production costs only in the comparison of average search costs among the various on-line and CD-ROM services.

Production costs for CD-ROM services are figured simply by dividing the total cost of each subscription by the number of months in the year, and then by dividing that monthly charge by number of searches. The obvious point to make is that heavy use of these fixed-cost services will result in very low average search costs. For example, October 1986 was UVM's busiest month in the ARC. There were 594 logged searches, of which 368 were on the CD-ROM ERIC service. The prorated monthly cost for the service is $312.50, so that the average cost for a search of that service during October was the astoundingly low figure of $.85. During that single month, 368 users logged 184 hours of time on the ERIC service. In FY86 the total hours of usage for ERIC in the librarian-mediated service was 33 hours, with significantly fewer users served.

UVM has been able to gather comparative data on end-user services (CD-ROM and dial-out) for slightly more than three months. Table 4 shows the average costs for each type of service month by month. Table 5 shows an average cost for each service over the entire period. Unfortunately, no effort has been made to capture comparable cost data for the use of corresponding print sources at this institution.

A final point that should be made about CD-ROM products is that institutions may see costs come down because CD-ROM subscription prices are being lowered. In January 1987, Silver-Platter announced a price reduction in its ERIC product, at least in part due to competition for ERIC services from two other vendors (DIALOG and OCLC). Purchasers of CD-ROM services will want to do comparative shopping before buying a system.

The average search cost for the end-user dial-out services is disproportionately low ($7.12), skewed by the inclusion of searches done on WILSEARCH, a service that has a very low cost per search. Table 6 breaks down the data by individual service: BRS/After Dark, Knowledge Index and WILSEARCH.

The University of Pittsburgh study on end-user searching reported an average search cost for BRS/After Dark (over a ten-month period) of $11.66, and an average search cost for Knowledge Index searches of $11.62 (over a two-month period).[6] Certainly those costs are comparable to those observed at UVM: BRS/After Dark - $9.39; Knowledge Index - $12.16. UVM's reported lower average search cost for BRS/After Dark is likely accounted for in one of two ways: users selected less expensive databases to search, or they printed fewer citations (users are limited to forty citations in any half-hour session). It is interesting to note, however, that at UVM the average BRS/After Dark search cost seemed to be on a downward trend each month.

The librarian-mediated service has consistently reported an average search cost of approximately $19.00 (for FY85-86 and again in fall, 1986). Most of the searches done are for graduate students and faculty and are of a highly complex nature — multiconcept, and searched in several databases. The searchers all have four of more years of search experience. The effect of the end-user search service is beginning to be felt in the librarian-mediated service. From October through December 1986, there was an observed drop in activity of 17% (of funds expended), a real dollar savings of nearly $700. It is likely that several patterns will begin to emerge in the next year: (1) very few undergradu-

Table 6

Average Search Cost by End-User Dial-Out Service, by Month and for Entire Period (Fall 1986)

Month	BRS/After Dark	Knowledge Index	WILSEARCH
September	not available	$17.37	$1.57
October	$13.93	14.84	3.06
November	7.79	5.89	2.03
December	6.76	11.21	2.39
Average for period:	$9.39	$12.16	$2.32

ates will use the mediated search service; (2) database use will change as users do their own searches in the standard databases in the ARC; (3) the average search cost, which has been quite steady over time, will increase as searchers are called upon to search unfamiliar, and often more expensive databases.

Instructional Program Design and Costs

In-house preparation of end-user instructional information is the norm. Librarians generally have found vendor training materials unsatisfactory — usually because they are too detailed. For instance, the end-user manual for Knowledge Index is well over 100 pages — excellent, thorough, and not likely to be used by someone learning to search in a library-operated service. Silver-Platter's help screens, which are also very well done, number 61, and are not easily reached via the index screens.

Brevity is the single most important point to consider in the preparation of end-user instructional materials, or sessions. There had been enough of this intimated in the "invisible college" to influence UVM's decision to devise the simplest possible instructional apparatus for training end-users. This, coupled with issues enunciated by Gavett in a paper presented at the meeting "Optical Publishing '86," governed the reference department End-User Task Force's recommendation to use computer-aided instruction:

> Other libraries have successfully used multisession workshops and printed instructional materials for training end-users. We expected very strong demand for searching privileges and, therefore, for training. With no planned staff increases, the workshop was not a feasible alternative. On the other hand, we felt that some form of tutorial feedback, a primary virtue of the workshop format, was essential. Computer-aided instruction (CAI) offered both the possibility of practice with feedback and adaptability to large numbers of learners without heavy commitment of staff time.[7]

The development of a CAI package to train end-users is further detailed in Gavett's paper.[8] It took him about 56 hours to develop the tutorial. In addition, there were modest costs associated with the purchase of the software used to create the CAI package. Total software development costs, then, were about $750.

The reference department has relied heavily on the package for training. It takes users from 20 to 30 minutes to complete and introduces them to the concepts of end-user searching, Boolean logic, and database organization. Future modules will address search strategy formulation, system command language, and other fine points of searching. During fall 1986, 478 end-users were trained using this method, as compared to 79 who were trained in workshops (14 separate sessions averaging six people per session). The workshops took 1.25 to 1.5 hours, where trainers quickly covered the concepts of end-user searching, Boolean logic, and database organization, and then concentrated on search strategy formulation and the command structures of the various systems available in the ARC. An effort was also made to demonstrate a "live" search, whether projected using a large-screen video projector or by direct sign-on by individual learners. This method is labor intensive, but provides excellent training. However, it is not surprising that users chose the CAI package, which took much less time to complete than a workshop, to fulfill the requirement for training.

If one costs out the expense for training by the two different methods employed during the period in question, CAI training cost $1.35/person (excluding overhead, equipment, etc.), and the workshop cost $4.80/person (figuring only the librarian's time at about two hours per session). If this had been the only method of training, and the size of the group was held at ten participants, it would have taken 113 hours of professional time (three full weeks of labor), and would have cost the institution over $1500.

In December 1986, the reference staff decided to write a workbook that would continue training users where the CAI package left off. The stated objectives were to help users learn to:

1. Formulate a workable search strategy;
2. Assign a subject area to a topic;
3. Divide research topics into their main concepts;
4. Assign synonymous or related terms to each concept;

5. Employ wildcards appropriately to search variant forms of a word stem;
6. Use Boolean operators to construct simple search statements;
7. Recognize the command languages of several different end-user systems;
8. Modify a search strategy when search results are unsatisfactory.

A 16-page workbook was written addressing these objectives, and will be tested in its draft form during the spring 1987 semester. Writing and editing took approximately 75 hours, or two full weeks of professional time, and cost around $1040. Printing is currently being done in-house, and costs the institution about $.82 per workbook for supplies and staff time. There is a possibility of eventually translating the workbook to CAI, in which case additional developmental costs would be incurred.

Table 7 details the costs of the various instructional methods in use in the ARC at this time.

There are advantages to each training method, and clearly some individuals respond to one type of training better than another. If the CAI modules could be completed, very interesting

Table 7

Costs of Various Instruction Methods
Employed in the Automated Reference Center

Method	Hours of Staff Time	Costs	
		Developmental	Continuing
CAI	56	$750	----
Workshop	2[1]	----	$29/session[2]
Workbook (January 1987 ->)	75	$1040	$.82/copy[3]

[1]Hours per workshop: .5 hours for preparation; 1.5 hours class time.
[2]Staff and printing costs
[3]Expense of copying: supplies and staff.

data could be gleaned about the effectiveness of a variety of training methods in an end-user search setting.

The CD-ROM systems offer a powerful training tool, as yet untapped at UVM. Some discussion has been given to introducing "structured searches" using the CD-ROM's in the mix of training methods, perhaps in lieu of the workbook. One of the reference librarians is designing a pilot project to explore this possibility.

Continuing Hardware and Supply Costs

Following the initial hardware investment, the reference department has confronted continuing hardware and supply issues. The first issue concerns upgrade of two AT&T 6300s to IBM PC-AT compatibles with hard discs, in order to utilize some of the newly announced CD-ROM publications, such as Dissertation Abstracts and OCLC CD-ROM reference publications. Because the AT&Ts have not always worked with IBM-based software, two new IBM PC-ATs will be purchased for the ARC, in order to eliminate compatibility problems and to ensure that any CD-ROM system can be used on the workstation; the AT&T 6300s will be moved to offices which were scheduled to receive new microcomputers.

The original configuration of dial-out workstations included a security board which made it impossible for students to "get at" the passwords. Users select the on-line database from a menu, and the system software then dials out automatically and provides the password without it showing on the screen. The security board kept users from getting into system software code to view the password. Unfortunately, the security boards are not compatible with other software packages which the reference department staff wishes to use and have become a hindrance rather than a help. Thus, the security boards have been removed. Since the room is monitored at all times and since these services are free to students and faculty, staff has experienced no problems with users trying to gain access to the passwords.

The most startling continuing cost for the ARC has been for printing. Each workstation has an attached Hewlitt-Packard Thinkjet printer, selected because they are very quiet. Based on usage during fall semester, a cost projection for supplies was made for FY88. For Thinkjet supplies, printing costs would have run $9,911 per year ($7,310 for heat-sensitive paper, and $2,601 for ink bladders). A cost-comparison using Epson products indicated that costs could be lowered to $5,100 per year ($3,570 for standard paper, $1,530 for ribbons) if Epson FX-86e printers were used; although noisier, the FX-86e comes with a built-on hood to minimize the noise. Thus, Epson printers will be substituted in the ARC and the Thinkjet printers moved to areas where quiet is mandatory or into offices where the volume of printing and attendant supplies will be much lower.

Impact on Other Public Service Programs

Mention has already been made of the effect that end-user searching is having on the mediated-search service at this institution. The impact, of course, does not stop there. The new information services have begun to influence the interactions at the reference desk, the design of sessions in the library instruction program, interlibrary loan activity, and use of collections (most notably microforms). Three months is certainly not enough time to make definitive statements about impact of these new services, but some general observations are in order.

Reference Desk

UVM has chosen what some would view a conservative method of offering end-user searching. Individuals must be trained before they are allowed to search, and they must make half-hour appointments for use of all systems (except INFO-TRAC). Users of the dial-out services must complete a search planner and have it reviewed by a reference librarian before doing their searches. This obviously has meant that reference librarians spend a fair amount of time discussing search strategies with end-users, as well as helping them determine the most suitable database(s) for a particular search.

On a busy evening, this translates to about 40 to 50 minutes spent counseling end-users, in addition to the regular traffic at the reference desk. Furthermore, this counseling seems to demand a priority, as it is the rare student who appears much in advance of his or her scheduled appointment to discuss the search planner. It would not be an overestimate to say that end-user issues absorb at least one hour per day of staff time at the reference desk, to which one could actually affix a cost.

Interlibrary Loan

Koch says, "A frequently cited cost related impact of on-line searching is an increased demand for document delivery. The effect that this will have on interlibrary loan activity will depend on the size of a library's periodical collection and the ease of access to more extensive collections."[9] UVM has begun to track interlibrary loan requests which use computer searches for verification. From January through August 1986, there were 260 requests using a search as a means of verification. From September through December 1986 (during which months end-user searching was available) there were 240 requests generated as a result of a computer search. It does look as though end-user searching will increase the interlibrary loan traffic significantly at UVM, but more data have to be gathered before this can be proven conclusively.

In a year's time, INFOTRAC searches alone have resulted in an additional five requests per month, most of them for journals that are not likely candidates for subscription at UVM. In addition, there have been more than five requests for several titles, and as a result, copyright restrictions have come into play (preventing the interlibrary loan staff from making further photocopy requests for these titles). The only recourse has been to use a tear sheet service, to purchase or borrow specific issues, or to request permission to photocopy directly from the copyright holder. All of these choices add to the time for and the cost of supplying the item.

UVM is also monitoring the number of unfilled requests to see if these increase over previous years. If they do, a likely correlate will be the use of computer searches to identify sources of information.

Bibliographic Instruction

Institutions that offer end-user searching are seeing it become a dominant theme in instruction sessions.[10] In fall 1986, about one-third of UVM's instruction sessions focused on computer searching, either as part of a continuum of information resources or as the sole topic under discussion. That figure promises to be higher in spring 1987.

Collection Issues

Decision 9 Hs to purchase CD-ROM and other optical systems are, at least in part, based on knowledge of use and availability of collections. It would be a mistake to purchase an ERIC CD-ROM system if there were not a backfile of ERIC documents available in-house. Purchase of INFOTRAC will have ramifications which the purchasing library will have to be prepared to meet; it may even result in the need to acquire the full-text service designed to accompany INFOTRAC.

The presence of these powerful new reference tools appears to have increased the use of parts of the collection at UVM. While impressionistic, periodicals and microforms staff report that ERIC document use is up by at least 33% and that there is increased use of popular, business, and psychology journals, which staff will try to document statistically in the future. Greater use of collections is a desirable state, but one that has costs associated with it, such as for staffing, increased demands for copying services, and a full litany of other items that are familiar to librarians.

Staffing Implications

Institutions have tried a variety of approaches to offering end-user services. The most common scenarios are: placing the service(s) close to the reference desk so that monitoring can be done by reference personnel, or placing the service(s) in a separate area that is monitored by wages personnel, usually student assistants. The first situation is more demanding of staff time, and may require provision of back-ups at the reference desk on nights and weekends to help counsel and guide people through the mechanics of searching. Reference departments may be able to absorb this; if not, at least one new staff position may result. One additional reference librarian was added to the department in 1985 in anticipation of increased demand for service. Experience has proven that the additional staff was necessary.

Services monitored by wages personnel are costly. UVM expects to spend between $13,000 and $14,000 dollars a year to keep the Automated Reference Center open (figured at slightly above minimum wage for 93.5 hours/week during the fall and spring semesters, and at 42 hours/week during intersessions and summer sessions). The library received no new funds for this purpose; funds were reallocated within the existing wages budget.

The demand for mediated searching may well drop off, in which case reference or search service staff time can be diverted to other projects—presumably counseling users of the end-user systems. Some staff time will be redirected to training and bibliographic instruction. It has already been suggested that as much as one-third of the bibliographic instruction sessions at UVM are being devoted, at least in part, to end-user training. Finally, increased interlibrary loan traffic and increased use of collections may result in the eventual need to add staff or wages personnel.

FUNDING SOURCES

Costs for the ARC have been funded through a variety of sources. One-time start-up costs were taken from profits from photocopy machines, end-of-year library budget savings, and capital funds for building modifications. A permanent annual budget increase of $12,000 was added to the Bailey/Howe Materials and Access budget by central administration, equivalent to the costs for mediated searching the previous year. Since mediated searching is dropping, the savings are used for optical end-user systems. Some publications have been cancelled, such as the microform *Magazine Index,* for an approximate savings of $2,050. Supplies are paid from the library's supplies budget. The remainder comes from the Materials and Access Budget; these services compete for base funding with all other publications.

CONCLUSIONS

Experience with the Automated Reference Center, though brief, has affirmed the validity of providing electronic publications as part of the library's basic collection. In order to contain costs, optical systems will continue to be favored, due to their fixed annual costs and their capacity for intensive local use to obtain lower per search unit costs. Since the only additional staff which might be anticipated will have to come from staff reallocations as NOTIS (an integrated automated library system) is implemented in other departments, end-user education must also be economical and will continue to be based on self-paced instruction such as CAI packages, expert systems, and workbooks.

The response to the ARC has been very positive on campus. In fact, many people filling out the evaluation questionnaires have indicated that they have never used the equivalent printed sources, nor were they users of the mediated search services. Use of the library's collections seems to be increasing, and some faculty report that student research papers have improved in quality. Thus, the library staff believes that the expenses associated with these new services are justified. It is anticipated that the reference department librarians will spend increasing amounts of time instructing end-users rather than doing searches themselves.

NOTES

1. *A Strategy for Library Development: University of Vermont, Vermont Department of Libraries, Middlebury College: Preliminary Report* (July 15, 1983), pp. ii, iii, 29-30.

2. Ethel Auster (ed.), "Part 5: Financial Considerations," in *Managing Online Reference Services* (New York: Neal-Schuman Publishers, Inc., 1986), p.159.

3. Jean E. Koch, "A Review of the Costs and Cost-Effectiveness of Online Bibliographic Searching," in *Managing Online Reference Services* (New York: Neal-Schuman Publishers, Inc., 1986), p.165.

4. Jean E. Koch, pp.163-4.

5. Jean E. Koch, pp.167-70.

6. Anne Woodsworth (ed.), *End User Searching: An Experiment at the University of Pittsburgh* (Pittsburgh, PA: University Library System, University of Pittsburgh, May 1986), p.43.

7. Franklin Gavett, "Optical Databases and Dial-Up Services in an Academic Library End-User Search Facility: Hardware and Software Issues," a paper presented at *Optical Publishing '86* (New York: Learned Information, October 1986), p.3. (Paper

available from the author, in care of Colgate University, Everett Needham Library, Hamilton, NY 13346).

8. Franklin Gavett, p.3.

9. Jean E. Koch, pp.170-1.

10. As reported by discussants at "End User Searching: Issues in Instruction, System Selection & Funding and Administration," a program sponsored by ACRL STS Section, ACRL BIS Computer Concerns Committee, and the RASD MARS Direct Patron Access Committee (New York: American Library Association Annual Conference, July 1, 1986).

Budgeting for Reference Services in an On-Line Age

Charles R. Anderson

SUMMARY. Budgetary considerations involved in integrating the use of on-line database searching as a ready reference tool are examined. A distinction is made between the use of on-line searching for ready reference at a public desk and computerized literature searching in academic or special libraries. There are suggestions for developing a methodology to analyze the relative cost-effectiveness of using on-line and print sources. The author implies that the use of on-line databases for ready reference is philosophically no different than the use of any other type of reference source, therefore, special treatment in budgeting for on-line searching used in support of ready reference is unwarranted and antithetical to a full service policy.

Currently budgeting practices in most public libraries probably do not take into account the effects of on-line searching. Significant amounts of resources may be allocated to standing orders for print sources in order to "stay current" without any rational certainty these sources are cost-effective. Judging from the literature and discussions at library gatherings, on-line resources have not had a significant impact on the print budget of small or medium-sized libraries, although some large institutions have dropped extremely expensive print sources such as *Chemical Abstracts* in favor of the on-line equivalent (Rollins, 1983). At conference panel discussions on on-line searching, a frequent question asked is, "Have you canceled any print sources?" Very seldom does the panelist answer, "Yes."

Charles R. Anderson is the Head of Information Services, Northbrook Public Library, 1201 Cedar Lane, Northbrook, IL 60062.

This paper will discuss how on-line searching can supplement, and in some cases supplant standing orders for some print materials. First, however, some background and rationale is needed to explain the utility of adding on-line database searching to reference services.

A clear distinction should be drawn between use of on-line services in a ready reference setting and the literature searches done in academic or special libraries. Because many librarians and some writers in the field tend to consider on-line searching as if it were one monolithic type of service, there exists a perception, particularly in smaller institutions, that on-line searching is expensive, is not justified, and would have very little utility in their libraries.

However, a close parallel can be drawn between reference service policies that provide manual reference help but exclude comprehensive literature searches of print indexes and policies that permit ready reference on-line searching but prohibit extensive on-line literature searching (unless patron-reimbursed). Exactly the same process is involved in ready reference on-line and manual searching. Only the source used is different. Ready reference searching involves "quick and dirty" searching, *not* extended question negotiation and lengthy research. Public libraries traditionally never have attempted to provide extensive bibliographic research — literature searches — for patrons at no charge. There probably have not been many instances where this lengthy kind of searching was done for a fee. Staff limitations usually limit any extensive research commitment, although some library systems with backup (second or third level reference services), have tried to provide more extensive research coverage.

On-line searching to fill a stated need of the type, "I have to know about all the research that has been conducted on the thermodynamics of thiotuomaline, particularly as applied to water interactions," clearly differs from questions such as, "I remember reading a story several weeks ago in one of the business magazines on a new type of bubble memory chip — where can I find the story?" The former type of question probably requires at least a minimum amount of chemical knowledge on the part of the searcher, perhaps a good amount of experience with chemical databases, and an intelligent negotiation of the question with the patron. The latter category of question can be searched on-line in a quick and dirty mode by any reference librarian with a knowledge of search techniques, i.e., the mechanics of on-line searching—logging on, bringing up a database, entering terms, and printing results.

To treat both types of questions as if they involved the same level of reference service and required the same type of expertise is to badly misunderstand the nature of ready reference on-line searching. With limited funds and staffing patterns, small and medium-sized public libraries would find it very difficult to conduct literature searches. But there is no reason why many of these libraries should not use on-line databases as ready reference tools. In some cases, these on-line databases may be more cost-effective than print sources, even for small libraries.

On-line sources have one benefit of great significance for smaller libraries—they are a pay-as-you-go service. Unlike high-priced indexes or other print reference sources, you can do on-line searching and only pay when you use the service. Unfortunately, the precise billing furnished by a database vendor at the conclusion of a search has focused an inordinate amount of attention on the cost of answering a question using an on-line database. What has been lost in this flurry of attention is the cost of answering a question using a print source—an expense that is almost a total unknown.

ANALYSIS OF PRINT SOURCE USE

What does it cost to use a print source? This question has not been well-addressed in the literature. Some reference cost studies have been, in effect, on a macroeconomic level—in some cases limited to computing total reference budgets, staff costs, and numbers of questions answered, and in others attempting to quantify time spent on individual questions.

At Northbrook we conducted a three-month long study of in-library use of 40 reference books. The dollar cost of standing orders to these sources was $6294.25 in FY 1986/87. We followed the principles suggested by *Output Measures for Public Libraries*, however we tallied individual use for each book for a total of 13 weeks and then estimated annual usage. The particular books chosen were selected because: (1) they all required annual (or more frequent) updating, and (2) while they were all standard sources that library reference classes suggest should be in many libraries, we did not have any solid evidence of how frequently they were being used. We thought some at least might be potential candidates for cancellation. We eliminated from the study books such as Standard & Poor's *Register of Corporations* which is consulted almost daily in our library. We acknowledged several limitations on the accuracy of the data collection. There might be an underestimation of use from some patrons reshelving books being studied despite prominent notices on the cover of each book saying "PLEASE DO NOT RESHELVE THIS BOOK." Also, measuring unattended use does not at all measure benefit to the user, since, unless the patron asks, there is no way to know whether desired information was found. However, *Output Measures* has given an accepted validity to measurements of in-library use of materials.

The sample items were then tabulated into a frequency distribution (see Figure 1). In a variation of the Pareto Rule, 11 of the 40 sources (27.5%) accounted for nearly 80% of the uses. The annual cost of these 11 sources amounts to $2719.28, or 43.2%

Items	Use Freq.	Cum. freq.	Cum. %
19	0	0	0.00%
7	1	7	3.89%
1	2	9	5.00%
2	4	17	9.44%
4	5	37	20.56%
3	7	58	32.22%
1	9	67	37.22%
1	16	83	46.11%
1	34	117	65.00%
1	63	180	100.00%
40			

FIGURE 1. Frequency of use of selected reference materials.

of the total cost for the 40. To put it in more depressing terms, better than 50% of this part of the reference budget is being spent to satisfy less than 20% of the demand for items in the group. Besides calling for a reevaluation of the usefulness of some of these sources, this is a perfect illustration of the inherent problems of allocating funds in advance for unknown information needs.

In order to arrive at some idea of an annual cost per use of this group of books, it is necessary to project the sampled use pattern over the course of one year. Using only those sources which had measurable use during the period of study, and *Output Measures* as a guide (which recommends calculating annual use on the basis of 50 weeks), we arrived at an annual estimated use for all sources of 692 or an average per item use cost of $9.10. The individual cost per use factor ranged from $1.81 for the *IMS Directory of Publications* to $58.50 for Moody's *OTC Manual*.

Interestingly enough, a survey of any listing of database searches in a heavily used search service will show this same pattern of widely varying costs. The significant fact is that if *any one* reference source is considered on an individual basis in a cost/use study, it is possible to find sources that are extremely expensive to use and sources that are very cheap. The same thing holds true for on-line database searching. In planning allocation of resources the important question to ask is at what point does it become impractical in terms of return on cost to continue to purchase a reference source, and whether there are alternatives to access the information needed. These questions are examined in the next section.

ALTERNATIVE REFERENCE SOURCES

The subset of print reference sources used in the preceding paragraphs for cost studies can serve as paradigms for examining alternative on-line methods of answering questions. Of the 21 sources listed in Figure 2, we identified six (indicated with an asterisk preceding the title) containing information that might reasonably be findable on-line. However, the total annual cost of these six print sources totals $1754.64, or 42.68% of the annual expenditure for the entire group of publications. It could be sig-

	Cost	Use (13 weeks)	Use (annual)	Cost /use
Acronyms Dictionary (Gale)	$166.00	1	4	$43.16
American Library Directory	119.69	1	4	31.12
Best's Property & Casualty	363.82	4	15	23.65
Bowker Annual	70.57	1	4	18.35
Broadcasting Yearbook	85.00	5	19	4.42
Commercial Atlas	189.73	7	27	7.05
*Dir. of Corp. Affiliations	247.90	34	131	1.90
Druggist Blue Book	24.53	1	4	6.38
Dun's Consultants Directory	225.00	9	35	6.50
*Facts on File	85.52	5	19	4.45
*IMS Dir. of Publications	111.22	16	62	1.81
*Million Dollar Directory	895.00	63	242	3.69
*Moody's Industrial Manual	190.00	7	27	7.06
*Moody's OTC Manual	225.00	1	4	58.50
Municipal Year Book	64.65	2	8	48.75
Official Museum Directory	86.00	4	15	5.59
Political Handbook of the World	81.24	1	4	21.12
Rand Mcnally Bankers Directory	158.40	5	19	8.24
Shepard's Acts and Cases	190.58	1	4	49.55
Wiesenberger Investment Co. Svc.	295.00	5	19	15.34
Working Press of the Nation	236.51	7	27	8.78
Totals	$4,111.36	180	692	

FIGURE 2. Use factors for selected sources.

nificant if it were possible to determine what it might have cost if on-line sources were substituted for these six print sources. In investigating this possibility, we created a comparison ratio called the On-line/Manual (O/M) ratio consisting of the projected on-line search cost for a question divided by the projected print search cost. The on-line cost is composed of the sum of connect time, citation royalties, communications charges, and librarian's time. Similarly, the print cost is a summation of the cost of buying, processing, storing, and in some cases (if the librarian is involved) accessing the resource. For the purposes of these comparisons, an assumption was made that, ceteris paribus, capital costs and overhead could be ignored. The ratio is also used to compare salary costs alone in on-line versus manual searching.

In trying to analyze use on this micro level, however, there is a large unknown in the use pattern that must be acknowledged. To use the *Directory of Corporate Affiliations* as an example, while DIALOG's file 516, *Dun's Market Identifiers*, can identify a parent company — one of the main reasons for consulting the *Directory of Corporate Affiliations* — the mere fact that we observed the print source in use doesn't tell us *how many* different companies a patron might have been looking up. A typical successful on-line search on file 516 usually costs us around $3.25 in search costs and $.90 in staff costs. If the observed use of the print volume was only for one company, then at the observed rate of use the O/M ratio would be:

$$\frac{C + R + T + L}{B + P + S + [L]}$$

where C = connect time; R = citation royalty; T = telecommunication costs; L = librarians time; B = book cost; P = processing costs; and S = storage cost (if one could obtain perfect knowledge of all costs).

The question of processing and storage costs opens doors to realms of calculations that would delight an econometrics fanatic. Accurate dollar values in this area are extremely difficult to obtain. Surveying the literature leads one to conclude that the only way to be certain of your own processing and storage costs is to do your own study — a time-consuming and expensive technique. In an extremely detailed study done at Washington State University, automated processing costs ranged from $3.024 per unit for materials cataloged via the on-line system, to $15.06 per unit for materials requiring original cataloging. If we assume our library could process the *Directory of Corporate Affiliations* for the lower figure, and we ignore the storage cost, the ratio computes to 2.2, i.e., using an on-line source would be about 2.2 times as costly as a print source if the print source use were limited to one company. The true ratio is of course less than this because the addition of storage costs, including such things as insurance, will increase the value of the denominator in the equation. It is obvious that each additional company lookup in the print version would rapidly make the print source far more cost-effective. Looking up four companies on-line versus manually would produce an O/M ratio of about 8.1 (some on-line economies accrue in batching searches).

Even when a librarian's time is factored into the equation for using this print source, it remains obvious that an on-line file can't economically substitute for this manual source in our library. However, if the use pattern had been completely different, for example only 24 projected uses in a year, for a manual per use cost of $10.33, the relationship changes dramatically, giving us a 0.4 O/M ratio. Now it would be nearly half as costly to use the on-line resource for a single consult, and the breakeven point would come at about 3 companies being checked at one time. We have only a reference librarian's intuition to work with as far as guessing the number of companies people tend to look up at one time, but experience suggests it tends towards the lower end — one or two companies — rather than a long list of affiliations.

The above is a very superficial examination of cost factors and is intended primarily to illustrate how important it is to consider individual patterns of use when making judgments about the utility of on-line versus manual searching. For example, consider the projected per use cost of Moody's *OTC Industrial Manual* — $58.50. This is an expensive tool to maintain at this use rate if an alternative is available on-line. DIALOG's File 555, *Moody's Corporate Profiles*, according to DIALOG's "Blue Sheet," "provides essential, concise, descriptive and financial information on 3,600 of the most important publicly-held companies. This includes all companies on the New York Stock Exchange and American Stock Exchange plus 1,300 of the most active companies traded over-the-counter." The print version of Moody's *OTC Industrial Manual* includes about 3300 over-the-counter companies. Thus, if the on-line source were used as a substitute for the print copy, about 61% of the over-the-counter companies would not be findable in File 516. However, 10-K extracts could probably be found in a more expensive DIALOG database — File 100.

In actual practice, it seems reasonable to theorize that the probability of patron disappointment because the company being searched was not in the on-line version would probably not be as high as 61% because of a likely connection between most active companies and patron interest. This is speculation of course, but a potential savings of $225 in up-front subscription costs is perhaps worth some consideration of potential alternatives. Retrieving information on one company from file 555 if the searcher goes in armed with the D-U-N-S number (a unique number for each company obtainable through Duns *Business Identification Service*) should cost around $4.25. The O/M ratio in this case becomes 0.073. Even if one observed use of the print version meant a patron was looking up multiple companies, on-line searches would be more cost-effective up to the point where 13 to 14 companies were being checked at one time by the patron.

The thesis intended by the above is not that a great deal of time should be spent in trying to analyze in specific detail the in-library use of print resources. As noted, collecting this sort of data is susceptible to error. But if the reference staff does not already have a good knowledge of use patterns of many of these costly print sources, it could be well worth the time to try to collect some hard data, possibly leading to some substitution of on-line sources for print. This is not a new idea, of course. Crawford (1979) described the results of putting similar ideas into practice in an academic library that considers on-line searching as simply an alternative reference source; does not charge for searching; and uses the on-line databases at the librarian's discretion.

It seems quite probable from observation of a number of reference departments that some standing orders are maintained simply because they are considered "standard" sources that "ought" to be in a library of a certain size, or from a belief that a certain source is the only way to answer a question that *might* occur at some unknown point in the future. Allocating reference resources on this basis of "might be used" is getting to be a luxury that many libraries can not afford. This is what makes on-line searching so attractive — except for equipment, which a library may already own, there is no up-front cost, nor are any funds spent for information before it is needed. And in a number of cases, it may be more cost-effective to use on-line sources even if the print equivalent is in the library.

COST-EFFECTIVENESS
OF ON-LINE SEARCHING VS. MANUAL

Only a few writers have dealt with comparisons between the cost of answering questions manually versus on-line. Mick (1979), in an extensive literature review, reports several cost-effectiveness studies comparing manual and on-line searching, but these papers are nearly ten years old. Furthermore, they deal with literature searching, while this paper focuses on ready reference uses. Two more recent articles perhaps come closer to the ready reference experience being studied here. Roose (1985) and Rollins (1983) have calculated some comparative costs in two situations — the Deerfield, Illinois and Houston, Texas public libraries.

Deerfield is a small public library in an affluent north suburban Chicago community and spent over $6000 in just under five years of on-line searching. Houston Public, in the Rollins article, had a yearly search budget of close to $20,000. Roose reports a per question cost at Deerfield of $1.83 for printed resources and $4.17 in salary costs ($6.00 per question total) for answering questions using manual sources. The on-line costs given for Deerfield are $5.30 per question, plus a suggestion that the labor cost per question may be only $.83 for a total of $6.13. Since Roose extrapolates the labor cost at Deerfield from Rollins' Houston labor comparisons, there is insufficient data to put too much emphasis on this labor figure. Also, Deerfield's cost estimates admittedly do not include overhead or fringe benefits. When all these factors are included as in Figure 3, we found a very narrow spread in costs at Northbrook. There is a wider difference in the Houston study — $15.75 for on-line and $22.50 for manual searching, although the Houston study omits a number of associated costs such as resources and overhead.

A more detailed breakdown of costs at Northbrook is given in Figure 3. These numbers differ from the above calculations because they are derived from a broader consideration of cost figures. The salary cost is calculated by totaling the full- and part-

	With Databases	Without Databases
Questions	49000	48400
Salary cost of questions	$1.44	$1.46
Resource cost of questions	.76	.65
Operating Cost of questions	1.57	1.59
Total cost	$3.76	$3.71
Net difference	$.05	

FIGURE 3. Cost factors in answering questions.

time salaries plus fringe benefits, multiplying the result by a factor representing the proportion of total hours spend on the reference desk and the proportion of these total hours spent on reference transactions as distinguished from directional transactions. The result was then divided by the number of questions to arrive at a cost per question. Similarly, the resource cost is based on total reference book budget (which ignores the resource costs of circulating materials and periodicals). The operating cost was derived from the total operating budget of the library and expenses of the on-line catalog multiplied by factors representing the portion of the library occupied by the reference department and the number of public and staff on-line computer catalog terminals in reference. The unit operating and salary costs are slightly less when on-line searching is included because this increases the total number of questions answered. On this generalized level, it appears that adding on-line searching does not materially affect the overall cost of answering reference questions.

When on-line searching is used primarily as a ready reference tool — resulting in a high proportion of quick and dirty searches, the labor costs drop dramatically. For example, an examination of the search logs for the 600 Northbrook questions used in this study reveals that 90% did not require extended (defined as 0.5 hour or more as in the Rollins study) librarian time in searching or question negotiation. Rather, the time spent in question negotiation was about 2 minutes. The average time spent on-line per question was 4.36 minutes. Thus the maximum labor cost for most of the questions was about $1.14 (at $10.80/hour including fringe benefits).

The average cost per minute for database connect time, citation charges, telecommunications, and dedicated telephone line was $1.84 in this period, or $8.02 per question. (See Figure 4 for a complete breakdown of search costs.) Therefore the total cost for quick and dirty type searches was $9.16 – about two-thirds of the reported cost at Houston – which no doubt reflects the greater use of on-line services for extended research questions at Houston. By comparison, answering the kind of reference questions searched on-line using print sources in the Rollins study cost $22.50 per question (labor costs). If Rollin's ratio of 5 to 1 in terms of manual versus on-line search time requirements is used, a comparable time spent on these questions at Northbrook would be about 32 minutes, or $5.76 in salary costs. This produces an O/M ratio for labor costs of 1.14/5.76 or 0.198, i.e., the on-line searching option is extremely cost-effective in terms of labor. Whether on-line searching is more cost-effective in terms of print acquisition costs, as has been seen previously, depends on the frequency of use of the print source.

COST ANALYSIS VALIDITY

In the breakdown in Figure 3 only resources added to the collection in the year of counting questions are considered. It might be argued that using manual sources is different than on-line because when you buy a book, you can re-use it in later years. But you also have to consider that each year it is necessary to add or replace print sources, therefore it is legitimate to analyze costs on the basis of one year's questions and expenditures. However, how meaningful is this analysis?

If one simply divides an annual reference book budget by the number of questions answered, a very low resource cost is produced – $.65 per question in the example from Figure 3. But typically the entire resources of the library may be called upon in answering questions manually, including circulating books, periodicals, on-line book catalog if available, and even the telephone. There seems to be no practical way to gain perfect knowledge of all costs involved in manual searches, i.e., to attribute a

1985/86	DIALOG Connect Hours	Cost	BRS Connect Hours	Cost	Vu-Text Connect Hours	Cost	WilsonLine Connect Hours	Cost
May	3.051	$384.73	1.267	$49.08	-	-	-	-
Jun	1.299	$194.77	0.683	$39.06	-	-	-	-
Jul	1.915	$50.20	0.848	$60.72	-	-	-	-
Aug	1.953	$260.49	1.172	$82.17	0.25	$32.15	-	-
Sep	2.000	$249.38	2.377	$98.79	0.57	$72.13	-	-
Oct	1.618	$186.00	2.273	$175.35	0.61	$76.23	-	-
Nov	1.622	$196.40	1.734	$134.86	0.41	$41.00	-	-
Dec	1.742	$210.90	1.112	$80.88	0.71	$71.00	0.079	$2.15
Jan	1.881	$244.75	0.986	$64.77	0.42	$42.00	0.064	$3.62
Feb	1.544	$301.43	1.192	$64.91	0.30	$30.00	0.078	$4.71
Mar	1.916	$297.43	2.130	$108.05	0.37	$36.90	0.110	$5.72
Apr	1.600	$267.24	1.061	$57.39	0.50	$50.00	0.124	$7.07
Totals	22.141	$2,843.72	16.835	$1,016.03	4.14	$451.41	0.455	$23.27
Averages	1.845	$236.98	1.403	$84.67	0.46	$50.16	0.091	$4.65
Avg./hour		$128.44		$60.35		$109.04		$51.14
Avg./Min		$2.14		$1.01		$1.82		$0.85

Total Connect Hours	Telephone Line Charges	Total Cost	Average Cost per hour	Average Cost per min.
43.571	$472.68	$4,807.11	$110.33	$1.84

FIGURE 4. Online search costs.

portion of the total resource budget to the actions used in answering questions. Furthermore, in our experience at least 30% of on-line searches could not be answered at all using print sources. Studies of specific database usage indicate at least this many of our on-line searches involve business sources—files such as D&B's *Market Identifiers* or the ABI/INFORM database—for which there are no print counterparts.

We are left therefore, with any attempt to analyze print search costs being based on studies of individual questions and sources used. And this method, as we have seen earlier, can produce widely varying costs depending on the source used and the number of uses. The classic example, which frequently turns up in articles about manual searching, is *Grove's Dictionary of Music and Musicians*. Many libraries bought this because it is a classic, even though it may be years before the cost/benefit ratio even begins to approach on-line searching.

ALTERNATIVE BUDGETING PATTERNS

We can use the breakdown of costs in Figure 3 as a model in which varying options of budgeting can be analyzed. The data in this table assumes that two categories of expense are fixed, i.e., it is a given that we would have spent the same amount on salaries and operating expenditures whether database searching was used or not. The only significant difference, then, in costs is in the resource column. Considering the on-line searching budget as another resource expenditure produces a net difference in cost per question of about $0.05 to include database searching. If some of the factors in the model are changed to reflect a decision to cancel little or unused print sources and substitute on-line searching for sources with a projected annual cost/use of more than $5.00 there is no appreciable effect on this cost difference— the increased number of searches is balanced by the savings from canceled print resources. However, we can be certain that money expended in this way could go directly to provide useful information, not for standing orders that might or might not be of use someday.

Drawing a distinction between on-line and manual searching, which can lead to the above type of calculations, may be a moot point. As far as our patrons are concerned, questions are questions. Information is the desired product, and the channel by which this produce is provided is usually immaterial to the user. If the information can not be provided, then the significance of the channel may become important. For instance, in almost all cases in those libraries lacking a backup reference service, many of the 600 database questions analyzed earlier would simply have been turned away—there would have been no way to answer the majority of these without using a database. The questions that were answered using a database are no different than any set of questions that need a specific type of resource to answer. If a significant need exists for certain resources to provide information, it is the responsibility of the library wherever possible to budget to fill these needs. The exact form of the resources should depend on the best judgment of the librarians involved—not on irrelevant criteria such as what format the information is stored in—print or electronic.

CONCLUSION

It is easy to watch standing order budgets grow as print resources become more expensive each year. Checking a renewal notice for many expensive sets of reference tools is certainly simpler than reevaluating the use these sources are getting and trying to answer hard questions about their value. It is also easy to avoid new ways of providing information, requiring training and new skills, with the claim that the new on-line methods are too costly. But at some point it is going to become very hard to explain to an increasingly sophisticated information consumer that we have been making rational allocation decisions to buy books no one is using, or investing in public access computer catalogs that are very difficult for the occasional library user to master, while we have avoided offering access to hundreds of databases with precise needed information—information that is both current and cost-effective. It is our responsibility to start thinking now about changing some budget priorities to take maximum advantage of this on-line age.

REFERENCES

Crawford, Paula J. & Judith A. Thompson, "Free online searches are feasible." *Library Journal* 104 (April 1, 1979), 793-95.

Druschel, Joselyn, "Cost analysis of an automated and manual cataloging and book processing system." *Journal of Library Automation* 14 (March, 1981), 24-49.

Mick, Colin K., "Cost analysis of information systems and services," *Annual Review of Information Science and Technology* 14 (1979), 37-64.

Rollins, Gene, "Some economies of online searching: Experience at Houston Public Library." *Public Library Quarterly* 4 (Summer, 1983), 13-18.

Roose, Tina, "Online or print: Comparing costs," *Library Journal* 110 (September 15, 1985), 54-55.

Zweig, Douglas & Eleanor Jo Rodger, *Output Measures for Public Libraries*. Chicago: American Library Association, 1982.

Multiple File Computer Searching: Can Trends in Use Be Predicted?

Jean E. Crampon

SUMMARY. This research project examines on-line searching data to determine if there are criteria which can identify the frequency of multiple file searching for use in predicting costs. Five years of data from the searching records of an academic medical research library were reviewed to identify the number of search requests answered using one, two, three, or more specific numbers of databases. Searches used for the study included all interactive subject requests and ready reference use. The data revealed some seasonal variation and a lower volume of multiple file searching than is reported in other research. The months with higher levels of search requests did not result in higher multiple file use, but in higher single file use.

The on-line search literature has numerous articles on setting up a search service, fee versus free discussions, selecting and training search intermediaries, training end users, and comparing intermediaries and end users. This research project tries to answer two questions: (1) Are there criteria which can be used to identify frequency of multiple file searching? and (2) What are the costs for this type of complex, and presumably more expensive, searching?

Jean E. Crampon is Head of the Hancock Library of Marine Biology and Oceanography, University of Southern California, Los Angeles, CA 90089-0371. The data were collected while the author was Head Reference Librarian, Southern Illinois University School of Medicine, Springfield.

BACKGROUND OF SIU-SM LIBRARY SERVICES

Southern Illinois University School of Medicine (SIU-SM) Library was established in 1970 with on-line searching of the National Library of Medicine's MEDLARS system being provided by the first reference librarian beginning in 1971. SIU-SM began as a three-year, community-based medical school with the first year basic science courses being given on the main campus of the system in Carbondale, and the clinical materials, clerkships, and residency programs taught in Springfield. Four Family Practice residency programs in central and southern Illinois also are affiliated with the School. The SIU-SM Library supports all of these educational programs as well as research in the basic sciences and some basic science graduate study. School of Medicine faculty are on 12-month contracts, so faculty, students, and residents are requesting service 12 months a year, not just the nine months of the standard academic year. All personnel, faculty, staff, residents, students of the School of Medicine and patient or educational needs of the affiliated hospitals are provided computer searching without charge to either the requester or the department. The entire cost has been part of the Medical Library's budget.

Southern Illinois University's main campus and general academic library are 200 miles away in Carbondale; therefore, in addition to the obvious medical information needs the Medical Library provides both reference support and materials for administrative needs, a graduate extension program in higher education, and general subject needs upon request. The Medical Library also serves as backup to provide service to the School of Medicine personnel in Carbondale.

The School changed to a four-year curriculum in 1983 with the basic sciences of anatomy, physiology, and biochemistry remaining in Carbondale and most of the curriculum in pharmacology, medical microbiology, and immunology moved to Springfield. This has resulted in increased time allotted to required and elective clerkship rotations through clinical and some humanities support departments, classroom teaching, and research with a corresponding increase in demand for support by the Library to these areas in addition to maintaining their support of basic reference services. There has been an accompanying increase in the Medical Library's faculty teaching responsibilities.

During the first two years of the study there was a close tie to the School of Nursing at SIU in Edwardsville (100 miles away) with searches being provided to nursing faculty and students at no charge. There was also an active RHEC (Regional Health Education Center) program which enabled hospitals in central and southern Illinois to obtain library service, including searching, without charge for the first three years of the study. SIU-E now provides searching for its own faculty and students including the nursing program. Former RHEC institutions now have the same status as other external requesters whose search requests have always been billed for the cost of searching. Other semiregular requesters have included students and faculty from other academic institutions and state agencies in the Springfield area who have need of health science information. This includes some support of programs in nursing, health administration, and medical technology both academic and hospital-based.

The librarians have faculty rank at the School of Medicine and over the five years of the study have increased the percent of time devoted to faculty responsibilities such as research, publishing, service to professional organizations, teaching, and administrative duties. Reference staff available to do searching ranged from three to five persons during the study. All faculty have teaching responsibilities. One searcher is a paraprofessional and had neither administrative nor teaching responsibilities during the search study time. No one does only searching. In all cases the searchers had additional teaching, library, or administrative responsibilities. The people available to search or do other reference functions ranged from 1.5 to 3.35 full-time equivalents with a maximum of one-half of a single person's time being devoted to searching.

Based on one study of searching on the National Library of Medicine using MEDLINE,[3] one FTE searcher should be able to do between 1400 and 1600 searches per year with search defined as equivalent to database access. If this is calculated as SIU-SM Library was staffed, this should have enabled 1050 to 1200 searches to be done when the staff was at the 1.5 level (.75 available to search) or 2345 to 2680 to be done when the staff was at the 3.35 level (1.675 available to search). As can be seen in Table 1 the highest rate (1600 per searcher year) was met three years out of the five in the study and the lower rate (1400) was met for an additional year as though staffing was at the 3.35 level for four out of five years. In reality staffing was at the 3.35 level for only 12 months during the entire time with 11 of those months in FY83. Staffing was at the 1.5 level for four months of FY86. Based on these figures, I feel that the 1600 rate is more appropriate for planning purposes for an academic library. Table 1 includes all searching activity by purpose of the search including automatically updated searches, or SDIs, in the research category. This total is higher than that of the searches included in the study due to the study excluding certain categories (See Data Collection.)

DATA COLLECTION

To obtain the data for this research project, five years of search request records from July 1981 through June 1986 were reviewed from the files of an academic medical research library. It was decided to include all interactive search requests and all reference searching requests from this time period although all searches were examined. The author reviewed all data to ensure that the criteria were applied consistently to include search requests indicated as being for the purposes of research, teaching, grants, or patient care. Backfiles were not counted as separate files

Table 1

Total Search Requests by Purpose
Rank Order

	FY82	FY83	FY84	FY85	FY86	Total	Percentage
Research	1172	1148	1372	1676	1542	6910	51.8
Pt. Care	283	348	317	392	374	1714	12.8
Teaching	277	366	338	253	309	1543	11.6
Verify	150	245	242	229	236	1102	8.3
Reference	86	156	206	253	274	975	7.3
Admin	97	211	171	187	195	861	6.5
Grant	18	43	32	20	28	141	1.1
Other	14	32	18	28	4	96	.7
Total	2097	2549	2696	3038	2962	13342	100.0

searched. This included 6149 search requests with 9320 databases accessed.

The definition of "search" here used was what some prefer to
call a "search request": the use of as many databases as necessary to answer an information request which generally results in a
computer-derived bibliography. This is not the same as the general definition used by this Library, and other academic health
science libraries, for statistical purposes to be compiled in the
*1984-1985 Annual Statistics of Medical School Libraries in the
United States & Canada* the "Houston Survey." According to
this Survey the definition is "the number of times current files of
on-line databases are searched for the specific purpose of obtaining a bibliography or other data in response to a specific inquiry
from a client. An inquiry involving the searching of two files—
e.g., MEDLINE and SCISEARCH—should be counted as two
accesses."[4] In common with this Survey backfile accesses and
SDI profile searches are excluded. These last two criteria are
used because in those instances the search strategy can be at least
partially saved and executed without complete rekeying. Contrary to the above mentioned Survey, search requests which are
considered to be for ready reference use are included.

In reviewing the data, searches performed for Library use: verification, cataloging, etc., were excluded. Searches for training
purposes also were excluded, e.g., use of the MEDLEARN or
INTROMED databases. (MEDLEARN is a computer assisted instruction program and INTROMED is a practice file intended to
be used with a training program and workbook.) Using these
criteria for inclusion accounted for 69.9% of all databases accessed during the five years reviewed for the study; however, it
accounted for 93.9% of the total searching costs. Informal review of searches run for administrative purposes has shown, in
this library at least, that the cost for these searches generally is
about 5% of total searching costs. SDI's account for the remainder of the searching costs at SIU.

Searches were run on NLM's MEDLARS, DIALOG, BRS,
ISI, and NYTIS systems by six different searchers who had varying levels of searching, library, and reference experience. On-
line search experience ranged from beginning searchers to
searchers with five or more years of experience at the beginning

of the study. All searchers had the capability to search more than one search system with the maximum of all five systems. NLM's MEDLARS was used by all searchers, either BRS or DIALOG by three searchers, and all five available systems were used by three other searchers. All of the searchers added at least one new system during the five years reviewed for this project. Four of the searchers had major responsibility in reference for a substantial portion of the study time; three searchers had at least half of their responsibilities in another area of the library, such as circulation or interlibrary loan, for some portion of the time.

The author reviewed search request forms and individual searcher's logs for all searches done during the five year period in order to obtain the data. The logs include brief information for requester of ready reference, departmental affiliation, topic searched, on-line time, citations retrieved, searcher, databases used, and estimated cost. The logs also include verification, search training, and other searching for the Library's purposes which was readily eliminated. The search request forms included all of the information listed above as well as purpose and notes on search strategy. In most cases complete strategies were available for review. Requests were identified as multiple file searches if they had files added within one month of a first request. Data analysis for this study was performed using *pm-Stat*[1] and SuperCalc 4.[2]

SUMMARY OF SEARCHING

During the five years of this study a total of 6149 interactive subject and reference searches were conducted (see Table 2) with an average of 102.48 of these searches per month. This ranged from one month with a low of 46 searches to a high of 143 searches. On average 1.52 files were used in each search with an average of 2.48 files used in each multiple file search. Table 3 presents a frequency distribution of the number of files used for each search. For 65.3% of all searches only one file was used. For the remaining 34.7% of the searches, the majority (72.2%) were run on two files. The highest number of files used in one search was 17. For the 2136 searches which used more than one file, an average of 2.48 files were used per search.

Table 2

Average Search Activity

Number of Search Requests	6149
Number of Databases Used	9320
Searches Per Month	
Average	102.48
Standard Deviation	23.85
Lowest Month	46.00
Highest Month	143.00
Files Per Search	
Average	1.52
Standard Deviation	.98
Files Per Multiple File Search	
Average	2.48
Standard Deviation	1.16

Table 3

Files Per Search
5 Year Total

	Frequency	% Total Searches	% Multiple Searches
Single File	4013	65.3%	
Multiple File	2136	34.7%	100.0%
2 Files	1563	25.4%	73.2%
3 Files	370	6.0%	17.3%
4 Files	100	1.6%	4.7%
5 Files	52	.8%	2.4%
6 Files	17	.3%	.8%
7 Files	7	.1%	.3%
8 Files	10	.2%	.5%
9 Files	7	.1%	.3%
10 Or More Files	10	.2%	.5%
Total	6149	100.0%	

These findings relating to overall searching activity support the findings of previous research. Cooper found an average of 1.5 files per search in his research, which compares with the average of 1.52 files per search found in this study.[5] Although the Northern Illinois study[6] found that only 49.6% of all searches were single file searches, he found that the multiple file searches were more common in the social science disciplines. In the medical disciplines, which at NIU was defined as nursing, allied health, and communication disorders, he found that 69% of all searches were single file searches which is comparable with the 65.3% found in this study.

During the course of this study a maximum of 52 different databases were used in any one month to fulfil search requests with an average of 32.5 different databases being accessed each month. As would be expected in a medical library the most common database used was MEDLINE which accounted for 48.1% of all databases accessed. An additional 30.6% of the total were run on these databases: EMBASE, BIOSIS PREVIEWS, HEALTH, PSYCINFO, ERIC, SCISEARCH, CANCERLIT, CATLINE, and TOXLINE. Therefore, ten databases accounted for 78.7% of the all the databases accessed. At the other end of the spectrum, databases such as American Men and Women of Science, Harvard Business Review Online, Standard & Poor's, Biography Master Index, Disclosure, Standards and Specifications, and Artbibliographies Modern were accessed at most one or two times per year.

For the multiple file searches the two file searches tended to be in a predictable pattern depending on the nature of the original search request. Examination of the original data shows these to be run on highly related files according to the question asked, e.g., MEDLINE and EMBASE for a question in clinical medicine; MEDLINE and CANCERLIT for a cancer question; MEDLINE and HEALTH for a question dealing with health administration; ABI INFORM and Management Contents for a management question; MEDLINE and PSYCINFO for a psychiatric question or PSYCINFO and NCMH for general mental health questions; ERIC and PSYCINFO for educational administration; etc.

The average cost per search for this five year time period was $9.30, and the average cost per file searched was $6.14 (see Table 4). The median cost per database was closer to $5.00 due to the high number of relatively low cost searches using

Table 4

Average Cost Per Search

Average Cost Per Search	$9.30
Average Cost Per Database	$6.14

MEDLINE. These cost figures compare favorably to other research which found costs of $5.30 per database and $9.67 per search request in a public library[7] and an average cost per search being between $7.97 and $10.00 in an academic library.[9]

PATTERNS IN SEARCHING

In examining the patterns of search activity in order to determine if the data from the past five years can be used to predict future search activity, two major questions were addressed. First, was there a relationship between the total number of searches, the percent of multiple file searches, and the average cost per search; and second, was there a seasonal variation in the number of searches and multiple file searches which could be used for staff scheduling?

Table 5 presents the correlations between the total number of search requests, the percent of these requests which represent multiple file searches, and the average cost per search. It was found that as the number of searches per month increases the percent of these searches representing multiple file searches tends to decrease ($r = -.42$). In other words, the higher the level of search activity in a given month the lower the percentage of times more than one database was used to answer the search question. Although further study needs to be carried out to identify the actual cause of this negative relationship, one possible interpretation of these data is that when the searchers have fewer

Table 5

Correlations
Monthly Activity

	Total Searches	% Multiple Files	Total Cost	Average Cost
Total Searches Per Month	1.00	-.42	.56	-.53
% Multiple Files	-.42	1.00	.06	.49
Total Cost Per Month	.56	.06	1.00	.38
Average Cost Per Search	-.53	.49	.38	1.00

requests they have more time to devote to complex multiple file searching.

Since multiple file searches tend to cost more than single file searches (correlation of .49 between percent multiple file searches and average cost per search), a negative correlation was also found between the total number of searches per month and the average cost of a search during that month ($r = -.53$). Thus, although the total cost increases with an increase in search activity (correlation of .56), the average cost per search tends to decrease. Again, although future study is needed, one possible interpretation is that given the additional time available during the low volume months, the searchers can carry out more complex multiple file searches which, while providing the user with more complete information, also result in a higher per search cost.

Given the above relationship between the number of searches per month, the percent multiple file searches, and cost per search it is useful for planning purposes to determine in what months these activities occur. Table 6 presents the seasonal indexes for these three variables. In respect to the total number of searches carried out per month it was found that the highest level of activity occurred during the late winter and early spring with March tending to have the highest level of search activity (averaged 122.01% of an average month). On the other hand the lowest level of search activity occurred during the late summer, fall, and early winter with December being the lowest month with only

Table 6

Monthly Indexes

	Total Searches	% Multiple File Searches	Cost Per Search
Jul	105.63	94.40	91.83
Aug	90.80	113.97	100.79
Sep	89.92	93.52	88.41
Oct	99.96	99.49	88.41
Nov	96.00	116.21	105.46
Dec	72.45	98.30	100.40
Jan	109.98	76.31	87.17
Feb	112.72	97.26	99.64
Mar	122.01	80.99	83.81
Apr	113.83	114.92	95.57
May	95.36	112.35	115.76
Jun	91.43	102.29	125.09

72.45% of the average monthly searches being performed. Thus, for planning purposes this library needs to recognize that a heavy searching workload is going to be placed on the reference staff during the spring, while during the fall the lighter search load may provide additional time for activities which could be postponed from the spring. This might be atypical from a general academic setting due to the 12-month rather than the 9-month academic year, but, if true, could be useful for those institutions which have a heavy fall orientation schedule.

In turning to the percent of multiple file searches, the months of high and low activity do not correspond to the months of high and low activity for total searches. For example, for the month of April both the expected number of searches and percent multiple file searches were higher than the average month (indexes of 113.83 and 114.92 respectively). For the months of July, January, February, and March the total number of searches was predicted to be above average (greater than 100), while the percent of these searches representing multiple file searches was below average (less than 100). On the other hand, during the months of August, November, May, and June the average number of searches per month was below average while the percent multiple file searches was above average. In September, October, and December both the total number of searches and the percent multiple file searches were below average. Thus, for planning purposes in this library, one can predict the lowest level of search activity to occur in September, October, and December while the overall highest level of activity occurs in the spring.

The seasonal index numbers for average cost per search per month are presented in the last column of Table 5. Overall the findings here tend to correspond with the findings for the percent multiple file searches with the highest average cost per search occurring in the spring and the lowest during the fall.

APPLICATIONS FOR THE ADMINISTRATOR OF ON-LINE SEARCHING

Other academic libraries may wish to examine their patterns to identify high total search and high multiple file search months for assistance in administrative decision making for the on-line searching section. First, the administrator must be aware that at SIU searching is an integral part of the reference section, although this is certainly not true at all libraries.

Identifying search activity volume may assist in two ways: (1) Supporting requests for increased total staffing needs can be calculated at 1600 per searcher per year, and (2) Deciding how to schedule staff for particular predicted heavy or light searching times per year can be coordinated with other needs of the staff and the library such as teaching. Average on-line searching costs may assist in (1) Predicting future budget needs for searching and (2) Monitoring the budget during the year and estimating needs for the remainder of the budget year, *i.e.*, can we finish out the year with the budget already 60% spent at the end of December with the heaviest cost months still to come? Probably we need to identify more income to pay the costs. For institutions which charge all users this will not be quite the problem as for those like SIU which only charge external requesters.

For searchers themselves, we must determine and be aware of user needs by time of year as well as by request. Is it possible to give partial results for a long-term project and postpone additional files until such time as the expected volume will decrease? How do we know when to stop? Quint has discussed this problem in more detail than this study for the opinion side and includes her suggestions for decision making.[8]

Further study will be needed at other academic settings to determine if these data hold true and if the reason for the decreased percent of multiple file searching always follows the increase in total search requests.

NOTES

1. Crampon, William J., *Pm-Stat*. (Springfield, IL), 1986.

2. *SuperCalc 4*. (San Jose, CA: Computer Associates), 1986.

3. Werner, Gloria, "Use of on-line bibliographic retrieval services in health science libraries in the United States and Canada," *Bulletin of the Medical Library Association* 67(1)January 1979, pp.1-14.

4. Annual Statistics Project Staff. *1984-1985 Annual Statistics of Medical School Libraries in the United States & Canada*. 8th ed. (Houston: Association of Academic Health Sciences Library Directors and the Houston Academy of Medicine-Texas Medical Center Library), 1986, p.15.

5. Cooper, Michael D., "Usage patterns of an online search system," *Journal of the American Society for Information Science* 34(5)September, 1983, pp.343-9.

6. Hurych, Jitka, "After Bath: Scientists, social scientists, and humanists in the context of online searching," *Journal of Academic Librarianship* 12(3) July, 1986, pp. 158-65.

7. Roose, Tina, "A month of searches," *Library Journal* 110(4)Mar 1, 1985, pp. 66-7.

8. Quint, Barbara, "Cross-system/cross file searching: Should you stop after 5 search services and 35 databases?" *Online '83 Proceedings*. October 10-12, 1983, Chicago, pp.244-250.

9. Markee, Katherine M., "Economies of online retrieval," *Online Review* 5(6) December, 1981, pp.439-44.

Financing and Managing Technology-Based Reference Services in the Undergraduate University Library

Rodney M. Hersberger

SUMMARY. Technology-based reference services are creating exciting and challenging opportunities for libraries in offering their basic service: access to information. This paper examines some of the possible approaches to high tech reference and how to manage and finance technology-based reference services. The focus is on the academic library which supports basically undergraduate level education but which is not a research library, i.e., one supporting large amounts of doctoral level and faculty research.

INTRODUCTION

Technology-based reference services create significant opportunities for academic libraries in offering their most basic service to students and faculty: access to information and, hopefully, knowledge. Although searching on MEDLINE, Dialog and SDC became commonplace in academic libraries by the late 1970s and the entrepreneuring people at SUNY started BRS in 1976, it is the technology of the 1980s which is serving a creative smorgasbord of possibilities for expanded reference services. Some of these technologies are, of course, powerful microcomputers and modems, laser and videodisc technology,[1] fibre optics, linked systems protocol to name some. Even while reference librarians are striving to integrate new reference services into the library's informational programs, they must at the same time preserve the

Rodney M. Hersberger is Director of Libraries, Cal State — Bakersfield, 9001 Stockdale Highway, Bakersfield, CA 93311.

traditional in many cases. The current challenges in reference services are to rethink and redesign the delivery of programs and services, to develop programs for instructing and educating our users and to find reasonable methods to finance all these projects.

All libraries face some common challenges in implementing technology-based public services. Other issues are unique to public or academic libraries which may be further differentiated by size, mission, location and other environmental factors. Our discussion will examine libraries at smaller universities and colleges; libraries which are clearly academic in nature but which are not and do not intend to be research libraries supporting large amounts of doctoral work. These are academic libraries which have as their main clientele the large body of undergraduate students but which serve faculty and limited numbers of graduate students as well. (Undergraduate libraries on very large campuses may also fit this definition well.) Some would argue that a major difference between smaller academic libraries and larger academic research libraries is the emphasis on programs and services in the former versus the emphasis on collections in the research library. This argument may well be borne out in the smaller library's ability to introduce technology-based reference services.

TRADITIONAL APPROACH

Students in the primarily undergraduate university have information and research requirements which are more homogenous than the esoteric interests of doctoral students. In the past the undergraduates research needs have been met by the traditional array of indexes and bibliographies typically found in most academic library reference departments as well as through the book collection accessed via the card catalog. Through structured programs of bibliographic instruction, both general and specific, and through class assignments requiring library use, reference librarians focused their energies on teaching the undergraduate how to use the bibliographic resources in "that" library. Although always available for specific or continuing consultation with students, our goal was eventual self-sufficiency for the student. In many ways the introduction of technology-based reference programs does not alter the approach. The sophistication required to master high tech information resources is certainly within the grasp of many of our students. In fact they are usually more adept than we in grasping new techniques. There are barriers, however, along the path toward making true end users of our students. Among these barriers are our reluctance to admit students have the abilities and capabilities of becoming bonafide end users, the development of necessary programs to train end users and the costs of these programs.

On-line searching traces its origins back more than 30 years.[2] When universities began on-line searching in earnest in the 1970s, it was thought that our major audience would be faculty with grant money to pay for the searches or graduate students who could not afford not to search because of the payoff in bibliographic results as well as the time saved. As the price of databases came down or alternative pricing schemes were introduced by the vendors, we found many undergraduates were interested in the marvels of on-line searching and willing to pay for them. The debate continues, of course, over charging fees. Increased undergraduate use of on-line searching services was often less the result of programmatic initiatives on the part of librarians but rather on the very success of on-line searching which was spread by word of mouth. Now we anticipate self-service "end user searching" and are facing the first wave of videodisc technology.

INTRODUCING NEW TECHNOLOGY
IN REFERENCE SERVICES

Whether or not a particular library's administration embraces an entrepreneurial approach to management or adopts a wait and see attitude toward new programs and services may well indicate its posture toward technology-based reference services. New technology can be expensive and there is, of course, an element of risk. Both our students and our library staffs, however, need as much exposure as possible to new and different types of information resources. A modest investment in public service technology can return impressive dividends in the form of user satisfaction. We also have a learning curve, which if properly fed, can rise more steeply over the long run. Some investment in technology is necessary if we are to gain experience in evaluating the importance and usefulness of programs and products which may come later.

The launching of Information Access Corporation's INFO-TRAC is a good case in point and is providing empirical data on which future decisions can be made. INFOTRAC was first demonstrated at the ALA Midwinter meeting in Washington in January 1985. Laser produced discs from several vendors were prominently on the scene for the first time at that trade show. INFOTRAC was one of the first, if not the first, vendor to offer laser produced disc technology for general library public service. Other early products based on this technology were primarily directed at technical service programs. INFOTRAC was first shipped in late summer or early autumn of 1985. Cal State-Bakersfield began using INFOTRAC in January 1986. The introduction of INFOTRAC as part of our reference services was easily the most popular information program ever offered in this library. To a sophisticated searcher, the searching approach on INFOTRAC is simplistic if not naive. To the undergraduate library user, a service-like INFOTRAC is a dream come true. After a few well-chosen minutes of searching, the student can emerge with a reasonable bibliography of citations to find, hopefully, and read.

There is much criticism in library circles of the quality of database, the coverage and the accuracy of INFOTRAC as well as other developing high tech media.[3] Much of this criticism, while valid, fails to recognize the embryonic stage in the life cycle of not only the individual product—INFOTRAC in this case—but of the industry—optical video technology. Part of the entrepreneurial spirit mentioned earlier comes into play here. To gain experience and to offer dynamic programs to the undergraduate, a library manager must be willing to invest in something new, learn from it, and presumably, be more enlightened about the program and the technology when the next opportunity arrives. We should be properly concerned about the lack of technical standards for videodisc technology, although there is progress on some standards in the compact format.[4,5] However, bringing new students into the library is reward enough for investing in new technology. Since many of our students have reached their early adulthood through a path of video games, VCRs and other electronic stimuli, they have every reason to expect a library to offer information utilizing similar technology.

Another high tech reference program which is also popular with students is BRS After Dark. Searching is at much reduced rates after 6:00 p.m. Eastern time and on weekends. It is eminently affordable even if the student is contributing to the charges. Our program is aimed at MBA students who have been extremely satisfied with the results from BRS After Dark. For a cost of usually no more than $3, we can offer the student good search results to start his research project.

In our own case, again after analyzing the need with the chemistry department, it was decided it would be more cost effective to purchase CHEMICAL ABSTRACTS (STN INTERNATIONAL) as an on-line service rather than in paper format. The savings have been justified. Student access to on-line access to CHEM ABSTRACTS can be controlled in this case. Working with chemistry faculty to identify research needs, students in particular upper division courses can have access to CAS through our regular program of on-line search services. This example may not work well in some institutions but in most cases a decision on any bibliographic source can be made on a programmatic basis.

In all instances cited, the initiative came from the library. The programs were either introduced with only modest publicity, as with INFOTRAC, or through diligent work from the reference department staff in marketing the program to appropriate faculty and students, as with BRS After Dark. In the CHEM ABSTRACTS example there was a trial period to determine the ability of the on-line service and library searchers to deliver the product cost effectively, which they did.

Programmatic Decisions

Programmatic decisions about the presumed utility of a high tech reference service can be made in most instances. The decision should hinge more on the value to the user of the service rather than the cost of the service to the library. Library managers are now faced with multiple choices of high tech reference services either to purchase or evaluate for possible purchase. For example, at the time of this writing, Information Access is offering a Government Documents index. Another company, Silver-Platter, is marketing ERIC, PSYCHOLOGICAL ABSTRACTS and is proposing other databases like SOCIOLOGICAL AB-STRACTS in compact disc format. Bowker is also marketing BOOKS IN PRINT and ULRICH'S INTERNATIONAL PERI-ODICALS DIRECTORY on CD-ROM.[6] H. W. Wilson Co. not only sells WILSON ONLINE and WILSEARCH, it is also developing CD-ROM products.[7] Dialog demonstrated its first CD-ROM-based service at On-line 1986.[8] The author is not promoting compact disc over other technologies; CD is simply being used now as a medium by many of our information suppliers and is in widespread use in the consumer audio market. Other new technologies like RDAT (Rotary Digital Audio Tape, with four times the capacity of compact disc) may well challenge compact discs soon.[9]

These and other products are not inexpensive, to be sure, and neither are on-line services. However, when gauged on a per use basis, high tech reference products may have a relatively modest cost. Many printed reference tools are rather expensive too. In every library there are reference works consulted so frequently they are worn out quickly. There are many titles, on the other hand, whose condition remains pristine through lack of use. While it may be impractical, of course, to make a decision about every title even over a long period of time, there are sets and indexes for which alternatives exist. Some were mentioned earlier like CHEM ABSTRACTS ONLINE, WILSON ONLINE, INFOTRAC, ERIC and PSYCHOLOGICAL ABSTRACTS. Even directories like THE FOUNDATION INDEX or THE EN-CYCLOPEDIA OF ASSOCIATIONS are available on-line through Dialog. The frequency of client consultation of some of these titles and the quality of answer provided, may suggest them as an alternative to print.

Many libraries now have either a terminal or microcomputer at or near the reference desk. Reference librarians can often provide cost-effective answers on-line to simple reference questions. However, one suspects few libraries have analyzed the cost redundancy inherent in duplicating on-line and printed reference services. On-line may be used more to "dazzle" clients rather than based on a philosophy of providing the most effective and efficient service for the client. What is really wanted is a commitment to genuine information service where the needs of the student comes first. Perhaps the need is hierarchical in nature such as the search for a term paper topic, followed by a brief, introductory bibliography, some manual literature searching and concluding with a more extensive on-line or disc-based search. Three of these four steps can be done using high tech reference products. The fourth, manual searching, remains necessary because of incomplete databases, user inexperience and librarian time.

End User Searching

Few libraries are yet set up to permit direct end user searching on remote databases where direct charges are accruing each minute, i.e., the more time in the database the greater the total cost. Of course, the opposite occurs with locally controlled data sources, notably discs; the more they are used the less they cost on a per use basis. Naturally, we hope to see these user stations at full employment to justify their subscription cost. There are some examples of end user searching or experiments in end user searching which we can cite. Most librarians agree that end user searching, to some extent under some definition, is not only inevitable but desirable, but that expert searching will still be done mainly by librarians, at least in the near to medium term.

One example of an end user searching experiment at Penn State University was documented in the literature recently as reported by Linda Friend.[10] Graduate students in education were trained as end user searchers on BRS After Dark. Two class sessions were devoted to the training, one a group presentation and the other individual discussions between trained searcher and student. By and large the reported results label this Penn State study as successful. About half the students, after gaining experience, felt they could continue searching without having a librarian-consultant present or available. The other half did want a librarian but would prefer someone who had some subject background in education, as well. (An interesting extension of the original study would be to follow up these user perceptions using controlled groups which did more end user searching but at intervals of varying lengths.)

Friend also advises novice users to try end user searching through their library rather than contracting on their own with BRS or another service. Her cautions for the unaffiliated novice include lack of access to detailed manuals and thesauri, problems with choice of terminology, lack of proper understanding of Boolean operators, lack of information on how to make a search more precise, system problems and minimal information in the end user system manuals supplied by the vendors.[11]

We also know from the literature of end user studies at University of Ottawa[12] and the University of Wisconsin-Stout,[13] among many others by now. Results are generally similar to the Penn State study. In reporting the UW-Stout study Trzebiatowski delineates five end user education needs: (1) analyzing concepts in a search strategy; (2) gathering appropriate terminology; (3) creating sets and using Boolean operators effectively; (4) selecting appropriate databases and (5) on-line evaluation of results, recognition of errors and strategy modification if necessary. She concludes by observing that the menu driven approach is only an interim solution to effective end user searching. "The truly user-friendly search system will be an artificially intelligent or knowledge-based system that will be totally interactive and offer on-line user assistance. It will allow users to enter natural-language search statements, and it will be able to relate synonyms and variant spellings and allow end users to choose or specify which concepts are most important and/or least important in the search statement."[14]

It can be presumed that many universities and their libraries will run similar experiments and report similar results for the next several years, some without ever making a decision. The more aggressive, entrepreneurial driven libraries, however, have or will soon make a firmer commitment to some type of end user searching or will reject end user searching for the time being on philosophical, managerial or financial grounds. This latter group will certainly revisit the issue before the decade expires.

An example of a very aggressive approach to end user searching backed by both a managerial and financial commitment is the one being offered at Cal Poly-Pomona. Here the library has dedicated space for end user searching, supports the operation with well-trained paraprofessional staff and fully underwrites all costs. The room is open and staffed 36 hours per week. In 1985-86 the Cal Poly library supported 2281 end user searches at a direct cost of $13,463.43 plus staff costs at $27,987.96.[15] This is clearly an example of a major commitment to end user searching.

Other libraries can start more modestly by building on experience gained by end users on captive cost videodisc-based systems. Admittedly at this writing the videodisc-based systems do not allow the more complex search strategies of on-line, but they do allow the potential end user to be comfortable with machine-based searching and to begin thinking about future steps in the bibliographic world.

At the 1986 ALA conference H. W. Wilson unveiled a promising next step to more complete end user searching. The product, WILSONDISC, apparently combines CD-ROM access and on-line access in the same workstation. In addition to data on the CD, Wilson claims users will be able to connect with 22 Wilson databases on-line through four access modes to meet differing levels of user experience and expertise.[16] SilverPlatter's prototype "MultiPlatter" (a multiuser CD-ROM system) also claims it will add a "seamless" interface with Dialog, BRS and other on-line providers. The new Dialog disc system is said to be headed in the same direction. The obvious advantage to the library in Wilson's, SilverPlatter's or Dialog's approach is the ability to offer on-line access to a variety of end users and for the library to maintain substantial control of the searching costs.

Financing Hi-Tech Reference Services

The explosive growth of publishing and information sources, the demands on our libraries to provide more materials and more access, and the great reduction of libraries' purchasing power from inflation and recession a few years back are well-chronicled elsewhere. Yet here we are discussing new forms of access and publishing and practically insisting a progressive library cannot afford to be without an ever increasing amount of technologically-based reference services and programs.

The hardware costs are generally much easier to rationalize and deal with than the material or service costs for high tech reference programs. On the upper end of the price spectrum, the IBM PC XT remains fairly expensive. The basic PC and a host of serviceable compatibles, however, are quite modest, ranging at the time of writing from about $1300 up to $2000. For on-line searching a decent smart modem and printer can add another $800 to $1000 to the above costs. For CD-ROM or videodisc the players are normally quite modest and, of course, hook up to a personal computer. For disc-based systems the vendor's software and connections may be separately priced or part of the subscription. Our dilemma is the incompatibility among some systems and the furious speed at which vendors are throwing products at us. Surely we do not desire one each of stand alone CD-ROM systems for Bowker, SilverPlatter, OCLC, Wilson, etc. yet that may well be the only choice for libraries entering the game early.

Only the very poorest of libraries could not afford the basic equipment mentioned. There are usually options for basic equipment purchases if the equipment line cannot support a PC or two and the other necessary peripherals. In some cases, a vacant position might be held open a month or two to free up the monies for equipment. Sometimes a computer center on a campus might have some discretionary funds to supply a PC, especially since the PC is essentially for student use in this case. PCs have been around long enough now that some computer centers are upgrading their equipment and might have a perfectly serviceable but lower powered model that could work for a library's purposes. In the realm of noninstitutional support perhaps the library's friends or a similar group could either donate or raise the money for some searching equipment. Local businesses, whether in the computer trade or not, are often willing to donate funds or equipment in return for some simple recognition. Equipment costs, however, are only the beginning of the commitment to high tech reference services and a much lesser cost than the information sources or the access to the information sources.

Financing or funding technology-based reference sources is clearly the topic of the moment. In fact in any entrepreneurial driven library, the question is not whether high tech reference, but how. Funding technology-based reference services seems to be replacing the fee or free issue of on-line bibliographic searching which has consumed so much print and conference time this past decade. An RASD MARS daylong program at the 1986 ALA Conference, for instance, was devoted to the theme: "Dollars and Sense: New On-line Technology." Although we have heard this threat before, one speaker warned that if libraries continue to treat on-line services as optional or exotic, someone else will fill the void. Other speakers identified cost considerations (start-up costs, search and citation charges, training costs, subscription charges, the impact on interlibrary loan and microform services, etc.) and when to expand services. Except for advice to try to convince funding agencies that on-line sources are normal information sources rather than something elitist, the speakers failed to offer any real proposals for funding.[17] Another speaker, Dolores Meglio of Information Access Corporation, indicated that an IAC survey found "the cost or perceived cost of searching is the single greatest barrier to the routine retrieval of full text material on-line." Yet, Meglio echoed something we suggested earlier under "Programmatic Costs" that most libraries have no idea of the costs of their print retrieval services, so there is really nothing against which to measure the cost of on-line retrieval.[18] We do, of course, know the price our libraries pay for a reference source or a serial subscription, but no one knows the cost of print retrieval on a per use basis. However, again as mentioned above, cost should be measured in terms of value to the user rather than price paid by the library for a book or service.

A more useful discussion of paying for high tech reference is to be found in Poole and St. Clair's article.[19] The authors claim, correctly in my judgement, that information provided by on-line services satisfies legitimate educational need and should be funded from the materials budget. They argue further that historically materials monies have been spent on a principle known as "probable need." Yet it is widely accepted that in an academic library normally about 20% of the titles held supply 80% of the demand. Probable need, these authors implicitly suggest, has not proven to be a very accurate method of selecting materials. (This problem may be of less concern to the large, academic research library than it is to academic libraries fitting the definition used for this discussion.)

Funding on-line services from the materials budget, Poole and St. Clair continue in their reasoning, should proceed in an inevitable fashion. First, they argue could be the purchase of those few journals and related items that are published only in the on-line format. The second logical step would be to provide for on-line indexing and abstracting services even when there are paper alternatives. In my estimation these two propositions can evolve fairly simultaneous and, in fact, the second — indexes and abstracts — may generate the first — full text data. Poole and St. Clair posit that the library's materials budget will be more wisely applied because "the user's need is expressed before it is met."[20]

This type of discussion invariably leads to cost control, staff commitment to provide services, "gate keeping," etc. Poole and St. Clair acknowledge these issues but do not provide any insight for us to address them. A promising approach for now was mentioned earlier in this paper: a combination of videodisc-based searching and on-line. This combination when properly programmed and sequenced can work to great advantage for both the client and the library. Most searching is done on the videodisc database with its captive cost and low cost per use. The user switches into the on-line mode for the most recent data using the search strategy and protocol already established in the local videodisc search. On-line interaction is kept to a minimum and therefore charges are better contained. When the software allows sophisticated manipulation and Boolean searching of the videodisc database without the clock running every minute, we are more likely to embrace end user searching with greater enthusiasm.

COLLECTION DEVELOPMENT –
OWNERSHIP VS. ACCESS

Is it indeed appropriate to use the library materials budget to purchase high tech reference services? *Absolutely!* As Poole and St. Clair suggest, it is wise to proceed in a logical, systematic fashion when applying the materials budget to technology-based reference services. Caution is necessary, however, and change, as well as growth, in services and procedures must be well-planned and measured. One should start with something manageable like a videodisc-based system or an expansion of on-line services in inexpensive programs like BRS After Dark. These progressions in service and access can and should be funded from the materials budget.

One then expects to hear the question, what will we be giving up to use our book budget this way? Probably nothing. First, if a library is enjoying some budget growth, even modestly, the library administration could commit all new funds for three years, for instance, to increased services in technology-based reference. After that time the services and programs can probably be regularized into the budget. Another approach, and one we use at Cal State, is to allow some flexibility for purchasing nonprint materials to academic departments in their library allocations. We have for several years had an unofficial policy of permitting academic departments to use up to 10% of their library allocation for nonprint. We can simply expand the definition of nonprint to include optical and digital formats whether owned or simply accessed. Appropriate control is assumed. Thirdly, librarians can make some intelligent collection development decisions and recognize that much of what we purchase is not used. Perhaps we can buy fewer books in certain areas and we certainly can buy fewer expensive journals which are seldom used. As suggested earlier we can make some programmatic choices about our reference services and examine critically some of the unused or seldom consulted reference services. A library might reduce some standing orders as well as individual purchases, especially if there are an on-line alternatives. Of course, we will make mistakes but our purchasing judgement now is fairly faulty. We need not be threatened by not buying print. Conversely we should be aggressively making plans to expand our bibliographic horizons with high tech reference and actively marketing our improved products.

CONCLUSION

Academic libraries that do not use technology-based reference sources are already being left at the starting gate. No one yet has synthesized the proper or most cost-effective approach to high tech reference but the game is still very young. With all the talk about end user searching and all the product development surrounding CD-ROM, librarian directed on-line searching remains the most effective technology-based reference service. It can be costly for the direct charges but need not be. The day is soon at hand when all reference desks should have a decent personal computer coupled with a smart modem and librarians should answer the majority of ready reference questions on-line. Longer or more difficult searching may not be available on demand, but the first, positive contact with the requestor can be made.

We need not be afraid of being aggressive about high tech or its relative costs. By making some fundamental judgements about the direction of our reference programs, by making some decisions about the real or relative value of some of our print sources and by making some strategic investments, we can not only improve our services, but our image as well. We will stumble occasionally, as will our suppliers, but that should not deter us from moving forward into high tech reference.

NOTES

1. For a brief, but useful, discussion about the differences between digital videodisc, CD-ROM, and optical digital disk see "Electronic Technology and Serials Publishing," *Library Systems* 6(11): 81-84, (1986).

2. Frederick G. Kilgour, "History of Library Computerization," *Journal of Library Automation* 3(3): 200, (September 1970).

3. William O. Van Arsdale & Anne T. Ostrye, "InfoTrac: A Second Opinion," *American Libraries* 17(7): 514, 515, (July-August, 1986).

4. William O. Van Arsdale, "The Rush to Optical Discs," *Library Journal* 111(16):53-55, (October 1, 1986).

5. "NISO Completes Work on CD ROM Format Standard," *Advanced Technology/Libraries* 15(12): 1-2, (December 1986).

6. "Bowker Introduces Books in Print, Ulrich's on CD-ROM," *Advanced/Technology Libraries* 15(7):1, (July, 1986).

7. "H. W. Wilson Shows WILSONDISC," *Advanced/Technology Libraries* 15(8): 3, (August, 1986).

8. "Dialog Introduces Dialog Ondisc CD ROM Line," *Advanced Technology/Libraries* 15(12): 1,8,9.

9. "Digital Tape Creates Wave of Excitement, Controversy," Los Angeles Times (January 12, 1987) part IV, p.1. (Technology was also reportedly first demonstrated by several vendors at an October 1986 electronics show in Tokyo.)

10. Linda Friend, "Independence at the Terminal: Training Student End Users to Do Online Literature Searching," *The Journal of Academic Librarianship* 11(3): 136-141, (July, 1985).

11. Ibid., 140.

12. Richard V. Janke, "Online After Six: End User Searching Comes of Age," *Online* 8(6):15-29, (1984).

13. Elaine Trzebiatowski, "End User Study on BRS/After Dark," *RQ* 23(4): 446-450, (1984).

14. Ibid., 450.

15. Information supplied by Harold Schleifer, Director of Libraries, California Polytechnic and State University, Pomona.

16. Op.Cit. *Advanced Technology/Libraries* 15(8):3, (August, 1986).

17. "ALA Speakers Discuss Funding Online Services," *Advanced Technology Libraries* 15(8):1, 8-9, (August, 1986).

18. Ibid., 9.

19. Jay Martin Poole & Gloriana St. Clair, "Funding Online Services from the Materials Budget." *College and Research Libraries* 47(3):225-229, (May, 1986).

20. Ibid., 227.

InfoTrac:
Is It an Appropriate
General Reference Tool?

H. Julene Butler
Gregory M. Kortman

SUMMARY. A survey was conducted at Brigham Young University to determine the usage rate and level of user satisfaction for InfoTrac, an offline bibliographic database developed by Information Access Company. This article describes that survey, its methodology, and findings. The findings from the survey indicated that two InfoTrac computer terminals were in use 54.0% and 40.4% respectively of the time the library was open to patrons. Over 64% of the patrons using the system were in the junior/senior category; over 90% of the system's users indicated they were satisfied that InfoTrac met their research goals.

INTRODUCTION

Bibliographic databases have typically been stored in the memory of a mainframe computer and accessed through telecommunications lines from remote locations. On-line charges and complex search techniques have limited end user searching in most libraries. With the development of laser disk technology, resulting in the ability to store large amounts of data on plastic coated aluminum disks, the marketing of bibliographic data is changing significantly.

Information Access Company (IAC) recently developed Info-Trac™, a computer-assisted indexing system that uses a 12-inch

H. Julene Butler is Chairman of the General Reference Department, Lee Library, Brigham Young University, Provo, UT 84602. Gregory M. Kortman is a graduate student in the university's Industrial Education Department.

laser disk to store bibliographic data. Each disk holds as much as 800 million bytes of data, equivalent to the amount of information that can be stored on 5000 flexible disks (those commonly used with personal computers).

At the time of this study, InfoTrac provided access to articles from 774 journals dating from January 1982 to the present. A careful review of these titles shows that InfoTrac accesses 118 of the 183 sources covered by *Readers' Guide to Periodical Literature* (64.4%). It also accesses the past 60 days of the *New York Times* and the *Wall Street Journal*. Because IAC formerly produced *Magazine Index* and *Business Index*, the focus of InfoTrac is toward general-interest and business-related titles. Indexed information is updated monthly with a new disk.

IAC provided Brigham Young University (BYU) with two modified InfoTrac systems so that BYU could evaluate them in its business and main libraries. Because of InfoTrac's business orientation, there was little doubt about the utility of InfoTrac in the business library. However, because of some doubt and concern for the system's utility in the general reference area of the main library, a study was proposed, designed, and conducted to determine if InfoTrac was an appropriate reference tool that should be added to the general reference collection.

To focus the intent of this study and achieve its goal, to determine if the library should purchase InfoTrac, four research questions were formulated:

1. Is the usage rate high enough to justify including InfoTrac in the reference collection?
2. Which library patrons does InfoTrac serve?
3. Do the library patrons using InfoTrac perceive that this reference tool meets their research needs?
4. Are the citations provided by InfoTrac available at the library?

METHODS AND PROCEDURES

Commercial InfoTrac systems have four personal computer stations. IAC installed a modified two-computer system in the main library for a three month trial period, to determine if it should be purchased. IAC also provided a questionnaire that was made available to patrons who used the system from its installation in December until about mid-January. When these forms were gone, another was prepared, with minor differences in the questions asked. In a subsequent review, it was determined that both forms were worded in such a way that patrons would be inclined to favor the system; neither instrument allowed patrons to fully communicate their opinions regarding InfoTrac to the library staff. The results of these two questionnaires are summarized in Table 1. The numbers shown in Table 1 represent the percentage of the total responses.

A new questionnaire was prepared (Figure 1). It was used at the library from 14 February 1986, starting at 5:30 pm, to 28 February 1986, ending at 5:30 pm. The questionnaire consisted of 13 questions and was printed on three colors of paper. This helped to ensure that the responses from the three categories of InfoTrac users (i.e., the forms at each of the two computers and the forms used during the interview with those who did not complete a questionnaire after using InfoTrac) would not become mixed. Questions 1, 2, and 7 were also included to keep the questionnaires in order during analysis. This procedure worked well. Only descriptive statistics were used to analyze the remaining ten questions; no attempt was made to correlate the information among the various questions.

Some errors in the questionnaire were not corrected because a pilot study was not conducted. Questions 8 and 9 should have been formatted with inclusive number choices (see question 11), because some respondents circled two adjacent numbers when their situation was bracketed by the choices provided in the questionnaire. When this occurred the higher response was used in the analysis of the data. Also, even though the acronym CARS (Computer-Assisted Research Services) was defined in question 6, it became a source of confusion for some patrons when they answered question 13. Repeating the definition for this acronym in question 13 might have lessened this confusion.

Patrons using InfoTrac were not compelled to complete a questionnaire. Therefore, a small sample of persons not completing the questionnaire was interviewed to determine if their responses were significantly different from those of patrons choos-

Table 1. Preliminary Questionnaires

InfoTrac QUESTIONNAIRE NO. 1

These numbers are the percent of 54 completed forms.

	Agree Strongly	Agree Some	Neither	Disagree Some	Disagree Strongly	No Response
No Training Needed	83.3	16.7	0.0	0.0	0.0	0.0
"Help Screens" Work	53.7	24.0	13.0	0.0	0.0	9.3
Achieved Goals	75.8	14.8	1.9	0.0	5.6	1.9
System Easy To Use	83.3	14.8	1.9	0.0	0.0	0.0
Preferred Reference Tool	81.5	11.1	5.5	0.0	0.0	1.9

	Student	Business	Staff	Faculty	Other
User Status(*)	79.7	11.1	0.0	5.1	3.4

InfoTrac QUESTIONNAIRE NO. 2

These numbers are the percent of 195 completed forms.

	Agree Strongly	Agree Some	Neither	Disagree Some	Disagree Strongly	No Response
No Training Needed	87.2	11.3	0.0	1.5	0.0	0.0
Achieved Goals	68.7	23.1	2.6	4.1	0.5	1.0
System Easy To Use	89.7	9.3	0.5	0.5	0.0	0.0
Preferred Reference Tool	82.6	12.3	3.6	0.5	1.0	0.0

	Student	Staff	Faculty	Other
User Status(*)	93.9	0.0	2.0	4.1

(*) Some respondents listed more than one status.

ing to complete the form. This information was also used to determine what percentage of InfoTrac users were completing the form. To collect this information, one observer watched both computers for one hour, and a second person interviewed the

InfoTrac QUESTIONNAIRE

Please answer the following questions as accurately as you can. This information is important for determining the utility of InfoTrac within the context of the BYU library system. Your cooperation is appreciated. Thank you.

GENERAL INFORMATION QUESTIONS

1) What is today's date? _____

2) What is the present time? _____

3) What is your grade level at BYU? Freshman, Sophomore, Junior, Senior, Master's Candidate, Doctoral Candidate, Faculty, Other

4) How many times have you used InfoTrac? 1 (this is my first time), 2, 3, 4, 5 or more

5) Which library resources would you have used if InfoTrac had not been available to you? _____

6) Are you familiar with Computer-Assisted Research Services (CARS)? yes, no

QUESTIONS FOR THIS CURRENT SESSION ON InfoTrac

7) Which computer terminal did you use in this session with InfoTrac? 1, 2, 3, 4

8) During this session with InfoTrac, how many minutes did you have to wait to gain access to the computer? 0, 5, 10, 15, 20 or more

9) During this session with InfoTrac, how many minutes did you spend using the computer? 5 or less, 10, 15, 20, 25 or more

10) During this session with InfoTrac, how many topics did you search? 1, 2, 3, 4, 5 or more

11) During this session with InfoTrac, how many citations did you obtain? 0, 1-3, 4-6, 7-9, 10-12, 13 or more

12) Are you satisfied with the results from this session with InfoTrac? 1 (highly satisfied), 2, 3, 4, 5 (not at all satisfied)

13) Did this session with InfoTrac replace your use of CARS? yes, no, not applicable

Figure 1. Final InfoTrac questionnaire.

nonrespondents after they left their computer station. They were interviewed out of sight of the computer so that this activity would not affect the natural tendency of future patrons to either complete or not complete the questionnaire. The hour from 11 am to 12 noon on the second Thursday of the study was chosen to sample the nonrespondents. This hour eliminated any chance of ambiguity in reviewing the forms, since the library closed every night at 11 pm, and an am/pm confusion could not occur.

As mentioned, there were two purposes for interviewing a small sample of InfoTrac users who chose not to complete the questionnaire. The first was to determine if those not completing the questionnaire were markedly different from those who did. The second was to estimate the actual usage of InfoTrac, recognizing that all the patrons using the system did not complete a questionnaire. After collecting the questionnaires from the two groups of patrons (those voluntarily completing the form and a small sample of those choosing not to), questions 3, 4, 5, 6, 9, 10, 11, 12, and 13 were used to determine if the two groups were different. The reasoning was that if the two groups were found to be the same, then a procedure could be developed to estimate the total usage of the InfoTrac system. Counting the number of patrons who used InfoTrac during the one hour nonrespondents were interviewed gave the actual usage for that hour. By summing the questionnaires collected between 11 am and 12 noon on each of the 12 days of the survey, and dividing this total by 12, the average number of questionnaires completed during that hour was obtained. Then, dividing this number (which represents the average number of patrons using the system who completed a questionnaire) by the actual number of patrons who used the system for that one hour they were counted, and multiplying by 100, the percentage of users who completed a questionnaire was obtained. Once again, if there were no significant differences between those who completed the questionnaire and those who did not, then the population using InfoTrac could be assumed to be of sufficiently similar orientation that this percent could be applied to each hour the system was in use, to yield the total usage rate of the system.

PRESENTATION OF FINDINGS

During the 12-day data collection period of this study, 350 patrons responded to the questionnaire. Their responses are presented in Table 2. In the one hour that nonrespondents were interviewed, nine patrons used the system, and none of them completed a questionnaire. Of these nine nonrespondents, eight were interviewed; their responses are also reported in Table 2. One of the nine persons left the library before he could be interviewed. Each of the numbers shown in Table 2 is the percent of the total responses for the various items presented. The third line of information shown for question number 3 is the percent distribution of the student population at BYU obtained from the registration office on the last day of the survey. Using the information presented in Table 2, the following observations were made:

(1) The student population of those completing the form was not significantly different from those who did not complete the form. By looking at questions 3, 4, 5, 6, 9, 10, 11, 12, and 13, and recognizing that each nonrespondent represents 12.5% of the total of nonrespondents interviewed, this comparison shows no significant differences between the two groups. Therefore, the patrons using InfoTrac were assumed to be homogeneous.

(2) The two terminals in the main library were in use 54.0% and 40.4% respectively of the time the library was open to patrons. The average number of patrons who used InfoTrac and completed a questionnaire during the 12 days of the survey, between the hours of 11 am and 12 noon, was 3.17. Since nine patrons used the system during the designated hour, dividing 3.17 by 9 shows that 35% of the patrons using InfoTrac completed the questionnaire during that designated hour.

Question 9 allowed the patrons to select usage time in five-minute intervals from 5 to 25 minutes or more. Multiplying these responses by the number of patrons in each category gave a total time of usage for terminals one and two of 2,155 and 1,610 minutes respectively. An estimate of the total hours of use for each terminal can be made by assuming that each of these two times represents 35% of their total usage. Therefore, the total usage for each of the two terminals was calculated to be 6,157 and 4,600

Table 2. Summary of Final Survey

These numbers are the percent of 350

survey respondents and 8 of 9 non-respondents.

Question 3. Student population distribution:

	Fre	Sop	Jun	Sen	Mas	Doc
Survey	13.7	11.4	25.1	39.7	6.3	1.7
Non-Resp	12.5	12.5	37.5	37.5	0.0	0.0
BYU Popul	20.8	19.4	20.5	29.5	6.7	3.0

Question 4. Number of times using InfoTrac:

	1	2	3	4	5 or more
Survey	48.0	20.3	9.1	8.3	14.3
Non-Resp	37.5	25.0	12.5	12.5	12.5

Question 5. Library resources replaced by InfoTrac:

	Readers Guide/ General Indexes	Indexes/ Abstracts	Computer- Assisted Research	Card Catalog/ Online Catalog/ Reference Books
Survey	61.2	12.0	3.9	21.1
Non-Resp	50.0	0.0	0.0	25.0

Question 6. Familiar with CARS:

	Yes	No
Survey	34.9	64.6
Non-Resp	25.0	75.0

Question 8. Minutes to wait to use InfoTrac:

	0	5	10	15	20 or more
Survey	45.7	29.4	12.9	5.7	4.3
Non-Resp	12.5	50.0	37.5	0.0	0.0

Question 9. Minutes using InfoTrac:

	5	10	15	20	25 or more
Survey	32.3	36.6	17.1	8.9	4.6
Non-Resp	50.0	12.5	12.5	25.0	0.0

Table 2 continued

Question 10. Number of topics searched:

	1	2	3	4	5 or more
Survey	38.0	20.9	18.6	9.7	12.6
Non-Resp	37.5	25.0	12.5	12.5	12.5

Question 11. Number of citations obtained:

	0	1-3	4-6	7-9	10-12	13 or more
Survey	5.7	14.9	12.6	11.7	12.0	41.1
Non-Resp	0.0	25.0	12.5	0.0	12.5	50.0

Question 12. Satisfaction with InfoTrac:

	1	2	3	4	5
Survey	59.9	22.5	10.4	2.5	4.2
Non-Resp	62.5	25.0	0.0	0.0	12.5

Question 13. CARS search replaced by InfoTrac:

	Yes	No	Not Applicable
Survey	14.3	18.0	67.1
Non-Resp	25.0	12.5	67.5

minutes. In the 12 days of the survey, the library was open and InfoTrac was available to patrons for ten week days (16 hours each) and two Saturdays (15 hours each). The system was available for patron use a total of 11,400 minutes. Therefore, InfoTrac terminals one and two were in use 54.0% and 40.4% respectively of the time the library was open. There was no system down time for either computer during this 12 day survey.

(3) Over 64% of the patrons using InfoTrac were in the junior/senior category. The student population distribution (Table 2, question 3) was obtained from the registration office on the last day of the survey. The small difference in undergraduate usage, compared to student population, perhaps reflects the fact that juniors and seniors tend to write more research papers than do freshmen and sophomores. Although graduate student usage was

low, it was closely aligned with the population of this group of students.

(4) Over 90% of the patrons using InfoTrac were satisfied with its performance. The responses patrons could choose from, when answering question 12, ranged from 1 (highly satisfied) to 5 (not satisfied at all). Responses 1, 2, and 3 were considered to be favorable responses to this question, and when added together, the survey shows that 92.8% of the survey respondents and 87.5% of the nonrespondents found InfoTrac to be satisfactory. From the two preliminary survey forms, the corresponding response was found to be just over 98%.

The high level of satisfaction expressed by InfoTrac users could be the result of short wait times to gain access to the Info-Trac computer, short search times once on the system, or the number of citations recovered during the search. Only 10% of the users waited 15 minutes or more to gain access to the system (see Table 2, question 8). Questions 9 and 10 show that the 350 patrons spent 3,765 minutes on the system, for an average of 10.8 minutes per user. These 350 users searched 830 topics, for an average of 2.4 searches per user. Dividing the average time on the system (10.8) by the number of searches (2.4) shows that a typical search was completed in 4.5 minutes. Finally, responses to question 11 show that 64.8% of the users obtained seven or more citations and that 41.1% of those users obtained 13 or more citations.

Considerable concern was expressed by some BYU subject librarians that the convenience and novelty of InfoTrac would make it the patron's first choice when a specialized index might be more appropriate. Thus, question 5 was included and InfoTrac users were asked which library resources they would have used if InfoTrac had *not* been available to them. Responses to this question showed that most users selected this database appropriately since over 61% used InfoTrac rather than *Reader's Guide to Periodical Literature* and, of those who indicated they would have used other indexes, 1.9% would have selected either *Business Index* or *Business Periodicals Index*. However, 10.1% cited an index that was more specialized than the scope of InfoTrac (e.g., *Psychological Abstracts*, or *Science Citation Index*) and 3.9% indicated they would have used CARS if InfoTrac had not been available to them. This last point conflicts with the data compiled from questions 6 and 13. For these two questions, 14.3% of the respondents and 25% of the nonrespondents selected InfoTrac rather than doing a CARS search.

Of significant interest was the fact that 21.1% of the respondents and 25% of the nonrespondents allowed InfoTrac to replace their use of the card catalog, the on-line catalog, or other unnamed reference books. These responses, combined with the inconsistency of the CARS data, indicate a lack of patron understanding of the scope and purpose of InfoTrac. This suggests a need to train library patrons in the use of automated library services.

(5) Over 70% of the cited references in the system are currently available at BYU. InfoTrac contains a database of 774 journals, periodicals, and newspapers. To determine how many of these titles were in the library collection, and therefore immediately available to the patron using InfoTrac, each was checked against the BYU Periodicals and Serials catalog. Of the 774 titles, 544 were found to be in the library collection. So patrons had at their disposal 70.2% of the titles indexed in InfoTrac's database.

CONCLUSIONS

The findings from the survey led to answers to the four research questions, and the following conclusions were reached:

1. The population of InfoTrac users is homogeneous to the point that those not completing the questionnaire are shown to have the same response to InfoTrac as those who completed the form.
2. Two InfoTrac terminals are in use 54.0% and 40.4% of the time the library is open to patrons.
3. Over 90% of the users of InfoTrac report they are satisfied using this system to achieve their research goals.
4. The survey indicated that InfoTrac is used predominantly by undergraduates, juniors and seniors accounting for over 64% of the system's usage.
5. With 70% of the journals cited by InfoTrac available in the

library, the users have a good chance of obtaining the materials they might want to read.

6. Over 61% of the users chose InfoTrac as an appropriate replacement for other library sources.

On the basis of these findings and conclusions, the library administration accepted the recommendations generated by this study and subscribed to InfoTrac. Because the test system provided by IAC had two terminals, and 90% of the users gained access to the system within ten minutes, the decision was made to purchase one InfoTrac system with its normal configuration of four terminals. Since its permanent installation in early March 1986, usage has been high enough to justify subscribing to several journals indexed on InfoTrac not previously in the library collection. As budgets allow, additional titles will be added.

Is InfoTrac an appropriate general reference tool? We believe that the results of this survey suggest it is.

FURTHER READING

Beltran, Ann Bristow, "Use of InfoTrac in a University Library." *Database* 9 (3): 63-66 (June 1986).

Carney, Richard, "Information Access Company's InfoTrac." *Information Technology and Libraries* 4 (2): 149-153 (June 1985).

Carney, Richard, "InfoTrac: An In-House Computer-Access System." *Library Hi Tech* 3 (2): 91-94 (1985).

Carney, Richard, "InfoTrac vs. the Confounding of Technology and it's Applications." *Database* 9 (3): 56-61 (June 1986).

Dorner, Joe, "InfoTrac: Storing Periodical References By Laser." *Byte* 11 (5): 236-237 (May 1986).

Ernest, Douglas J. & Jennifer Monath, "User Reaction to a Computerized Periodical Index." *College & Research Libraries News* 47 (5): 315-318 (May 1986).

Herther, Nancy, "Access to Information: An Optical Disk Solution." *Wilson Library Bulletin* 60 (9): 19-21 (May 1986).

Herther, Nancy, "Point . . . and Counterpoint: Can Performance Match Industry 'Hype'?" *Online* 9 (6): 22-23 (November 1985).

"IAC Introduces Videodisc System." *Information Technology and Libraries* 4 (1): 70-71 (March 1985).

"Information Access Company's New InfoTrac." *Wilson Library Bulletin* 59 (6): 379 (February 1985).

InfoTrac Handbook. Belmont, CA: Information Access Company, n.d.

Kesselman, Martin, "Online Update." *Wilson Library Bulletin* 60 (4): 40-41 (December 1985).

Krismann, Carol, "InfoTrac." *Colorado Libraries* 12: 31-34 (March 1986).

Littman, Jonathan, "Optical-Disk Databases; Off-line Searches Save Users Money, Complement On-Line Offerings." *PC Week* August 13, 1985, 31-33.

Pemberton, Jeff, "'Shooting Ourselves in the Foot' . . . And Other Consequences of Laserdisks." *Online* 10 (3): 9-11 (May 1986).

Stephens, Kent, "InfoTrac: Laserdisc Technology Enters Mainstream." *American Libraries* 17 (4): 252 (April 1986).

Fee-Based Business Research
in an Academic Library

Mary McNierney Grant
Donald Ungarelli

SUMMARY. The Center for Business Research (CBR) is a department of an academic library in a private university and it houses a special business reference collection. It had a unique origin that led to providing business research for a fee in addition to its primary function of academic support. Its present management, organization, collection and marketing concepts are still under development. Fee-based service in libraries is a popular topic that is perceived differently by librarians in particular situations. In this particular situation, the CBR conducts fee-based business research as a cost-reduction benefit program, however, this business activity imposes many nontraditional library management problems, and marketing of fee-based services requires major attention. Pricing these services is one of the elements of marketing and the rationale is based on compensation of services diverted from primary academic support function and on competition from other brokers of reference service.

ORIGIN OF THE CENTER
FOR BUSINESS RESEARCH (CBR)

Some 20 years ago, a group of librarians and business professionals developed a concept for an advanced reference library to be centrally located on Long Island. The rationale for this concept was most likely motivated by the fact that the Nassau County and Suffolk County areas on Long Island are, in effect,

Mary McNierney Grant is Manager of the Center for Business Research, Schwartz Memorial Library, C.W. Post Campus, Long Island University, Brookville, NY 11548. Dr. Donald Ungarelli is University Dean of Libraries, Long Island University, Brookville, NY 11548.

metropolitan areas without a large central public library capable of supporting advanced research. In 1970, Nassau County made space available for establishing a research library in an unused firehouse on what was a WWI military airfield in the middle of the county. It was named the Nassau County Research Library (NCRL) and had as its first and only director Harold Roth who had previously been the director of the public library in East Orange, NJ.

After a period of some five years spent on collection development, Mary McNierney Grant, a specialist in business information for many years, was appointed the first subject specialist and the library opened its doors for business research. By this time, a rather large business collection had been developed, including a complete holding of SEC disclosure documents on microfiche and many periodical collections on microfilm.

For what may be termed political reasons, Nassau County officials discontinued funding for the project. There were many efforts made to make NCRL self-supporting through federal and state aid, subscriptions, grants, and conducting business research for a fee. In 1978, these efforts culminated in the acquisition of the collection by Long Island University and it was installed in the B. Davis Schwartz Memorial Library on the C.W. Post campus, Brookville, NY, with Mary Grant as its manager. Then known as the Center for Economic Research, the collection was made available for academic support, public reference, and for research services conducted by a professional staff for a fee. After some initial adjustments to its academic environment and in consideration of faculty advice, the name was changed to the Center for Business Research (CBR).

Long Island University, the ninth largest independent university in the nation, is a private, non-sectarian, multi-campus university with more than 20,000 students and over 300 undergraduate and graduate programs offered at six regional campuses with faculties in business, public administration, accountancy, communications, computer and information sciences, education, pharmacy and health sciences, visual and performing arts. Since its beginning in 1926, it has had a tradition for developing and implementing many innovative and nontraditional programs to meet the demands of a changing society. It was one of the first schools in the country to create classes for evenings and week-ends and in 1970, a weekend college format was established at its C.W. Post Campus. Acquisition of the CBR was in keeping with the programs and traditions of the university.

Since its inception at C.W. Post, this special library has supported the business research needs of a wide range of university administration, faculty and students: undergraduate, graduate, and post graduate, and this is its primary function. General business questions may arise from or be stimulated by any of these academic patron communities.

The Library Administration has had a policy of open access to all academic, special, public and high school libraries. Our new university president, Dr. David J. Steinberg, views the libraries of the university as community resources and encourages university friends to use them, especially the CBR. It has been pointed out to the university administration that the CBR is doing its fair share to off-set costs with its fee-based services and is making new friends for the university. Over the last eight years, the CBR has been an effective specialized research service center for many corporations and has brought onto the campus many Chief Executive Officers and their staffs thus creating an opportunity for the university to build a pool of new friends for possible future corporate funding of special programs and projects. This is, in itself, a great public relations factor that should not be taken lightly and can reap rewards in the immediate future.

Staff organization of the CBR has remained as an informal structure. There are, at present, five full-time professionals and three secretarial-technical assistants. Additionally, several graduate assistants and a number of student assistants are employed for part-time help. With the informal structure, assignment of personnel is made to fit everchanging demands for volume or character of service support.

Business Library Concept

To understand the capabilities of the CBR it is necessary to understand that this special library is a complement of and is housed within the University's main academic library on the C.W. Post campus. Schwartz Library is comprised of eight major departments in a large building also housing the Palmer School of Library and Information Science, the School of Education, an Academic Computer Center, an Instructional Media Center and an Audio/Visual Center. The library's major departments include Reference, Cataloging, Acquisitions, Circulation, Rare Books, Periodicals, Government Documents Depository, the Center for Business Research, the Accounting/Tax Library, and a computerized Information Retrieval Service Center. The interdependent nature of these departments, faculties, and facilities presents a complex management problem for Dr. Donald Ungarelli, University Dean of Libraries, but their centralized location provides easy access to sources, services and facilities enabling better support for a wide variety of research problems.

The CBR collection and staffing is structured to take advantage of its unique location. For instance, Schwartz Library's large periodical collection with 5,020 periodicals and newspapers makes it unnecessary for the CBR to maintain supplementary subscriptions, and allows greater subject specialization with space for these titles in its immediate floor area. Similarly, the large reference and circulating collections eliminate the need for additional business book materials, thus reducing the costs associated with acquisition, processing, and services.

In addition, Schwartz Library has a Federal Depository Library with over 400,000 Federal documents and maintains, at the university's expense, a 75% selection policy with heavy emphasis on publications from the Departments of Labor and Commerce. After 15 years of well-known, professional management it has become a leading research center and is an enormously valuable source of business information, freely available to knowledgeable researchers. Because of the complexity of the Su-Docs classification scheme for government publications and the enormous amount of material, specially trained librarians are needed to realize the full potential of this library's capability. It is with the able assistance of these librarians that the business librarians can quickly and accurately obtain needed information and documentation.

The Academic Computer Center maintains many terminals throughout the building and these are networked to a complex center of high capacity, high speed computers with a wide variety of software available for database management, statistical work, word processing, and specialized application programs of use to library management. CBR librarians use these facilities for maintaining mailing lists and various word processing tasks. To keep abreast of the everchanging technology, training and education of the CBR staff is an ongoing activity.

Graduate assistants from the Palmer School of Library and Information Science, who have completed part of their training and education, provide a valuable pool of talent for part-time work in the various library departments. Here they receive additional on-the-job training, performing reference and technical support duties. Upon graduation, these people provide the library with a ready-made source of well-trained candidates for full-time employment.

Special Elements of the CBR Collection

In 1979 the Center had a collection of about 500 titles comprised of subscription services, controlled circulation periodicals, trade association serials and free publications. At the time Long Island University acquired the collection, it was valued at a duplication cost of over a million dollars, with an annual maintenance expense of about $100,000. Acquiring a resource of this size was a major undertaking, committing the university to an operation on the level of the largest institutions and corporations in Manhattan.

The back runs of the core serials collection on microfilm often range from Vol. 1, Number 1; the *Wall Street Journal* runs from 1889 and the *Oil and Gas Journal* from 1902 to date. Expansion of this collection was carefully planned by the staff. The intent was to have important representative titles for every major segment of business and industry. To be selected, a title must be indexed either in *Business Periodicals Index, Business Index, F&S Index* (a most heavily used tool) or one of the on-line databases such as *ABI Inform* or *Nexis*. Today, the Center's serials collection has grown to about 1,500 titles.[1] The collection also has expanded to include additional financial services and directories. Because we retain many of these sources we can provide historical background on companies. For example, our Moody's

Manuals go back to 1917 and our fiche collection of SEC filings to 1974.

The reference librarians scan all new materials for clippings to be inserted into our subject files, regional files and company files. With this work paralleled by eight years of continuous collection maintenance, the CBR has attained a unique position as the major business research center on Long Island.

Typical of many of our research projects utilizing multiple sources was the report we recently produced for a marketing consultant on the specialty cheese industry. This was accomplished by combining on-line searching with our hard copy indexes to find the data in our specialty trade journals and business journals, along with trade association data and Department of Commerce statistics on imports and exports. The client said that our research was superior to a previous study by an information broker and that they appreciated the speed of response.

CBR – PHYSICAL DESCRIPTION

The CBR occupies 6,000 square feet of floor space within Schwartz Library. Seating and desk space for a peak of 60 patrons occupies about a quarter of the space. Equipment for patrons is clustered in one area of this large room and includes two copiers, ten fiche/film readers – some of which print copies, and one *Business Index* reader. Stacks for periodicals, directories, and indexes use up peripheral space. Telephone directories, valuable for their yellow page sections, once occupied a 60 foot stack but were curtailed when access to the Electronic Yellow Pages on-line was deemed more practical.[2] This allowed better shelving for growing numbers of trade directories.

In a separate room with controlled access, there are terminals for internal access to the Academic Computer Center and for accessing on-line databases. Also, through the good will of Disclosure, Inc., there is an IBM PC with printer for accessing Disclosure On-line. This PC is capable of running separate application programs and has a modem for accessing other on-line databases. In this room there is also a copier for the exclusive use of our staff.

Four additional rooms within the CBR space are used for an

operations center, office spaces, technical work areas, and shelving for ready reference materials. Some of the office furniture and library equipment was acquired in the transfer of the collection from NCRL but much of the additional desks, letter files, vertical files, and fiche file cabinets were provided by generous donations from Esselte Pendaflex and Boorum & Pease.

In the operations center, there is one keyboard terminal for accessing the main catalog of Schwartz Library — locations for off-campus materials are readily determined within the limits of the system, comprised of a DEC computer separate from the Academic Computer Center. Input for this computer is maintained by the cataloging department which is currently served by a direct link to OCLC. The advent of new equipment in the OCLC system, and an updating of equipment in our cataloging department, will provide linkage with other research centers, a new utility for bibliographic searching that may supplant our usage of some of the commercial on-line databases.

Most Used Sources

We would advise against drawing a conclusion that our most used sources would serve as an acquisition guide for other business libraries contemplating fee-based research services. There are many other selection tools that point up the enormous variety and number of business information sources. Chief among these is *Business Information Sources* by Lorna M. Daniells, one of the most recent and comprehensive tools, and by virtue of its organization and treatment of business information categories, is recommended as a useful guide for any library.

We answer a greatly varied number of questions that are difficult to pattern. However, to help our users answer the most frequent business information questions, we published a collection of seven categorical bibliographies titled *Business Information Guide* highlighting about 200 of the many specialized books and periodicals in our collection. Like the Daniells book, it is an example for structuring research questions, and is a help reducing time spent in bibliographic instruction, hopefully allowing more time for the paying customers.

As a matter of interest for this article, six members of our staff were asked to list the 15 most frequently used reference tools in the CBR, and also to list most used databases. It is noteworthy that the list is comprised of only 35 print sources out of 90 possibilities and suggests some unanimity of opinion. Top selections in print media include *Business Index, Predicast's F&S Index United States, Standard and Poor's Industry Surveys, Annual Reports and 10 K's, Standard Directory of Advertisers* and *Value Line*. Databases most used include NEXIS, ABI/INFORM, Dun & Bradstreet's Market Identifiers, PROMPT and, as mentioned elsewhere in this article, Electronic Yellow Pages in DIALOG.

Probably the CBR's single most intensively used data bank for answering questions on companies is the Disclosure *Annual Reports and 10 K's* file on microfiche. This file has a full run of 10-K's, annual reports and proxies from 1974 to date. The CBR's Disclosure collection is unique to this locale as it is a full run subscription. Other academic systems in the area are limited in their business holdings and their students patronize the CBR.

Management Process

The manager of the CBR reports directly to the Director of Schwartz Library who, at this time, is also the University Dean of Libraries who oversees six other campus libraries. As the organization chart shows (see Figure 1), there is a newly formed Business Analysis Group with liaison access to the CBR through its manager. This group is housed adjacent to the CBR and uses its services on an ad hoc basis, paying fees for services rendered. Mutual liaison and access to the Academic Computer Center, the Library School Library, the Instructional Materials Center, and other Departments of Schwartz Library are also maintained through the CBR's manager.

Within the CBR, staff elements include Technical Support and the Marketing Coordinator. The latter is an MBA student majoring in marketing. Technical Support is provided by secretarial and clerical assistants who produce correspondence, initiate billing, handle mail, and keep records for acquisitions, claims, and budget control.

One of the five reference librarian positions is shared by two part-timers. All of the reference librarians teach various courses

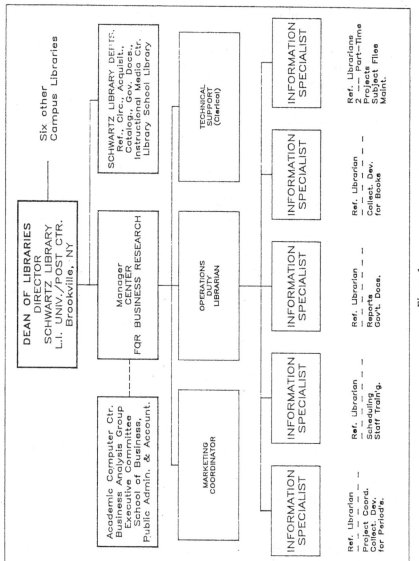

Figure 1

247

in the library's bibliographic instruction program and most of them do on-line searching. The operations office is maintained on a daily basis by a flexible scheduling—each librarian has a desk, a phone and file space. Projects are scheduled by one of the librarians, and operations duty time is scheduled by another.

An Executive Advisory Committee comprised of prominent business men on Long Island has been functioning since the inception of the CBR. The concept for this group was inherited from the NCRL and its purpose is to provide sound advice to the manager on policy, finances, public relations, marketing, and the recruitment of new subscriber members for the CBR. The value of this input is enormous and has helped maintain the CBR as an ongoing entity through difficult administrative periods.

Linking Corporate Research Libraries to CBR

Since 1984, Long Island University has been developing a multisite, multipurpose library network with a central database at the C.W. Post Campus. Four types of libraries are currently being phased into the network: college and university; corporate and scientific; high school; and museums in Nassau County. One level of networking involves terminal access to bibliographic data, and will take place with the CBR subscriber members mentioned above. They will be able to access CBR's vast business resources as well as the other participating library network collections.

In addition, borrowing privileges as well as direct courier service are being planned. This network is a high priority goal of the university and its president is fully committed to its implementation. At this time there are 12 companies represented on the Executive Committee and the CBR has 22 business member subscribers.

Character of Business Librarians

Administrative concerns in a business library are multiple and complex, a situation which seems to be more intense at the CBR. Basically, this library department is a resource for a wide variety of graduate and undergraduate students. Graduate students enrolled in the business school are largely part-time students who work at full-time jobs, who know what they want but always seem to be under pressure, and their information requirements can vary enormously from specific to general needs. On the other hand, undergrads require an enormous amount of coaching in the use of bibliographic tools, financial services and specialized directories.

Switching roles from a low key directing mode, then to a teaching mode and finally to that of providing a professional fee-based service to sophisticated business and industry clients with specific deadlines requires a very specific combination of personality, professional expertise, planning and versatility.

For many librarians, the ability to perform a triple role on a daily basis, with collection maintenance duties, schedules, and a myriad of unpredictable interruptions attendant in a public service department, is difficult. The situation is further complicated if salary structures are not competitive with other institutions (or are drastically lower than in private business). Turnover of trained staff can be continuous and, at times, almost devastating to all levels of service. For good reasons, skilled business librarians today are prized commodities — acquiring and holding good people is a major challenge.

Continuous recruitment of prospective staff members is an essential activity of the manager or department head. This involves close alliance with the library schools, professional associations, and other community contacts. Previous employment on Wall Street firms and teaching a course in Business Information Sources and Services for ten years at two library schools has opened up valuable sources of selective contacts for this manager to get outstanding trainees, full-time staff, and business clients.

A major characteristic of the Business Librarian/Information Specialist, as always, is that he or she must be *people oriented*. No matter how technologically advanced our profession becomes, there is no substitute for that rare ability to treat our patron/clients' information problems as if they were our own. The manager of the department should be a manager of people, problems and goals. To maintain a facility for training and education of staff, clientele and prospective clientele, and for marketing, requires exceptional verbal and writing abilities.

Training

Almost all of CBR's full-time and part-time librarians were outstanding students in the manager's course in "Business Information; Sources and Services," and have had previous special library experience or a strong interest to specialize. Our projects coordinator, who recently completed this course, was previously a Manhattan law librarian experienced in corporate mergers and acquisitions. She recently completed a $3,000 project on behalf of a lobbying group. As suburban employment is more compatible with her life-style at this stage in her family's development we may be able to hold on to this highly skilled, productive librarian.

Other members of the staff were attracted to us for the training, experience, and fringe benefits of an academic appointment and tuition benefits. Recent graduates of library school recognize that their CBR experience will make them prime candidates for higher-paid positions in New York City—corporations usually ask for two years of relevant business library experience because they do not have the time to train their personnel. One of our trainees, recently employed by a Manhattan firm said, "My training and part-time experience in the CBR has been invaluable to me in making a smooth transition into a full-time librarian position with a major New York City advertising agency."

Our success in getting and training good people has benefited the CBR and is also enjoyed by others. We are proud of our alumni: former members of our regular staff have been employed by Bell Communications Research Corporation, Bankers Trust Company, Ernst & Whinney, First Boston Corporation, and Morgan Stanley and Company. Former trainees are now at American Association of Advertising Agencies, DDB Needham, Dean Witter Reynolds, Ebasco Services, Goldman Sachs Company, Library of Congress, Price Waterhouse, and Queensborough Public Library.

SCOPE OF SERVICE FOR FEE-BASED RESEARCH

The following four tasks for a fee-based business research center have been deduced from a variety of business plans, our own efforts in writing budget proposals and annual reports, brochures and various seminar or educational talks.

1. Provide business subject research services in response to inquiries from the public, the business community, the academic community and government agencies for a fee.
2. Publish print and nonprint materials of general use to various client markets — public, business community, academic community and government agencies.
3. Conduct educational programs and symposiums to provide direction for acquiring business information and for the free exchange of ideas concerning the use of business information.
4. Promote products of major business information publishers and manufacturers of information processing facilities or equipment.

Marketing Concepts

Practically speaking, most of our business comes from the personal contacts and from referrals. There is nothing like a satisfied customer and we can claim them from many states and from overseas.

We have developed some strong out-of-state affiliations and repeat business with clients who had tried commercial information brokers and found their services costly and unsatisfactory. One particular connection was made through a small consulting firm which sought us out three years ago. The initial project involved finding specialty baked goods businesses that couldn't be located by SIC (standard industrial classification) codes. Our research results were successful and led to many more projects.

Ideally, if we had the time and resources we should market systematically.We can logically ascertain from the four *service elements* noted above that markets for our services can be listed as four major categories: public, corporate, academic and government. It also follows that each of the four *service elements* should be conducted concurrently within each targeted market (of the four market categories) for best effect. Since the purchasers in each of the four market categories have different characteristics and would require different marketing efforts, we should have 16 marketing programs going at the same time.

Practical considerations have limited our selection of markets and types of services to those with the most immediate needs for business research. But we have accomplished all of them at one time or another. We have furnished the kind of services noted above for a fee to many businesses, to individuals, to Nassau County, the Suffolk Cooperative Library System, and to several academic institutions.

Selection of markets and evaluation of marketing efforts should be based on continuous marketing research. In various marketing studies we have conducted for others, we have observed that descriptive research is a basic task and generally provides two types of information: physical attributes and attitudinal information. At the CBR we have developed a wealth of descriptive information about the companies on Long Island. In this respect, our market research activity is a by-product of our research project activity and helps us target our efforts.

Because of budget and personnel limitations we have combined marketing with public relations and promotions to get the best of each for the least cost. We have conducted educational seminars and breakfasts that lead to new business—but we haven't been able to keep these activities going on a frequency that would permit us to keep up with changes in the marketplace, to maintain momentum and to insure acceptance of our services.

We have observed in general that major corporate markets include finance, banking, manufacturing, real estate, insurance, travel and personnel services. Our project research efforts have produced mailing lists, names of individuals purchasing research services, immediate information needs, speed of response desired, cost expectations, need for selective dissemination of information, degree of specialization required, need for consultation, need for confidentiality, and the need for training or educational programs. All this information we have is valuable, but we have to dig it out of vertical files, company files, project files and in some cases, from the heads of our staffers. If we had the time, this information should be compiled systematically for better access and continuity.

As mentioned before, we get a lot of business from referral. To help this process along we have listed the CBR in various directories and have created very handsome facility brochures, mailing inserts, newsletters, handouts, and have engaged in various promotional activities. The latter includes a seminar on fee-based research; the proceedings *Fee-Based Research in College and University Libraries*[3] sold very well. We have also had some executive breakfasts, conducted continuing education courses for SLA and have published a number of bibliographies and small informational pamphlets. Do these help us get business? Undoubtedly—they create awareness and help maintain image, but who knows how long after the initial contact an actual purchase is made, or what motivated the action?

Almost every time our monthly *Business Alert* newsletter goes out, we get new business. In the past, after a lapse in publication, our business fell off. We have a mailing list of about 2,000 but this is small compared to the circulation of *Long Island Business*, a newsweekly that goes to about 10,000 executives. We have had occasional articles in this publication and in *Newsday* that have produced some leads, an activity that our marketing coordinators have attempted to maintain for a more productive communications effort.

Pricing Services

Pricing each service element is flexible and must be acceptable to both the client and to the producer; actual sales experience have provided guidelines. In the situation given, an academic library providing research services for a fee, commonplace evaluations of acceptable returns on investment are difficult, mainly because access to the library cannot be as closely controlled as in a private business activity. In the CBR, staffing for academic support is not separated from fee-based research service support. For this and other reasons, fee-based service is evaluated as a cost recovery program rather than a profit making scheme. However, the CBR estimates that time spent and costs incurred on fee-based service is very well compensated.

Pricing of research services is nominally based on the rationale of compensating the university for the diversion of effort from the main purpose of academic support. Time costs are derived from actual costs related to full utilization of personnel. There is, of course, no extra charge added for profit. This concept is in marked contrast to practices of information brokers who must derive profit from markup over cost, and cost is calculated from partial utilization of personnel and overhead. For example, if the cost of a full-time librarian is $10 per hour, the man-hour billing rate would be at least $20 per hour based on 50% utilization, plus overhead, plus profit.

Our personnel and facilities are available full-time for academic support. What we realize on fee-based services is compensation for professional services from a privately supported institution. This can be viewed as a diversion of effort from the main purpose, although, this business activity is conducted on a nonconflicting basis. We believe it to be analogous to the marketing of professional research at large universities and that the fees charged by their research libraries are not really comparable to ours, because we are operating in a different context. In other words, the CBR has an added dimension that puts it part-time in a special class of business activity. Our prices and quality of services have to compete with those of information brokers and other research activities.

Prices are also determined on the basis of what self-service would cost the client. For instance, if we provide a company with information from an expensive subscription service, what would the company have had to pay if its own personnel had to access the service? What is the company cost to get to the source? What happens in the reference process if the information obtained by self-service is unsatisfactory? We find these questions rather difficult to answer in any given case, but we can make approximations and this leads us to a more realistic pricing policy.

In a recent project, the CBR produced a report on the quality of life on Long Island for a national real estate marketer. The price was established by a letter of proposal and after initial discussions the job price was set. The CBR had made its estimate based on 60 hours of work at $40 per research hour. The actual job required 20 hours of research and 60 hours of writing. Although the CBR's estimate was low, the company was billed for the agreed amount. The actual cost of "diverting" 80 hours was $800 — the fee was paid and went into a restricted fund for use in improving library equipment and for reducing collection maintenance costs. The client had previous experience with another information service company and was well-satisfied with the CBR's service.

NOTES

1. About two-thirds of the periodical/serial titles are highly selective, free, trade association and regional bank letters.

2. As AT&T was subdivided or broken up it was no longer possible to receive current directories free of charge on a uniform basis. Furthermore, information brokers wreaked havoc on the collection, tying up copiers and leaving hundreds of directories for reshelving on a daily basis.

3. Conference on Fee-Based Research in College and University Libraries. Brookville, NY: Center for Business Research, 1983. Proceedings of the meetings at C.W. Post, Long Island University June 17 and 18, 1982.

High Priced or Over-Priced: They're Every Library's Problem

Nancy R. Posel

SUMMARY. During the eighties, the prices of many essential reference publications have increased at a rate far above those of other hardcover volumes and cost-of-living items. Many librarians are disturbed by this problem but have been at a loss as to the remedy. Based on the positive experiences of two publisher/librarian open forums, a fruitful option would be meetings with more publishers under the auspices of state professional associations and ALA. Together, publishers and librarians can arrive at more equitable prices and information resources which are more user-friendly.

Overpriced reference materials affect every library in the country. Regardless of size or type of institution, resources are finite. Professionals are becoming aware that unreasonable price increases are threatening our information priority. And as we attempt to devote more of the book budget pie to reference, our other service responsibilities are threatened.

Regardless of the type of library we work in, information is our primary activity. Pressures to hold down costs exist in school, special, academic and public institutions. Certainly many municipally supported facilities are being forced to examine carefully, salaries, operating costs and materials expenditures. Many large city libraries have faced egregious funding cuts. Surely academic institutions must confront rising costs as tuitions skyrocket. Every library director and reference department head faces the need to make the reference dollar go further.

Nancy R. Posel is Director of Libraries, Abington Free Library, 1030 Old York Road, Abington, PA 19001.

257

In a survey of public libraries in my district, it is apparent that most are spending a minimum of 33% of their book budgets on reference. This figure may be higher, as at my own library, if periodicals are included. The service objectives of each institution affect the percentages. How much is allocated in your library?

It becomes important to establish and control these figures when we discover that the costs of many reference materials have risen in recent years at a much higher rate than either the cost-of-living or the costs of other hardcover volumes. Who sets the allocation for the reference budget? If reference publishers eat up more and more of our funds, this fact will affect what we are able to spend on circulating materials, A-V, children's materials, or whatever else we must buy.

The titles listed in Table 1 were assembled by Mary Lou Ginsburg, Reference Department Head, Abington Free Library. We believe that these titles are "musts" for any busy reference department.

The figures are particularly shocking when we contrast the price increases for these high demand items with cost-of-living increases. Between 1981 and 1985, the Bureau of Labor Statistics' Consumer Price Index shows an increase of 14%; between 1981 and 1986, the CPI rose 17%. Bowker figures are available on the costs of hardcover book costs only for 1981 to 1985. Compare this increase of 18% to those on the must-have list.

ARE LIBRARIES BEING PRICED OUT OF THE INFORMATION BUSINESS?

One of the unique roles the professional librarian plays in each setting — public, academic, school or special library — is that of advocate for the end-user. If we do not act to protect the library patron's need to know, who will?

What is the effect on our users of skyrocketing reference prices? An alarming, perhaps unheralded effect, is that slowly, but surely, the information business may be getting so costly that we cannot meet our professional standards of providing the latest, most up-to-date material available. This may be unheralded because it is happening over a period of years and we have become conditioned. Some librarians I speak with seem to accept price increases as inevitable regardless of whether they are reasonable or unreasonable.

If we can afford to purchase certain core reference materials only every second or third year, what are the consequences for our clientele? The resulting degradation of our information capability is a matter which needs to be made a top priority by ALA, all librarians on the frontlines and the providers of our materials.

And what are the consequences when libraries drop titles permanently? How many libraries have had to drop the "New York Times" on microfilm and the index? If libraries can no longer afford to be in the information business, then we face a crisis which has profound implications for the American public as well as for our profession. The critical need for information in our society should make librarians key figures in every constituency they serve.

NEED FOR LIBRARY/PUBLISHER DIALOGUE

During my 30 or so years in public librarianship, I have heard, from time to time, that it would be beneficial to have publishers and professionals exchanging information. It is no longer merely desirable, it is absolutely essential. What could be accomplished by organizing open forums with reference publishers?

First, publishers who are wholly or primarily dependent upon library customers for their sales would have the opportunity to become aware of fiscal realities. Publishers could provide to their purchasers, the rationale for current pricing policies.

Second, librarians could provide greater input so that the scope and content of publications designed for libraries would more nearly meet our needs. Publisher sales would no doubt increase.

The present situation is that publishers are losing sales, librarians are angry and frustrated, and the library patron is not getting the latest and best information available.

One New Jersey librarian confessed that she felt she had been taken advantage of for years by the pricing policies of reference publishers. She said she felt ashamed that she had heretofore

TABLE 1

PRICE OF SELECTED REFERENCE BOOKS (year invoiced)

1981-1986

	1981	1982	1983	1984	1985	1986	% Increase
AMERICAN LIBRARY DIRECTORY	$ 49.50	$ 55.95	$ 89.00	$ 97.50	$125.95	$125.94	155
BOOKS IN PRINT (TITLES & AUTHORS ONLY)	$129.50	$149.50	$169.00	$185.00	$199.95	$225.00	74
CONSULTANTS & CONSULTING ORGANIZATIONS		$100.52		$275.00	not published	$275.00	175
CONTEMPORARY AUTHORS	$ 65.00	$ 68.00	$ 72.00	$ 82.00	$ 85.00	$ 88.00	35
DUN & BRADSTREET MILLION DOLLAR DIRECTORY VI & V2	$360.00	$460.00	$520.00	$570.00	$917.50 (now 4 vols)	$937.50	160
ENCYCLOPEDIA OF ASSOCIATIONS VI	$135.00	$140.00	$170.00	$185.00	$195.00	$220.00	63
EUROPA YEARBOOK	$180.00	Cannot Verify	$195.00	$210.00	$210.00	$210.00	17
FACTS ON FILE	$279.00	$299.00	$325.00	$340.00	$370.00	$395.00	42
INTERNATIONAL WHO'S WHO	$ 90.00	$105.00	$117.50	$130.00	$130.00	$145.00	61
McGRAW HILL SCIENCE & TECHNOLOGY		$675.00				$1260.00 by '87	86

TABLE 1, continued

	1981	1982	1983	1984	1985	1986	% Increase
MOODY'S LIBRARY PACKAGE 4 titles	$795.00	$895.00	$995.00	$1085.00	$1175.00	$1270.00	60
NEW YORK TIMES INDEX	$210.00	$395.00	$425.00	$475.00	$495.00	$515.00	145
NEW YORK TIMES MICROFILM	$595.00	$645.00	$695.00	$795.00	$835.00	$870.00	46
SOMETHING ABOUT THE AUTHOR	$44.00	$46.00	$52.00	$58.00	$64.00	$64.00	45
STANDARD & POOR'S CORPORATION RECORDS	$378.00	$465.00	$515.00	$570.00	$630.00	$800.00	112
STANDARD & POOR'S CORPORATION REGISTER	$215.00	$245.00	$270.00	$298.00	$330.00	$398.00	85
STANDARD DIRECTORY OF ADVERTISERS					$195.00	$220.50	13
STANDARD DIRECTORY OF ADVERTISING AGENCIES					$97.00	$125.00	29
TRADE NAME DIRECTORY		$175.00		$230.00	$210.00 (supplement only)	$230.00	31
ULRICH'S INTERNATIONAL DIRECTORY	$78.00	$89.50	$110.00	$125.00	$139.95	$142.45	82
VALUE LINE					$265.00	$395.00	49

261

done nothing to express her opinions. A questionnaire to my colleagues in Montgomery County, PA elicited replies from three who suggested an organized boycott, many who deplored the fact they could no longer purchase each year and some who had been forced to permanently drop publications and services which they had heretofore regarded as essential. Publishers would do well to be concerned especially about this latter group.

Librarians MUST be concerned about libraries whose information sources are being degraded as a result of excessive price increases. What action has our profession taken regarding the plight of libraries who can no longer afford basic reference tools?

PROTESTS WHICH DON'T WORK

Editor Bill Katz's instructions were to write about the "nittygritty" of reference service administration with a focus on budget and finance. I am suggesting that all reference librarians and library directors re-examine their traditional roles. We can no longer absorb out-of-line price increases in a passive manner. Herbert S. White has much the same message in his article, "Differential Pricing" which appeared in "Library Journal" September 1, 1986, on the subject of international periodical pricing.

The "nitty-gritty" of the reference situation is that protests by individuals will not work. "Value Line" is a much depended upon reference publication in my library and my neighboring libraries. From the kind and amount of advertising we receive, we believe they wish to sell to libraries. The abrupt end of the educational discount resulted in a price increase of 49% per subscription! A neighboring library director purchases three subscriptions for her three facilities. Her bill increased a total of $390.00! We pride ourselves on being good business persons who monitor our expenditures carefully and spend many hours planning. Such arbitrary increases knock the planning function into a cocked hat.

When letters were written to call attention to our problem, the replies bordered on the arrogant, even the ignorant. One library director was told that anyone who wanted to use "Value Line" could afford to purchase his own! This of course flies in the face of what we know: the majority of stock in this country, is, in fact, owned by the small investor. The thousands we serve each year are managing their own investments. They can not afford to purchase a $395.00 per year publication.

My letter to the president of Bowker in regard to preposterous price increases in the *ALA Directory* was apparently unworthy of any reply. I have also tried to interest publisher representatives in the plight of the library which cannot continue to absorb enormous price increases. This is such a new notion that this arouses no interest or concern of any kind (although my sample is not large). I have a sneaking suspicion, however, that even should such a matter reach the next sales meeting, it will go no further.

Well, we know what doesn't work.

DIALOGUES WITH PUBLISHERS PRODUCE RESULTS

"Orchestrated pressure" is what one academic library director called for. Our state and national organizations can in fact accomplish a great deal. This is where our strength lies.

After my article, "Pricing Us Out Of The Market," appeared in *American Libraries*, July/August, 1985, Sue Kheel, a New Jersey librarian with the same concerns, organized an Open Forum with Gale in May, 1986, at the New Jersey Library Association conference. That meeting was well-prepared by Gale, was constructive in tone and instructive to both publisher and professionals. Gale has also held an Open Forum at the Pennsylvania Library Association conference in November, 1986 (plans to have Wilson attend the Pennsylvania meeting unfortunately fell through). The same topics were uppermost at each: the expensive quantities of advertising librarians receive from Gale, lack of larger discounts on standing orders, changes in content and format without notification (or consultation), publication of high priced items only to be followed by a sale on the same volumes, not knowing how much information we are being asked to pay for, paying for information which we already have in numerous other sources, etc.

How Does Gale Respond to Library Concerns?

Gale is to be commended for their efforts to meet some of our problems. They have promised to provide more product information in their "Acquisitions Bulletin." They have announced they would "customize" mailings to meet the individual library's needs (just call them if you wish this also). And they have announced that they would not raise literary reference series' price last set in July, 1985, until 1987. They agreed to reinstate special discounts on back volumes of certain literary series, and they promised to hold future price increases to the rate of inflation or below. This is the beginning of responsible pricing; it is the beginning of mutually beneficial pricing policies.

All this happened with only one meeting. Of course there are still problems aplenty. Gale maintains that they monitor the cost of each publication separately—and charge accordingly. But several New Jersey academic libraries complained that they supported publication and updating of expensive sets, such as *Biography and Genealogical Index*, but receive no break on the cumulations. A very persistent librarian, with a $20,000 a year book budget, said she needed Gale publications, but could not afford "starter" sets. President Fred Ruffner said he would send someone to see what they could arrange. I hope that any special arrangements will be advertised so that all libraries in this category will benefit.

My conclusion, after attending this forum, is that Gale is indeed making an effort to respond to some very serious concerns. I could wish, however, for a better understanding of the key role they play in the information business. Our professional responsibilities are endangered when we are told to purchase less frequently if we can not afford their prices! Thus they do not seem concerned about selling fewer copies. This is an area of consciousness-raising which needs to be pursued with all those who publish primarily for libraries.

OTHER PUBLISHERS NEED
TO JOIN THE DIALOGUE

As the head reference librarian in our largest county library expressed herself, Wilson has a "hammerlock" on the field. There are many concerns as to scope and format as well as price, which need to be aired with Wilson, according to the Cumberland County, PA system administrator and the library director of Willow Grove, PA.

A director of a library serving 13,000 population with a book budget of $30,000 (one-third for reference) told me she HAD to buy the *McGraw Hill Science and Technology Encyclopedia* this year. Her patrons are just as badly in need of access to that publication as those in larger libraries whom we tend to think can absorb a $1260 invoice. She said she absolutely could not have purchased it without funds from a new program in PA (which may be only temporary).

My own library, serving 61,000, has been able to increase its book budget 26% in the last five years (to $94,000). But we can buy no other encyclopedia this year, except the McGraw-Hill, which has whomped us with an 86% price increase (since '82). Business references are among our most heavily used; the chart shows heart-stopping price increases.

A relatively small number of publishers serve tremendous needs in our libraries. It should not be difficult to begin to talk over our problems in state and national forums. One dialogue with one key publisher brought us the welcome news that price increases in the future will be tied to the cost-of-living. McGraw-Hill, Wilson, Bowker, "Value Line," and others would benefit from these open forums. If reasonable pricing policies result in more sales, all publishers will benefit. Publishers can learn more about the needs of information consumers from those who serve them. Future publications can be tailored to meet needs more specifically. Surely more sales will result from providing a better product.

ARE LIBRARIANS TOO BUSY
OR TOO PASSIVE TO BEARD THE LION?

Herb White, in "Library Journal," Sept. 1, 1986 (p.170) wrote that, in his opinion, higher prices for library purchases of serials result from librarians accepting whatever increases were passed along to them. We are now becoming aware that this may be taking place in reference tool publishing.

In 1984 I wrote to officials of the American Library Association when I began to be aware of run-away price increases in many reference materials. It was suggested that I submit an article to "American Libraries." This appeared in July/August, 1985, with a call to action to ALA. So far we have been very disappointed that ALA has not scheduled important dialogues with publishers as part of our annual meetings. A librarian from Wisconsin contacted me to ask what activity ALA was organizing. She was encouraged. She and her colleagues had long been discussing the problem. They felt that now something would be done by ALA.

All of us can be encouraged to act by our positive experiences with Gale. They have certainly been cooperative and should be commended for the steps they have taken thus far.

What would be the likely result of a series of hearings held around the country to dramatize the situation? Library directors and reference librarians would be able to take a much more active role in the information business. Reference publishers would become aware of the need to keep price increases reasonable. Thus their sales would increase. Competition would be encouraged. Our patrons would benefit as we take steps to make the library's book budget dollar go further.

CONCLUSION

The only agency in a community which can meet the informational needs of its citizens is the library. We do not have to elaborate on the critical importance of the library's role in aiding the job seeker, the career changer, the medical consumer, the information-needy electorate, etc. Geopolitics, commerce, the whole range of contemporary problems must be revealed, studied and analyzed. Librarians must fight to maintain the highest standards possible in the information business. There is no one else to guard the patron's right-to-know.

Certain professional publications seem greatly taken up with the question of "image" in our profession. When librarians begin to organize and concern themselves with problems which have profound implications for the entire community of library users, then we will no longer have an image problem.

ALA and state professional organizations are vital agents for organizing constructive, honest and instructive discussions between reference publishers and librarians. If we do not give high priority to this effort, our libraries will not be the vital agencies our citizens need them to be. There is no one else to do the job.

Managing Difficult People:
Patrons (and Others)

Helen M. Gothberg

SUMMARY. Coping with difficult situations or impossible people is all part of a day's work in the life of a reference or other public services librarian. Coping with difficult situations may require different approaches than dealing with a set of difficult patron behaviors. In some situations, it may be a matter of establishing policy, keeping emergency numbers available or helping librarians develop more assertive attitudes and behaviors. In the case of working with impossible patrons (or others), understanding what motivates human behavior and developing coping skills which consciously make use of specific kinds of interpersonal communication can improve staff performance in this area. In either case, library managers should recognize their own part in being role models for reference staffs and the need to provide opportunities for growth and learning in this area for library personnel.

Human relations can be the most rewarding part of a reference librarian's job except for those few times when difficult situations or impossible patrons make it otherwise. When these occa-

Helen M. Gothberg is Associate Professor, Graduate Library School, University of Arizona, 1515 East First Street, Tucson, AZ 85704.

sions do arise they may come forcefully to the attention of the head of the reference department and/or the library director. Reference staffs frequently need a better sense of how to cope with difficult situations and patrons in the library. Managers, librarians and other staff members can all benefit from a greater understanding of what motivates difficult people who can, from time to time, make our lives miserable. Sometimes these impossible people are patrons, but they may also be co-workers — or even the boss. Since the buck stops at the top, and public relations concerns are increasingly on the minds of budget conscious and politically attuned administrators, finding ways to cope effectively with problem situations and patrons in the library is an important area of concern for management.

INTERPERSONAL COMMUNICATION AS A TOOL

How we relate to one another in a public place such as a library is largely a matter of interpersonal communication style. Because human communication is learned and because we are each in control of how we communicate in any given situation, increased knowledge and awareness about human interaction is extremely useful in dealing with difficult situations or impossible people. There are, however, some cautions to note as we begin this exploration into the subject of human relations in the library. The first one is to recognize that there are no pat formulas that will turn every problem into a peak experience. Human behavior is never entirely predictable. The recommendations that follow may or may not work.

Second, we must not look at patrons (or others) as objects to be dissected, analyzed and then responded to according to some set of prescriptive actions. We would do well to heed Buber's words: "The world as experience belongs to the basic word I-It. The basic word I-You establishes the world or relations."[1] "I-It" dialogue between the reference librarian and the patron could be characterized as that which involves the search for information. It would be sufficient if this was only a matter of two machines communicating with one another. Because reference librarianship is (or should be) more than the transfer of information upon request, there is also a need to establish a world of relations with the patron. "I-You" dialogue is the humanistic aspect of library service about which Ranganathan[2] wrote so eloquently. If librarianship is to be viewed philosophically as a helping profession, library service must go well beyond the basic concern of settling problems amicably solely for reasons of public relations (PR).

Lastly, some spontaneity will be lost in developing coping skills for dealing with difficult situations and impossible people through the conscious use of specific types of communication behavior. However, what may be awkward in the beginning, can very soon become fully integrated into your own style. What coping does for the library is to permit those who are involved in its services to get on with the business at hand. Certain types of communication do work much of the time because they interfere with the disrupting function of difficult behavior.

DIFFICULT SITUATIONS

Late in the afternoon, on a warm summer's day in the reading room of the University of California's Berkeley Campus library, a disturbed young man walked up to a female patron. It was the early 1960s; he was black, and she was white; they had had a lover's quarrel. He pulled out a gun, shot the woman and then turned and walked out of the building. Everyone was in a state-of-shock including the writer who was in the building at the time. We are rarely prepared to deal with such a catastrophic event. Nor is this the kind of situation which requires some type of process intervention; it is a time for cool heads and quick action.

There is a difference between difficult situations such as the one described above and impossible people. Difficult situations may be dangerous, or they may only be a nuisance. Other dangerous situations that sometimes occur in the library include epileptic seizures, heart attacks, emotional breakdowns and other health related problems. Difficult situations which are also dangerous require a written policy about who to contact and what to do. Such a policy must be worked out with legal advice and should be reviewed with all library employees at least once a year. New library employees are to be provided with such information at the time of their orientation. Having up-to-date emergency phone numbers clearly posted at all public service desks is a must even if there is a guard in the building. Having one or more people on the library staff knowledgeable in first aid procedures, including CPR and the Heimlick maneuver, is also a very good idea.

There are difficult situations that are only a nuisance yet they take up staff time and often try the patience of even the best of professionals. A few examples of these types of difficult situations in the library are: the lonely patrons who come to the library frequently and talk endlessly. They are very often elderly people whose feelings you don't want to hurt. Or it may be the practical joker in the children's or young adult's areas. Patrons with bizarre clothing or extremely offensive body odors may pose a problem, but rarely a threat, to other patrons and sometimes to librarians. Anyone who has worked the public service desk of a large metropolitan library could add considerably to this list. Much of the time situations such as these can be effectively dealt with by using assertive, nondefensive communication.

THE ASSERTIVE LIBRARIAN

One of the reasons that nuisance situations get out-of-hand is because we do not want to confront people in a public place about inappropriate behavior. We are reluctant for the sake of good manners and our commitment to treating all patrons with courtesy to say: "You talk too much, and I have work to do," or "You're not funny, and if you do that again . . ." or "Whew! you smell—why don't you take a bath!" Nor should we—these are expressions of aggressive behavior. But we do have such thoughts at times, and repress them until an unspoken barrier may develop between the librarian and, not only the offending patron, but possibly all patrons.

Janette Caputo's[3] excellent book on the subject of assertiveness is recommended reading for all public service librarians. Caputo defines assertion as, "Standing up for your rights without violating the rights of others," while nonassertion is a matter of not standing up for yourself. Aggressive behavior, "is standing up for your rights without concern for (or conscious avoidance of) the violation of other's right."[4] No matter how much we may empathize with a lonely patron, there is work to be done, and while librarians need to be sensitive to the emotional as well as the intellectual needs of people, limits must be set. It may be a matter of setting some sort of mutually agreed upon general departmental guidelines, but it is more likely that members of the reference staff will need to develop specific ways to extract themselves from this type of difficult situation.

One of the first steps to take is to make a mental note that it is a difficult situation when loquacious patrons pin you down for too long a period of time and at the expense of other patrons or the work load. *You* have the right to change it. There is no one way that will work with all patrons, but attentive listening and a response that shows that you have heard and understood the chatty patron is a good second step. Don't feel anxious or rushed. (The library manager may need to reassure staff that it is ok to take some extra time with library patrons and to be interested in them.) Lastly, close down the conversation politely but firmly. If there are others waiting, say to the patron that you enjoy visiting with her, or that you found something he said enjoyable — or whatever positive *but honest* reinforcement is appropriate for the situation. It may even be acceptable to lightly touch the patron on the hand, arm or elbow. Then make direct eye contact as you indicate that you now need to help the next patron or do some other work and move away physically. Do not make excuses or apologize; do be straight forward and nonjudgmental in what you say and the tone of voice in which you say it. Keep in mind that you have the right to say "no" to inappropriate patron behavior and not feel guilty about it. There is no reason to be defensive.

Learning to develop a nonjudgmental communication style is not easy for professionals. We have been brought up to compete and to rank others in order to make ourselves feel more important. On the other hand, language and mannerisms that are too formal and aloof are not the answer. Such behavior lacks the human qualities that are important on both sides of the reference or public service desk. Jack Gibb's[5] article on "Defensive Communication," written in 1961, is a classic on the subject. He defines defensive behavior as that which occurs when an individual perceives a threat and uses energy to defend him or herself.

As a result, the object becomes not to understand the exchange of dialog for whatever purposes, but to win, dominate, impress or escape punishment.

The Gibb model is based on six pairs of defensive and supportive categories which are presented below. Behavior which the patron may perceive as having any of the characteristics listed in the left-hand column arouses defensiveness, whereas that which is perceived as having any of the qualities that are supportive reduces defensive feelings.

Defensive Climates	Supportive Climates
1. Evaluation	1. Description
2. Control	2. Problem Orientation
3. Strategy	3. Spontaneity
4. Neutrality	4. Empathy
5. Superiority	5. Equality
6. Certainty	6. Provisionalism[6]

Not only what we say, but the way in which we say it — that is, tone of voice and nonverbal communication may engender defensiveness in the patron if the librarian appears to be making judgements about his or her person. If we examine the problem with the juvenile practical joker along the lines of the Gibb model, several useful ideas come to mind. The first is that the librarian or other staff member has the right to be treated with respect and to ask for what he or she wants. (Ask does not equal demand.) The second step is to assess the situation carefully and not to overreact, but if the situation does need to be changed, then the next step is to describe to the young offender what has been observed. The second step is to explain why this is a problem.

A third step might be to ask the young patron how he or she might go about remedying the situation. The librarian might say for example: "Bob (or Alice), you can see that we have a problem here. What are *you* willing to do to change it?" Once the desired response is forthcoming (and don't take "I don't know" for an answer), the next step is to move with the patron in some way. Find out why he or she is in the library, what the youngster likes to read (watch or listen to). How long has he or she been there? Maybe a parent has a habit of dumping the child on the library as a free babysitter, which is going to mean dealing with the parent as well. The librarian should not say with certainty, "I know you can find something fun to do here if you just look around." Say instead (provisionalism), "I want to help you find ways to enjoy your trip to the library. Tell me something more about what you like to do, and we will explore your interests together."

RIGHTS AND RESPONSIBILITIES

Libraries have rules about behavior and sometimes dress. They are necessary to maintain an environment that is comfortable for the greater majority of their publics. These rules should be posted in the entry so that patrons know what the limits are. There are patrons who will not respond to a supportive climate. When this happens, then appropriate punitive action may have to be taken for the good of others. For example, a frequent and unwelcome visitor to a university library was an individual who would sit near the reference desk area and play with a knife. He also exuded a very foul odor. Patrons complained, and the librarians were nervous with the situation. The library director was the right person to deal with this situation, and he did. He told the person calmly that playing with the knife made the librarians uncomfortable, and that a number of patrons had complained about his body odor. He concluded with a statement that the individual would need to take care of both of these problems before he returned to the library. This unwelcome visitor, who was not using library resources but merely taking up space, did not return.

Librarians have a responsibility to respect other people even when they are different from themselves. They have the right to dislike a patron but a responsibility to not let those feelings interfere with the quality of the service provided. On the other hand, patrons have the right to ask questions (even stupid ones) and to have expectations about the services they receive and to understand how and why a library functions as it does. Patrons have a responsibility in turn to behave in ways that do not violate the rights of librarians or other patrons using the same resources and physical space. Librarians not only have the right, but also the responsibility to let people know when they have violated the rights of others, but to do it in ways that are nonevaluative or judgmental but rather descriptive and problem solving oriented.

THE DIFFICULT PERSON

All of us can be "difficult people" from time to time or find ourselves in a difficult situation which is of our own making. The difficult personalities described here are those individuals whose behavior is ongoing and habitual. They are frustrating to work with — sometimes as patrons, or as co-workers — or as people that you supervise. Other people tend to find the difficult person impossible to cope with, although there is no doubt that some kinds of behaviors one person will react to more vehemently than say another. There will tend to be general agreement, however, about certain behavior characteristics that make a certain individual(s) a problem in any workplace. Bramson[7] identified seven patterns of such difficult behavior:

Hostile-Aggressives. These individuals are among the most difficult patrons for librarians (or others) to work with in providing reference service. They try to bully and overwhelm staff by throwing their weight around or making cutting remarks.

Complainers. Although a nuisance, complainers are probably less of a problem as patrons than they are as co-workers. As a peer or a subordinate they represent a problem because their feelings of powerlessness cause them to shirk library responsibilities.

Super-Agreeables. This behavior trait may not seem at first glance to be a difficult one, but in this group the problem occurs when the individual is always willing to agree with whatever you say but will act contrary to what your expectations are. One of the worst positions for the super-agreeable person to be in is as a manager or supervisor. Staff hostility soon mounts to the boiling point when what they perceive to be an open communication style turns out to be an individual who is going to do whatever he or she pleases with little regard for the rights or opinions of subordinates.

Silent and Unresponsives. Reference librarians have reported to this writer that among the most frustrating patrons to serve are those who don't know what they want but believe that the librarian can, not only find the right book, but also discover what their needs are — even when the patron is not sure what they are. Getting reluctant communicators to speak up can be a very real challenge.

Know-It-All Experts. As co-workers, bosses, employees and patrons, this group is infamous for making you feel like an idiot by their condescending or pompous behaviors. The problem is that they may be right much of the time, although some are only bluffers.

Negativists. You don't want to ask people who fall into this behavior pattern if they had a good weekend on Monday morning. While they can be something of a problem as patrons, they are more difficult to cope with as co-workers or subordinates because their bad attitudes eat away at the esprit de corps of the organization.

Indecisives. As patrons they can't make up their minds about what they want from the library no matter how many suggestions are made to them about available resources. As co-workers, they drive others to the wall with their stalling because they want every decision to be free of risks and to always be perfect in what they do.

Coping with Difficult Behavior

What exactly does "coping" with difficult people mean? A first rule or guideline is to recognize that it does not mean changing the person; it only means coping with certain behavior patterns in ways that facilitate reference service or the smooth operation of the department. A second guideline is to try to understand the motivation behind the behavior, without pigeonholing people or trying to be pop psychologists. The basic purpose of coping is to keep difficult behavior sufficiently off balance so that both the patron (co-worker or boss) and you can function a well as possible.

Four of the seven difficult behaviors noted above are explored in more depth in relation to reference and other public services in libraries. Readers are encouraged to read Robert Bramson's book, *Coping with Difficult People*, for a more in-depth look at the subject as it relates to organizational management. The four types of difficult behaviors that are particularly troublesome in doing reference work are: Hostile-Aggressive, Silent and Unresponsive, coupled with Indecisives and Know-It-All Experts.

Coping with Hostile Aggressives

Bramson divides the hostile-aggressives into three subgroups which he christens: Sherman Tanks, Snipers and Exploders. Sherman Tanks come on strong; they have lots of power and regard others as their victims. Any evidence of rage or weakness in the librarian will often stimulate the Sherman Tank personality to continue the attack. These individuals have a strong need to prove themselves to others and are quickly angered when they perceive resistance to their way of thinking. The best way to cope with Sherman Tanks is to stand up to them without fighting. You can give them a little time to run down, but you must get their attention — even through rude, interruptive behavior if necessary. Assertive behavior is very useful with Sherman Tanks. Be forceful but don't argue. Put yourself in a power position by standing up if you are sitting, or get the Tank to sit down. Be sure to maintain eye-contact.

Don't apologize for library rules and policies. For example, if a patron blows up over the fact that he can't take out a reference book, say firmly: "Mr. Sherman, reference books are not checked out of this library, partly because of the high cost of replacement, but also because they need to be available to *all* of the public on call. We have other books on the subject which you may check out, or we have a copier that you can use if there are certain pages you want from that particular book." Don't be surprised if Mr. Sherman turns out to be very friendly the next time he comes to the library — and even seeks you out to help him. It is part of the character of Sherman Tanks to respect those people they can't run over.

Snipers are like guerilla fighters. They don't use an open show of force but rather hit and run tactics. They take pot shots at you; make not so subtle jokes and then retreat behind comments such as, "I was only teasing, can't you take a joke!" Snipers have strong feelings about how others should behave and when things don't go the way they expect, they become aggressive. The best way to cope with snipers, according to Bramson, is confrontation. Let them know that there are other points of view besides their own. Focus on problem solving and call in reinforcements from other reference staff or patrons.

Let's take Miss Betty Snipey for example. She always talks down the branch library you work in and compares it unfavorably to another branch that she also uses. You know from visiting with your co-workers at the other branch that she does the same thing there. The next time she complains about never finding what she wants, say to her: "We have material on that subject. I'm sure that it is not all checked out. However, I can also call the X-Branch and have some books sent over for you." Reach for the phone right away and dial the branch. Or say to a nearby patron: "Do you have problems finding the materials that you want in this library?" And then pleasantly to the sniper: "We do believe in meeting our patrons' needs as much as possible in this library system."

Exploders do just that—they have adult or adolescent (in the case of young adult services) temper tantrums. Do not try to placate them. This writer knows of one instance where an exploder, who was not handled well in a reference department, hit the librarian over the head with a book after a long tirade involving the location of some books he had donated to the collection. Temper tantrums in adults have the same motivation as they do in children. They are a tactic designed to cope with fear, feelings or frustration and helplessness. In coping with exploders, do give them a sufficient amount of time to run down and regain some self-control. Try to get them into a private area where you can talk things over in a quiet nonthreatening way. Because such individuals may be potentially harmful, it may be well to get another librarian or supervisor to join you. Then take the person seriously and try to work out the problem to the best of your ability. Sit down, use an open and supportive body posture, such as gesturing toward the person while talking. Keep eye contact brief but friendly. Lots of head nods and "uh-huh's" are useful as long as they indicate a sincere interest in what the exploder is saying.

Another way to look at all hostile aggressives is to keep in mind that their behavior is that of either a child or a parent. In these situations you do not want to complement the child by behaving like a critical parent, or like a child who turns anger back or is intimidated by harsh behavior on the part of the patron. The mature adult transaction can be used successfully in coping with hostile aggressive patrons. It helps to keep the undesirable behavior off-base — that is, not profitable to the impossible person at the reference or public service desk. You may also find it helpful to team up with a trusted fellow librarian to monitor one another in terms of how you come across with difficult patrons and the recommendations given here.

Coping with Silent, Unresponsives and Indecisives

Clams at the reference desk try the best professional's patience. Having once stated that they want something, any attempts to further determine the specifics of their request are met with "I guess," or "Maybe that will be ok," or some other unhelpful euphemism — or no response at all. As a concerned individual in a helping profession, you can appreciate the need not to invade the privacy of another person. At the same time, it can be almost impossible to conduct the reference interview with any degree of success without the cooperation of the patron. In some cases people are just shy, and you can only do so much to draw them out. These are the Stallers or Indecisives. They are fearful of making a mistake or of offending someone. You will need to move slowly with Stallers and try to develop their trust. The shy person is different from the more aggressive clam. You will recognize the difference by the degree of frustration this latter type of patron arouses in you. The reason that the clam is more of a problem is because his or her noncommittal ways are a means of expressing calculated aggression.

Coping with Unresponsives and Indecisives means getting them to talk. Using open-ended questions for either type of behavior is a useful coping method. Open-ended questions cannot be answered with either head nods or "yes-no" responses. For example, the reference librarian might say to a patron: "Tell me something more about the kind of exercises you are interested in. We have books, audio tapes and even video cassettes which you may want to see or listen to." If the patron decides on a video tape, express support about the decision, such as: "That seems like an excellent choice." Establishing an ongoing, friendly personal contact with Stallers will help in working with shy individuals the next time they come to the library.

Coping with the more hostile type of Clam means not only asking open-ended questions but also getting accustomed to long spaces of silence between the two of you. Wait with as much composure as you can muster. Let the patron know how much time you can spend with him or her if there are others waiting. After you have worked with an Unresponsive patron for a few minutes, you might say for example: "I will need to move on to the next patron in a few minutes." Keep your tone even and nonjudgmental. If this approach does not work, terminate the interview or other service-oriented dialogue and indicate that you will come back to the person when you can, but that there are others who need your help. Try not to appear frustrated or rushed.

Coping with Know-It-All Experts

Know-It-All Experts have all the answers, and they really don't like asking questions of librarians. They feel they should and do know how to use the library. A simple inquiry on the part of the reference librarian, such as: "May I help you?" may engender a curt reply. Bramson notes that Know-It-All behavior comes in two varieties: the Bulldozers and Balloons. The main difference between the two is that the former do know, and the latter pretend that they do. Bulldozers are successful people who act as though they have great personal authority and need others very little. However, when things go wrong you are going to hear from them in no uncertain terms — such as when a book is on the shelf that they received a notice about, or the copy machine is not working.

In coping with the Bulldozer, be sure that you do your homework or there may be a call to the President of the Library Board (or City Manager) at worst, or a letter to the Library Director at least. Be sure that you understand what Jan Bulldog may have just said about a certain library book being harmful and inappropriate for children to read. A listening skill called paraphrasing is helpful in coping with Bulldozers. After carefully listening to what the patron has said, rephrase it and give the information back to her. "Now let me be sure that I have understood you correctly," is a useful phrase to begin such a response. "You feel that you don't want *your* child to read this book, or are you making a value judgment about *all* young people having access to this title?" Avoid dogmatic statements, and if it is necessary to disagree, be tentative, yet don't equivocate — especially on issues of censorship!

Balloon behavior is motivated by a desire to be admired and respected by others. This is not a question of being liked, but more one of being viewed as a person of some importance. Balloons are really not that much trouble to the skilled reference worker in contrast to the Bulldozer, but it is important to recognize the difference. When Balloons really are influential within the community, college or school, it can spell real trouble if they misunderstand some comment or course of action that you as a librarian or manager may take. Coping with Balloons is not very different from coping with Bulldozers. What is most important to keep in mind with this type of patron behavior is to allow him or her to save face. Be prepared to deal with gaps in the conversation and make sure that you have really understood what the patron has said to you or feels about a certain situation before responding.

CONCLUSIONS

Coping with difficult situations or impossible people is all part of a day's work in the life of a reference or other public services librarian. Understanding human behavior and developing coping skills which consciously make use of specific kinds of interpersonal communication can make the job easier some of the time. While effective coping is useful to a library's public relations in that angry or dissatisfied patrons can be harmful, it is even more important to view such activity as a commitment made to a helping profession. Unless we view reference librarianship as something more than a switching job between people and information, many of the humanistic qualities that make it a profession — not just an occupation — will be lost. John Nesbitt made an important point in his book, *Megatrends*,[8] which has been noted by a number of other authors as well. He observed that as our world becomes more high tech, there is going to be a need in our society for high touch. High touch in the library may be increasingly a librarian who can cope with the difficult patron and/or situation. Library managers must be cognizant of changing needs and developing trends. Managers set a style and serve as role models for others. They also need to find ways to provide in-service training, counseling and the evaluation of reference and public services that take into consideration high touch skills. Florence DeHart, in her excellent book on *The Librarian's Psychological Commitments*, closed her final chapter with this compelling thought:

The power of response choice within the self and toward others — how great it is! It is the basis on the librarian's psychological commitments. And these commitments design the pattern of human relations in librarianship.[9]

NOTES

1. Martin Buber, *I and Thou*. (New York: Charles Scribner's Sons, 1970). p. 56.

2. S.R. Ranganathan, "Reference Service and Humanism," in Rowland, comp., *Reference Services*. (Hamden, CT: The Shoe Strong Press, Inc., 1964).

3. Janette S. Caputo, *The Assertive Librarian*. (Phoenix, AZ: Oryx Press, 1984).

4. *Ibid.*, p.3.

5. Jack R. Gibb, "Defensive Communication," *The Journal of Communication*. (September 1961). pp. 141-148.

6. *Ibid.*, p. 143.

7. Robert M. Bramson, *Coping with Difficult People*. (Garden City, NY: Anchor Press/Doubleday, 1980).

8. John Nesbitt, *Megatrends*. (New York: Warner Books, 1984).

9. Florence E. DeHart, *The Librarian's Psychological Commitments; Human Relations in Librarianship*. (Westport, CT: Greenwood Press, 1979). p. 188.

The Realities
of College Reference Service:
A Case Study in Personnel Utilization

Terrence Mech

SUMMARY. At a time when reference services are generally seen as a central function of college libraries, the activities of college reference librarians may indicate otherwise. This study examines reference services in four similar sized college libraries within a greater metropolitan area. Profiles of each library and reference department are developed. Interviews and data collection instruments were used to discover what tasks librarians providing reference services performed and the amount of time devoted to them. Interview data provides a look at some of the issues involved with sharing reference responsibilities among all librarians.

Differences between college and university libraries and their educational role and goals have been well explored by Farber.[1] But even among college libraries sharing similar educational roles there is great diversity. College libraries vary greatly in their services, operations, organization and levels of use. "The reasons behind that diversity are numerous and complex, and ultimately the best analysis of them will be qualitative rather than quantitative."[2]

Even among similar institutions there is diversity in what is expected of reference librarians. Differences in expectations are not always obvious because of obscured and concurrent vari-

Terrence Mech is Director of the Library, King's College, D. Leonard Corgan Library, Wilkes-Barre, PA 18711. The author wishes to thank Judith Tierney, Reference Librarian, D. Leonard Corgan Library, King's College, for her comments in preparation of this manuscript.

285

ations in the size and mix of the student body, size of the library collection and the status and professional recognition accorded librarians. These factors make it difficult to establish reasonable expectations or norms regarding reference librarians and the provision of reference services.[3]

Reference service for faculty and students is presently seen as a basic function of a college library, with emphasis on teaching library skills rather than just providing information. However, it was not always that way. Well into the 20th century the library was regarded as a faculty preserve where faculty could practice their art form of serendipitous research without the assistance of "technicians" (librarians). College faculty felt that librarians "did not understand and respect the accepted methods of scholarly research" and therefore faculty did not see a need to consult with librarians.[4]

College reference services were slow to develop partly because of expectations that faculty and students should be able to find their own materials and information. The scholarly community also felt that libraries should emphasize collection development and cataloging for subject access to materials.[5] By the 1940s and 1950s, because of changes in higher education and librarianship, reference services began to assume a more important role in college libraries. By the 1970s reference services were recognized as a major activity of college libraries. Although college reference services have not been around long they have developed certain traditional areas of activity: library instruction, providing specific information without instruction in how the material was obtained, providing a collection selected to meet local needs, and promoting the library's resources and services.[6]

Underlying these reference activities is the basic function of providing personal assistance to users. With the advent of computers, reference services are changing and evolving. However, the essential process of identifying and clarifying user needs, selecting information or resources to meet those needs, and assisting users in finding and using resources remains the same. The key to any personal assistance service is the staff that provides it.[7] Reference service by its very nature is individual and personnel intensive. However, even with the relatively recent establishment of separate reference services, reference librarians frequently had other duties assigned to them besides reference and library instruction. At times the demands of these other services: interlibrary loan, circulation, government documents, college archives or part-time cataloging were allowed to take precedence over the provision of reference services.[8]

Along with assigning other duties to reference librarians, librarians with other major responsibilities have been assigned reference duties. Because of relatively small staffs in college libraries, college librarians have generally done everything, with reference service seen as a basic service that all librarians should be able to provide. However, not all librarians want to or are suited by nature of their education, work experience, personality or temperament to provide reference services. A growing body of information indicates that reference librarians may have a preferred cognitive style or way of perceiving and thinking that affects the way they negotiate and answer reference questions.[9]

Even in college libraries where the emphasis is on service to the undergraduate, libraries must work with the available personnel resources. But in many cases the emphasis has been in simply covering the reference desk without a great deal of regard for the quality of reference service. This is unfortunate because the personal, professional and academic qualities of reference librarians and their directors have usually been a crucial factor in the kind and quality of reference service provided.[10]

THE STUDY

This descriptive study explores how libraries at four similar colleges utilize their personnel to provide reference services. It describes the duties of those librarians providing reference service and how they use their time. In October and November of 1986 library directors, heads of public service and reference departments, as well as those librarians who provide reference services at four college libraries were interviewed. Librarians providing reference services were asked to keep a record of their activities for five normal work days.

Because reference services and libraries in general are personnel intensive, effective use of personnel is important. For most college libraries personnel expenses are their largest single expenditure. The libraries in this study are no exception. See Table 1 for details. While most individuals agree that effective personnel utilization is important, very few college library directors really know what their librarians actually do. Because reference is a highly visible library service on a college campus, its perception and the image of its providers on campus have very important public relations and budget consequences. Reference librarians sorting mail and reading novels at the reference desk or not being at the reference desk because of meetings do not speak well for the library.

While the findings of this study do not extend to college libraries in general, they do provide an eye opening look at what goes on at four, not so unique, college libraries. To the extent that time utilization reflects individual and library priorities, this study provides a basis for examining and understanding the ac-

Table 1

Characteristics of Colleges and Libraries

1985–1986

	College A	College B	College C	College D
Undergraduate FTE	1,108	1,922	1,759	1,804
Graduate FTE	41	----	458	231
Institutional Classification	IIB	IIB	IIA	IIA
Highest Degree Offered	Master's	Bachelor's	Master's	Master's
Average Student SAT Score	N.A.	943	900	930
Average Salary Associate Professor	24,000	27,800	26,600	26,700
Average Salary Assistant Professor	20,000	23,500	21,900	22,300

	Library A	Library B	Library C	Library D
Volumes Held	73,438	132,586	176,568	188,922
Volumes Added	1,220	2,781	3,636	4,223
Circulation (Excluding Reserves)	11,667	28,228	59,061	24,928
Interlibrary Loans (Sent and Received)	475	872	902	1,327
Librarians FTE	3	4	9	9
Support Staff FTE	5	8.6	15.71	8.16
Workweek (Hours)	35	35	35	35
Salaries and Wages (Excluding Students) as % of Library Expenses	76.46	59.37	66.25	47.38

tual priorities of four college reference departments. It is hoped that this study will encourage other libraries to examine how they actually utilize personnel to provide reference services.

THE COLLEGES

The four colleges are located in a greater metropolitan area within 20 miles of each other. These four coeducational colleges are classified as II A and II B type institutions. II A (comprehensive) institutions are characterized by diverse graduate programs (including first-professional), but no significant doctoral level programs. These institutions grant a minimum of 30 graduate degrees in three or more graduate programs. II B (general baccalaureate) institutions are characterized by their primary emphasis on general undergraduate baccalaureate-level education. These institutions are not significantly engaged in graduate education. They grant fewer than 30 graduate degrees in fewer than three graduate programs.[11]

College A is a private college sponsored by a religious order of women affiliated with the Roman Catholic Church. College B is an independent college founded by a religious order of men. College C is a private college sponsored by a religious order of women affiliated with the Roman Catholic Church. College D is a private independent college. Students attending these colleges are mainly first generation college students. Additional information on the colleges is presented in Table 1.

THE LIBRARIES

The libraries in this study are not very large and have depended on cooperation and reciprocal borrowing arrangements to assist their students and faculty in finding what they want locally. Although this study did not gather information on reference activity levels, using Table 1 and existing research it is possible to estimate reference activity levels at these libraries. Previous research has shown that there is a positive relationship between circulation activity, other measures of library use and the level of reference activity.[12] However, in a study of private college libraries enrollment had a stronger correlation with the number of reference questions asked than did circulation.[13]

Library A: On Call

The reference and serials department at Library A is staffed with one librarian, one clerical worker and several student assistants. The librarian's time is partitioned approximately 40% reference, 20% interlibrary loan and 40% serials. The reference librarian is also responsible for the college archives, "a role given more lip service than time." As part of their faculty responsibilities, Library A's librarians also advise students. Advisement responsibilities occasionally consume some time. When asked about the variety and range of duties, the reference librarian indicated that it helped the time pass quickly.

The physical shape of Library A, long and narrow, is largely responsible for Library A not having a reference desk. Library A takes up the entire floor of an academic building. Individuals enter the library at its center. Circulation and the card catalog are located in the center of the library. Reference and serials are located at one end of the floor, with the collection at the other end. Offices are located along one side of the floor. Because of the library's arrangement and the huge amount of material housed in a small area there is simply no convenient place to put a reference desk. Earlier there was a reference desk towards the center of the library, but because of the distance to the reference collection and the librarians' other duties, it was difficult to staff it.

Reference services are provided by the reference and serials librarian and the other two librarians on the staff, the director and a technical services librarian. Reference services are provided on an "on-call" basis. Typically an individual seeking assistance approaches the periodicals return desk which is staffed by student assistants most of the hours the library is open. Library users are asked not to reshelve periodicals, but rather to return them to the desk for reshelving. At the periodicals return desk a student assistant or clerical worker will answer directional or informational questions. If additional reference assistance is needed, the librarian on call would be summoned. Individuals more familiar with the arrangement go right to the reference librarian's office, "the door is always open."

Library A offers on-line database services. However, the searches are not conducted at Library A. The reference and serials librarian conducts the interview and telephones the information into one of the local medical libraries where the search is conducted.

Library A is open: 8:00 a.m. to 10:00 p.m., Monday through Thursday; 8:00 a.m. to 7:00 p.m., Friday; 9:00 a.m. to 5:00 p.m., Saturday and Noon to 10:00 p.m., Sunday. All three librarians at Library A, work one night a week, every third Sunday and Monday night, plus two Friday nights per semester. Two support staff work on Saturdays. Sunday through Friday nights the library is staffed by one librarian and one support staff member and student assistants. The support staff member is stationed at the circulation desk. Librarians operate out of their offices. All support staff, except the director's secretary, have completed a basic reference course or two. Because of circulation's location across from the card catalog, circulation personnel handle most of the card catalog questions.

Library B: Days Only, But Double Coverage

One librarian and one student assistant, working 10 hours a week, form the core of Library B's reference department. Although the reference librarian is also responsible for the library's special collections and the college archives, only minimal time is devoted to these areas in order to keep up with the growing demands of reference. The two librarians from technical services also provide reference services. Library B has a long tradition of shared reference duties. The library director has no assigned reference responsibilities. Searching on-line databases is done by all the librarians providing reference services.

The reference staff's duties are streamlined as much as possible in order to concentrate on such primary responsibilities as reference, on-line searching and bibliographic instruction. While the reference department is an individual's first contact for interlibrary loan, the bulk of the interlibrary loan work is done by Library B's circulation department. The reference department screens the request to see if it can be filled locally or with alternative materials. Reference verifies the request and then sends it to circulation. However, more and more verification is being done by circulation. The reference department checks in current newspapers, a choice made by the reference librarian. Newspapers, located in the reference area, are the source of many questions like "Is today's paper in yet?" Filing of the major services is handled by other departments.

Because of strong feelings that Library B is a college library where students should expect only professional assistance, support staff and student assistants are not encouraged to provide reference assistance. A student's first contact with the reference desk is an important one. The ability to negotiate what appears to be a deceptively simple question and explain the use of library resources is important and timely when working with college students. College students do not readily distinguish between support staff and librarians; because they are all librarians to students. Student assistants and support staff, in their efforts to be of service, occasionally get in over their heads and give out misinformation. Librarians at Library B feel that no information is better than misinformation. When approached for assistance, support staff and student assistants direct individuals to the reference desk or ask them to come back when a librarian is available.

Library B provides reference service Monday through Friday 9:00 a.m. to Noon and 1:00 to 5:00 p.m. Currently no reference service is available evenings and weekends. However, because of a 36% increase in library use over three years, the library was advertising for a new position, a reference librarian to work 1:00 p.m. to 9:00 p.m., Sunday through Thursday. Over the last four years Library B's program of bibliographic instruction has grown. All freshmen at College B, as part of an English course, must complete a library workbook. The workbook contains a self-guided tour and asks students to demonstrate familiarity with basic library tools and equipment such as the *Readers' Guide* and microform reader/printers. Advanced subject workbooks are a formal part of biology and education courses. Several other courses contain less formal bibliographic instruction components. Additional bibliographic instruction is available upon request from faculty. However, the reference librarian indicated that if large numbers of additional bibliographic instruction sessions were requested the department would be in trouble.

Because of the demands generated by this program of bibliographic instruction, Library B attempts to provide double reference coverage from 10:00 a.m. to Noon and 1:00 p.m. to 3:30 p.m., Monday through Friday. Two reference desks are located outside the reference office to accommodate two librarians and their clientele. In order to provide this degree of coverage, the primary reference librarian spends about 28 hours a week at the reference desk. The two technical services librarians spend about 25 and 7 hours each at the reference desk. While desk hours are heavy, librarians are pleased with the double coverage. The second librarian in the reference area has resulted in a more relaxed approach to reference services. The lone librarian is no longer hurrying through one question and the stacks in order to get back to the next student pacing before the reference desk. Librarians report being able to comfortably spend more time with individuals and their questions. The sound of the telephone ringing no longer escalates blood pressure. No longer do librarians calculate if they can answer the question and still make the sprint from *Psych Abstracts* to the telephone in time.

Library C: First Stop Circulation

The reference department at Library C is staffed with one librarian and two student assistants, who work 14 hours a week each. Additional reference assistance is regularly provided by the circulation librarian. Library C provides reference service all hours the library is open: 8:00 a.m. to 10:00 p.m., Monday through Friday; 9:00 a.m. to 5:00 p.m., Saturday and 1:00 p.m. to 10:00 p.m., Sunday. Library C's policy is to have two librarians on duty when the library is open, one at circulation and one "visible" in the reference area. In order to provide this coverage, all nine librarians, including the library director, work one night a week and one Saturday and Sunday a month. Saturdays and Sundays are at the librarians' convenience and do not have to be worked consecutively. Previous to the new library director, one librarian had full-time responsibilities for providing evening and weekend reference services.

The circulation desk is located to the immediate left of the main entrance. Because of its location and activity, the circulation desk serves as the first point of contact for many individuals seeking reference assistance. The circulation department, staffed by a librarian, three support personnel and seven student assistants, serves as the "line of first defense" for the reference desk. Although you can see the front door from the reference desk, you cannot see the reference desk from the front door. Located to the immediate left of circulation, the reference desk is dwarfed by the circulation desk and its accompanying fleet of book trucks. Depending on the question, circulation personnel will either answer it or refer the individual to the reference librarian. Two circulation support staff have over 20 years of library experience. The other support individual in circulation holds an undergraduate degree in library science. Circulation's support personnel quite comfortably field directional, informational and ready reference questions. Located less than six feet from the front of the circulation desk, the card catalog is a frequent source of questions fielded by circulation personnel.

Because of circulation's prominent position, the circulation librarian is a trouble shooter or expeditor for reference and spends one to two hours out of a seven hour day providing reference assistance. The circulation librarian estimates that 75% of the average day is spent in circulation and 25% providing reference assistance. Although the split between reference and circulation varies, at no time has the circulation librarian spent more than 50% of the day providing reference assistance. The circulation librarian feels that in terms of the library's purpose, reference duties have a higher priority than circulation responsibilities.

Library C's reference department handles all interlibrary loan operations itself. Because of a growing volume of interlibrary loan requests, the reference librarian actually spends little time at the reference desk. Most of the reference librarian's time is spent in the reference office, immediately behind the reference desk, processing interlibrary loans or supervising student assistants, who are processing interlibrary loans. Between interlibrary loan and on-line searching the reference librarian does not "have the luxury of staffing the reference desk.'' A growing traffic in on-line database searching helps keep the reference librarian off the reference desk. Library C has four trained database searchers, two veterans with over three years experience and two rookies. Searchers are usually assigned on the basis of availability. An individual requesting a search frequently inquires at the circulation desk. A staff member attempts to identify which searcher is available. If searchers inadvertently walk by the circulation desk, the search is theirs by ''luck of the draw.'' The requester makes an appointment with the searcher. After the interview the searcher conducts the search and contacts the requester. Currently, the search load is heaviest for the two veteran searchers, the library director and the reference librarian. Two other librarians were trained in an effort to even out the searching work load.

Bibliographic instruction is handled as faculty request it, over 30 classes a semester. The bulk of the general or freshmen instruction is conducted by the circulation librarian and the library director. The reference librarian conducts no classroom bibliographic instruction sessions. Other librarians have specialized presentations that they have developed and presented over the years.

Library D: Visible Coverage

Library D's reference department is staffed with two librarians and student assistants. The two librarians, considered equals, report to the head of public services. The department's senior member works mainly days and is responsible for the coordination of faculty liaisons and development of the circulating collection. The junior member of the department works mainly nights and Sundays and is responsible for providing on-line database services. Because there is no clerical support, the reference librarians handle the departmental mail, file the services and maintain the reference shelf list, the vertical file and college catalog collection themselves. All interlibrary loan operations are handled by circulation. The reference department ''sandwiches in'' bibliographic instruction for its small cadre of faculty who regularly request library instruction for their students. Bibliographic instruction is provided basically on demand by the two reference librarians. Like all of Library D's librarians, the reference librarians serve as liaison to two or three faculty departments.

Library D attempts to provide reference service of some type most of the hours the library is open. Providing reference service is complicated by the fact that the reference desk, while on the same floor, is separated from the reference office. The reference desk and office are not visible to each other. Staffing the reference desk means "a body sitting at the reference desk, at the desk — not in the vicinity." When on duty, reference librarians are to be at the desk, not in the office or weeding in the stacks. The reference librarians are expected to spend 20 "visible" hours out of their 35 hour work week at the reference desk. Student assistants and librarians from other departments, with the exception of library director, also take turns at the reference desk. Four librarians from circulation and technical services, staff the reference desk from Noon to 2:00 p.m., Monday through Friday. These hours tend to be very busy ones at Library D's reference desk. In the beginning technical services librarians were unsure of their reference skills and a bit reluctant to staff the reference desk. However, they now reportedly manage to field reference questions, do their mail and catch up on their professional reading quite well.

Student assistants staff the reference desk during nonpeak hours: 8:00 a.m. to 10:00 a.m. and 4:00 p.m. to 6:30 p.m., Monday through Friday; Saturday, Noon to 5:00 p.m., and Sunday 4:00 p.m. to 6:30 p.m. Reference student assistants are selected by the head of public services and trained by the senior reference librarian. The use of "brighter" student assistants with some basic reference training was intended to "cut down on student frustration." Student assistants at the reference desk provide directional information as well as some basic reference information. Student assistants will also summon a librarian for library users. Most of the time during nonpeak hours there is a librarian in the building. Although student assistant coverage is admittedly superficial it is felt that "a student aide at the desk is better than no one at the desk."

When a librarian is supposed to be at the reference desk, but can not be there, a sign is placed on the reference desk directing students and faculty to ask for help at the reference office or the circulation desk, as indicated. The signs are intended to provide a contact for those individuals who "may just walk away if they do not see anyone at the reference desk." While the signs are hated by the librarians, the message is seen as better than an unattended reference desk. Because the reference desk is blocked from the view of the front lobby by a card catalog, regular library users frequently will ask at the circulation desk if a reference librarian is on duty before going to the reference desk.

RESULTS

Although the concept of the reference desk as a place where library users find the services and information they need has been questioned,[14] the libraries examined saw the reference desk as vital to their operation. Even the library without a reference desk was looking for a way to reestablish it. Two libraries examined were considering ways to make the reference desk more visible, central, and workable in the reference process by changing its location and configuration to take advantage of microcomputers and CD-ROM technology. The importance of the reference desk and its staffing stems from the tradition that college librarians are there for the students. As part of the education process it is the duty of reference librarians to help students learn how to find material themselves; it is part of the librarian's teaching function to help students use their own talents and energies.[15] In order to provide that type of personal assistance virtually on demand, college librarians have had to be visible and available.

Research has shown that reference librarians use their professional expertise and training only 10 minutes out of every hour they are at the reference desk. Although they are only answering a few real reference questions, it is difficult for librarians to concentrate on any other work at the reference desk because of frequent interruptions to answer other types of questions.[16] In this study librarians providing reference services were asked to keep a record of how they utilized their time. Although not all of the survey forms were returned or usable, it is possible to provide a brief sketch of how the primary reference librarians at three of the libraries utilize their time. For the primary reference librarians at Libraries B and D over 60% of their time was assigned to the reference desk. Please note that the data is self-reported and that the periods covered, mid to late semester, are not intended to be representative of an entire semester. With the cyclical nature of college reference work a much larger and extended study would be necessary to provide a complete profile of how librarians providing reference services utilize their time. Table 2 lists the major activities performed by the primary reference librarians at Libraries A, B and D. Incomplete survey forms made it impossible to provide a complete profile for Library C.

Library A

Because Library A's librarians are "on-call" the figures in Table 2 represent the major activities of their primary reference librarian. Survey forms for Library A's other two librarians revealed little or no reference related activities. Nearly 9% of the librarian's time is spent nursing an aged photocopier or showing a student the idiosyncrasies of a heavily used microfilm reader/printer.

The reference librarian indicated that "working reference 'on-call' isn't too bad. Interruptions are generally not too frequent. However, after the third interruption, in the middle of a five minute project that is now half an hour long, you tend to get a little testy."

Library B

Complete returns from Library B make it possible to provide a very good profile of how desk time is utilized. See Table 2. At Library B one primary reference librarian and two technical services librarians provide reference services at the desk. All of the librarians in this study took breaks or personal time away from the desk. At Library B breaks for all personnel are of uniform length and scheduled twice a day.

During the study, picking up the reference area was a major activity. The absence that week of the student assistant indicates just how much the reference department depends on student help. The student assistant's absence caused the reference librarian to devote almost 10% of the time to shelving books. Almost 24% of the secondary librarian's desk time is spent answering reference

Table 2
Major Activities Performed
By Reference Librarians

Library A
Reference and Serials Librarian

Activity	% of Time
Reference Questions	26.42
Interlibrary Loans	15.56
Meetings	9.63
Serials	9.38
Mail	9.14
Tending Machines	8.88
Breaks	5.43
Clerical	4.20
	88.64

Library B
Primary Reference Librarian

Activity	% of Time
Reference Questions	20.60
Reference Project	15.08
Interlibrary Loans	11.81
Meetings	10.80
Breaks	10.30
Pickup Reference	9.55
Special Collections	6.53
Mail	4.52
	89.19

Library B
Secondary Librarian
(Desk Time Only)

Activity	% of Time
Reference Questions	23.69
Cataloging	23.34
Reference Project	14.63
Meetings	13.94
Reading	6.27
Breaks	6.27
Online Searching	5.57
	93.71

Library B
Tertiary Librarian
(Desk Time Only)

Activity	% of Time
Reading	27.46
Class	21.15
Meetings	16.90
Acquisitions	10.56
Breaks	8.45
Reference Questions	7.75
Collection Development	7.04
	99.31

Library D
Senior Reference Librarian

Activity	% of Time
Reading	11.96
Meetings	11.04
Mail	11.35
Filing Services	9.51
Acquisitions	9.20
"Sitting at Reference"	8.28
Pickup Reference	5.52
Breaks	5.21
	72.07

Library D
Junior Reference Librarian

Activity	% of Time
Reference Questions	24.70
Reading	21.31
Online Searching	15.01
Breaks	7.75
Filing Services	7.02
Meetings	3.87
Mail	3.39
Reference Statistics	3.15
	86.20

questions. This individual is able to spend almost the same amount of desk time cataloging, the individual's primary area of responsibility. The third librarian spends most of assigned desk time in reading and professional development, spending only a fraction of time in reference related duties. The importance of the third librarian to the department cannot be overlooked. This individual provides coverage of the reference desk so that the other two may have some time away from the desk on a regular basis.

Library C

Although incomplete survey forms make it impossible to provide a complete profile for Library C, it is possible to provide information on interlibrary loan and on-line searching activity. Library C's reference librarian spends 35% of the time, 12.25 hours, on interlibrary loan related activities. Most of this activity appears to be clerical in nature: "writing up copyright records for articles reserved," "preparing notifications for patrons," "OCLC terminal, sending and receiving new requests," "checking requests against catalog and serials holdings," and "filing interlibrary loan records in office."

The time devoted to interlibrary loan may still be a reflection of Library C's previous administration's penchant for bureaucratic detail. With twice as many support staff as any other library this is not the best use of this librarian's time. Library C's reference librarian spends another 5%, 1.75 hours on on-line searching related activity.

Library D

Library D's senior reference librarian engages in a wide variety of activities, most of them during assigned desk time. The time engaged in reference activities at the desk is reported at 3.07% and ranked 12th out of 18 activities. Mail related activities was the second largest consumer of time. Because of overall responsibilities for services, collection development, and faculty liaison work, there is a fair amount of mail to be processed. Time devoted to mail means that almost another 5% of this individual's time is spent cleaning off the desk, "excavating desk top and mail tray."

Library D's junior reference librarian works nights and has few opportunities for meetings, yet meetings are ranked sixth. Almost 25% (24.70) of this individual's time is spent on reference questions or on-line searching. However, the individual spends 21% of assigned desk time reading, both professional (10.91%) and personal (10.41%). Both reference librarians at

Library D express a great distaste for filing services, it represents a major burden for them. Both librarians enjoy reading at the reference desk. However, it can be argued that almost anything a reference librarian reads is job related or potentially useful on the job.

Meeting and Desk Time

Reference related activity is the largest single desk activity for most of the librarians studied. However, the time given over to activities that take them away from the desk is surprising, but not an uncommon pattern. An analysis of the activities of public service librarians at a medium-sized research library indicated that meetings accounted for a significant amount of their time. Meetings were ranked third out of six activities and accounted for an average of 6.4 hours out of a 40 hour work week.[17] A time and workload analysis of 12 librarians at a medium-sized state university revealed that almost 21.4% of their time, an average of 9.5 hours per week out of a typical work week, was spent in committee meetings. Of those hours, 6.2 (almost 14%) were devoted to university and external meetings.[18] Although the four college libraries in this study are not large, meetings were listed as a major activity during assigned desk time. That means that individuals were away from the reference desk for a significant portion of the time they were assigned to staff it.

While there are many differences between college and research libraries, something may be learned from larger libraries regarding reference desk staffing. Research librarians made a subjective judgment that the average minimum, maximum, and optimum number of hours a week that an individual should spend on the reference desk was: 10, 20.43 and 14.64 hours respectively (with the qualification that fluctuations in user traffic would change their responses).[19] In a study of large and medium-sized academic and research libraries, nearly 90% of the libraries reported that their reference librarians typically work between seven and 21 hours per week at the desk. The reported desk hours per week are as follows: 5.5% work 7 to 9 hours; 16.4% work 10 to 12 hours; 41.8% work 13 to 15 hours; and 10.9% work 19 to 21 hours per week. None of the libraries reported weekly desk hours of less than seven hours. The most frequent weekday desk shift was two hours with evening and weekend desk shifts being longer. Librarians in these libraries indicated that " productivity falls off after two hours or so . . . and that longer shifts can cause excessive stress."[20]

In this study of college libraries, almost all of the individuals with major responsibilities in other departments worked less than seven hours a week at the reference desk. All of the primary reference librarians in this study have desk responsibilities in excess of 20 hours a week. This is not a good situation for college libraries to be in.

OBSERVATIONS

Many of the librarians studied have been with their institutions for most, if not all of their careers. The librarians typically are from the area, went to a local or regional library school and returned to the area. Second masters are the rare exception among the librarians studied. Many individuals in this study became librarians when librarians were in short supply. Wanting to get a job in the area meant that the would-be-cataloger had to become a reference librarian and the would-be-reference librarian had to become a cataloger. In some cases, with time and shared reference duties, everything worked out well. In other cases where the transition did not work out, closer supervision is evident and others are asked to "sort of cover for" or protect the individual.

The inescapable fact is that these libraries must work with the personnel resources they have. Libraries attempt to provide reference services in spite of some of the personnel they must work with. Efforts to work around specific individuals, personalities, and lack of technical expertise and motivation are clearly apparent. Efforts by some individuals to avoid public contact by doing, expanding or hiding behind other tasks were noticeable. Providing reference service is difficult, even in the best situations, but having to work around individuals or situations only compounds problems.

Among primary reference librarians their motivation, attitudes toward reference and use of time may be linked to how challenged, excited or satisfied they were with their work. Among the newer reference librarians, college reference work is still seen as glorious and the epitome of academic librarianship. Among veteran reference librarians, some may be "frustrated by the superficiality of what they have to know—no opportunity to really get your teeth into something. You also get to the point where all questions give you a feeling of 'deja vu.' You get to a point where few or no new questions come up. Nothing more to be learned." Some veteran reference librarians still feel they have the best job in the library but they recognize the need to seek greater variety and new challenges in order to maintain their positive feelings about reference work.

Part-Time Reference Responsibilities

Libraries in their efforts to provide reference services found it necessary to share the burden of reference. Nonpublic service personnel were pressed into service with mixed results. Technical services librarians felt that staffing the reference desk was a change and provided an added perspective to their jobs. While several librarians indicated it was important to take a turn at the reference desk in order to maintain contact with students and faculty, they did indicate occasional displeasure at having to do it. Resentment festered when individuals felt they were pulled away from their work to do something they were not particularly good at or prepared to do: namely reference. Technical service librarians may find answers in different ways from reference librarians. This concerned technical service librarians because they felt they should be able to do it just as fast and in the same manner as the regular reference librarian. However, that experience they wish to emulate cannot be gained by staffing the reference desk one day or night a week. A few hours a week on the reference desk does not provide the variety, repetition, depth and range of experience librarians felt they needed to feel confident in their abilities. Resentment was greatest among those who worked the reference desk only four to seven hours a week. Resentment grew, particularly if librarians had more exciting things to do, like automating technical services or bringing up an online catalog.

Technical service librarians with shared reference responsibilities also mentioned the importance of compartmentalizing work and preparing mentally for the reference desk. At the reference desk your time is not your own, you cannot budget it or plan it. Adjustment to interruptions is important. Individuals had to remind themselves that they had reference duty and that duty required a certain mind set and behavioral responses. The selection of tasks that could be done at the reference desk was important. The feeling was, "if I have to be at reference, how can I best use the time and get my work done?" One librarian automatically considered time at the reference desk as wasted and anything that got done was an unexpected surprise.

Reluctance to providing reference service might also be explained in terms of self-worth. Many individuals identify themselves in terms of their work. If librarians feel that they are not providing reference service the way they would like to, their sense of self-worth goes down. Very few people readily place themselves in situations where their sense of self-worth is assaulted. The psychological dissonance caused by the perceived "gap between our professional ideal and the reality of our practice is intensified by an increasing lack of confidence in our professional and technical knowledge, by the feelings that our own individual knowledge is mismatched with the situations we face."[21]

Reference librarians can usually help only one person at a time and when they are working with that individual they cannot really do anything else. There is an "opportunity cost" associated with reference work. In the daily fray, reference librarians do those things that need to be done, like putting up the newspapers, or threading a microfilm machine. However, in the course of doing their day-to-day work they may be sacrificing the chance to look for opportunities or potential problems within their environment. It is difficult to deal with larger issues like faculty relations when you are up to your chin in chemistry and marketing majors. As a result, the planning and direction that allow a department to lead rather than just react to its environment is lost to the daily fray.

If libraries are to effectively utilize personnel to provide reference services, they must reduce desk time for primary reference librarians. Libraries must also increase desk time for other librarians if they are to gain the experience necessary to provide real reference service. Libraries must also make better use of support staff if reference librarians are to be freed of the mundane paper and processing that drains their time and energies. Providing quality reference services is a library-wide effort, not just the concern of the reference department.

Priorities and Philosophies

Some of the personnel issues facing these libraries and reference departments can be traced to earlier budget or staff reductions. Unfortunately, levels of reference activity stayed the same or increased. Introduction of library instruction and on-line searching generated increase use of reference services. In trying to meet increased demands for services, the libraries studied have, for the most part, failed to truly examine their priorities, programs and how effectively they use their professionals and support staffs. In these libraries the importance of reference, in various degrees, is given more verbiage than actual support. The personnel resources to support reference services, a basic and highly visible function of a college library, does not appear to be allocated relatively well in these college libraries. It seems there is agreement in principle about the importance of reference, but an examination of where professional and support personnel resources are committed indicates that actual priorities may be different.

The examination of actual priorities is important not only for programs, but perhaps most importantly for its potential effect on personnel who provide the services. Most of the librarians studied have plateaued. For these individuals, their current jobs must change to provide them with the growth and challenge they need to remain motivated and effective. Where librarians feel that they can operate in an independent and professionally autonomous manner, they took the initiative. These departments appear to be marked by a more proactive approach to library services.

One cannot examine priorities without examining the real philosophy or lack of philosophy behind them. A library's approach to reference will determine how it uses its limited personnel resources. Many libraries try to provide extensive reference service. This usually means providing reference service most, if not all, of the hours the library is open. With this approach, extensive coverage of the reference desk generally entails finding a warm body, a student assistant, nonprofessional, inexperienced librarian, to staff the reference desk. This emphasis on coverage is reflected in some of the libraries studied. With this emphasis, small staffs are spread thinner, working evenings and weekends in an attempt to provide extensive reference service in addition to their other duties.

Another approach is to offer intensive reference service. The idea is to concentrate delivery of the service and maintain quality. This approach conserves limited personnel resources by limiting when reference service is available and who can provide it. At Library B it means only librarians at the desk and no reference service during its evening and weekend hours. Each approach requires a trade-off in what work is done and who does it. In each case a price is paid by the library and its users. Given the available resources it is up to library directors to determine the best possible use of those limited resources and make the commitment.

The delivery of quality reference service must have the support of the library director, if it is to work. All of the librarians surveyed have other responsibilities besides reference. Those other responsibilities are generally more measurable and visible than quality reference service. If interlibrary loans are not done or if books are not cataloged, it soon becomes apparent. "But if the reference assistance given is less than adequate or inaccurate, usually the only person who knows is the reference librarian. Even the student needing help will probably not be fully aware of its inadequacy."

College reference services are personnel intensive. Limited personnel resources must be actively managed and developed to maintain their vitality. Granted, some college libraries are understaffed and overextended, but unless their directors carefully reconsider current reference staffing practices, they may be slowly destroying one of their most important, visible and personal services to library users. If all librarians are to provide reference services they all must have the experience and adequate desk time to keep their skills sharp. Primary reference librarians must have time away from the daily fray in order to plan and do those things that separate quality reference service from just adequate services. Each library must also determine, for itself, what the appropriate role for its support staff will be. Limited college personnel resources should not be squandered providing unfocused, unrealistic or loosely defined reference services.

NOTES

1. Evan Ira Farber, "College Libraries and the University-Library Syndrome," in Evan Ira Farber & Ruth Wallings (eds.), *The Academic Library: Essays in Honor of Guy R. Lyle*, (Metuchen, NJ: Scarecrow Press, 1974), pp. 12-23. And Evan Ira Farber, "Limiting College Library Growth: Bane or Boon," in Daniel Core (ed.), *Farewell to Alexandria: Solutions to Space, Growth and Performance Problems of Libraries*, (Westport, CT: Greenwood Press, 1976), pp. 34-43.

2. Dennis Reynolds, "A Survey of Libraries in American Four Year Colleges," in William Miller & D. Stephen Rockwood (eds.), *College Librarianship*, (Metuchen, NJ: Scarecrow Press, 1981), p. 29.

3. Nancy J. Emmick & Luella B. Davis, "A Survey of Academic Library Reference Practices: Preliminary Results," *RQ* 24 (Fall 1984): p. 67.

4. Richard E. Miller, "The tradition of Reference Service in the Liberal Arts College Library," *RQ* 25 (Summer 1986): p. 463.

5. Charles A. Bunge, "The Personal Touch: A Brief Overview of the Development of Reference Services in American Libraries," in Sul H. Lee (ed.), *Reference Service: A Perspective*, (Ann Arbor, MI: Pierian Press, 1983), p. 3.

6. Miller, pp. 462-465.

7. Bunge, p. 12.

8. Miller, p. 463.

9. Kerry A. Johnson & Marilyn Domas White, "The Cognitive Style of Reference Librarians," *RQ* 21 (Spring 1982): pp. 239-246.

10. Miller, p. 465.

11. "The Annual Report on the Economic Status of the Profession, 1985-86," *Academe* 72 (March/April 1986): pp. 1-71.

12. Stephen P. Harter & Mary Alice S. Fields, "Circulation, Reference and the Evaluation of Public Library Service," *RQ* 18 (Winter 1978): p. 151; and John J. Regazzi & Rodney M. Hersberger, "Library Use and Reference Service: A Regression Analysis," *ERIC*, ED 129 219.

13. Terrence F. Mech, "Staffing in Twenty Midwest Libraries: Some Notes on Comparative Data, With Selected Library Statistics for 1982-1983," *ERIC*, ED 257 475.

14. Barbara J. Ford, "Reference beyond (and without) the Reference Desk," *College & Research Libraries* 47 (September 1986): pp. 491-494; and Thelma Freides, "Current Trends in Academic Libraries," *Library Trends* 31 (Winter 1983): pp. 457-474.

15. Guy R. Lyle, *The Administration of The College Library*, (New York: H.W. Wilson, 1974), p. 91.

16. Edward C. Jestes & W.D. Laird, "A Time Study of General Reference Work in a University Library," *Research in Librarianship* 2 (1968): pp. 9-16 as cited and discussed in Rao Aluri & Jeffrey W. St. Clair, "Academic Reference Librarians: An Endangered Species," *Journal of Academic Librarianship* 4 (May 1978): p. 83.

17. Anthony W. Ferguson & John R. Taylor, "What Are You Doing? An Analysis of Activities of Public Service Librarians of a Medium-Sized Research Library," *Journal of Academic Librarianship* 6 (March 1980): p. 27.

18. Eileen Hitchingham, "Academic Librarians' Workload," in Danuta A. Nitecki (ed.), *Energies for Transition: Proceedings of the Fourth National Conference of the Association of College and Research Libraries,* (Chicago: ACRL, 1986), pp. 135-136.

19. Scott Stebelman, "Characteristics of Public Service Staffing At ARL Libraries," *ERIC*, ED 220 090, p. 5.

20. Charles A. Bunge, "Reference Desk Staffing Patterns: Report of a Survey," *RQ* 26 (Winter 1986): pp. 171-179.

21. Charles A. Bunge, "Potential and Reality at the Reference Desk: Reflections on a Return to the Field," *Journal of Academic Librarianship* 10 (July 1984): p. 129.

In Search of Insight: Library Administrators Work the Reference Desk

Ralph E. Russell

SUMMARY. The paper identifies a means by which an administrator can derive feedback on library performance: work at the reference desk. This is consistent with much of current management thought which advocates closeness between management and the customer or consumer. The reference desk is suggested as the best vantage point from which to view the library and its users. Reasons why such desk service will benefit an administrator include the reaction of users to library policies, reality testing of library planning, seeing signs and communications from the users' viewpoint, appraisal of staff, administrator perceived as practicing librarian, acquaintance with collections' strengths and weaknesses, and insight into locally-developed tools and finding aids. Drawbacks include the possibility of feeling guilt over the few hours an administrator can work at the desk and the frequent necessity to admit ignorance. Reference desk service for administrators is advocated because it delivers the "end," while much of what we do daily is concerned with the "means."

Many crucial experiences and processes in our society are abbreviated for the casual, the hurried, and the dilettante. With emphasis on speed and convenience, our society is vulnerable to accusations of shallowness and superficiality. Manuals can give us management advice in one minute spurts; dial-a-prayer can provide solace on the fly for the hurried; the microwave can provide a "gourmet" meal in a matter of minutes; fast foods and their purveyors proliferate daily on freeways and neighborhood

Ralph E. Russell is University Librarian, Georgia State University, 100 Decatur Street, S.E., Atlanta, GA 30303-3081.

streets. This list is not exhaustive but illustrative of the cultural tendency towards quick gratification of various drives and desires. So, too, library managers pursue the means for quick assessment of their organizations. But performance feedback to the library manager is rarely so neatly labelled, taxonomized, and efficiently produced. The evaluative stream is polyphonic – but then, the library's clientele are equally diverse. The purpose of this paper is to identify a process through which a library administrator can get accurate, timely, and ongoing evaluations among other benefits from the library's clientele. In a word or two from Mayor Koch, we can quickly determine "how we're doing." My suggested means for assessment is readily and consistently available to all library managers: work the reference desk.

Among the hyped quickie manuals and popular publications, there are some which contain essential truths. *In Search of Excellence* is such a one. The book underscores the need for management to stay close to the customer for feedback and communication. This advice is buttressed with examples from highly successful companies and their executives. A specific application of this philosophy is that of A & P President James Wood cited in a *USA Today* article (August 27, 1986, B-1). He says that he learned an important principle as a stock boy in a grocery store in his native England: "You have to keep contact with the customer." If we accept the testimony of success, how can a library administrator "stay close to the customer?" And do so with a prudent expenditure of time?

In simplest terms, the administrator ought to be where the library users are to be found. Granted, some are to be found in the library administration office, but those are not necessarily a representative sampling of library users; their opinion certainly may not reflect that of the larger population of library users. It is my contention that the best vantage point to view use of the library is from the reference desk. That location is the juxtaposition of users and information sources; it is there that the locally-developed tools are taught and tested; and it is there that users frequently will return to give a report on their quest. The users provide the most important (some would say "only") performance assessment for the library.

But wait, you say – I have no time for reference desk service.

Besides, I am paid too much to spend my time on the reference desk. While that may be true, most administrators can find 2 to 3 hours in a week to be scheduled at the reference desk. Better yet, do not limit yourself to daytime hours only. Work an occasional night, Saturday, or Sunday. You will find that the users and the patterns of use vary greatly from weekdays to weekends. Before you discard the idea as impractical, let me give you my rationale for working at the reference desk. Although the explicit reasons are numerous, they can all be summarized as means of gathering insight. After all, effective administration is dependent on judgment and, frequently, the filter of experience.

WHY DO IT?

From the vantage point of the reference desk, an administrator may observe the reaction of users to library policies and procedures. A perfectly lucid procedure that sailed through the Library Administrative Council is perceived by the library users as off-the-wall and/or wacko. Many of our users are quite frank about what they perceive to be useless or silly regulations. It is a healthy experience to have to defend such policies and procedures. Occasionally, it may lead to change!

Change does not always culminate in a nirvanic conclusion. Have you ever planned and arranged furniture or equipment or collections—in the abstract, of course—and then been greeted by the disillusionment of reality? I have done so, and have found that dialogue with library users at the reference desk can be of immense help in grappling with the problem and finding the solutions. In my own case, I became quickly sensitized to a confusion in many users' minds about the arrangement of the periodicals collection. The solution is expensive and, in the short-term, disruptive. Having witnessed the confusion and its fallout of unsatisfied users, however, I am committed to resolving the problem.

Problems are not always solved by dollars and designs. With some effort and expense, graphics and signs are posted on every surface and wall in many libraries. Not only do we describe the location of various collections and services, most of us seize every opportunity to exhort our users to do some things and plead with them to refrain from doing others. I must confess that a favorite sign of mine paled in its luster when I noticed a pattern of derisive comments about it. The comments were offered as I accompanied users to the stacks. After all, for whom are the signs posted? Certainly not to provide me with the information! If my objective is to communicate with library users, I'd best speak their language.

Performance appraisal is difficult regardless of your language; so, too, the performance of library staff is hard to assess. For many of the library workers who handle "things," or process materials, quantification of their tasks may help. For public service staff, and for reference librarians in particular, performance appraisal is frequently very difficult. An administrator's time on the reference desk does not provide instant capability to evaluate reference staff; I do, however, appreciate the opportunity that reference desk service provides me to observe and to learn from consummately talented and informed reference librarians, most of whom deal compassionately and sensitively with a dazzling array of questions and questioners. I've observed them from closehand; they are impressive. Contact with other public service staff is beneficial because both parties see each other in a new light ("he actually works!").

The public perception of an administrator as a practicing librarian is surely a worthy goal for all of us. In the first place, it states strongly to teaching faculty and university staff that the practice of librarianship (as opposed to management) is important. It also states openly the priority which service to the information seeker enjoys—that we all join in the fray. That message, conveyed to the library staff, should not be muted nor minimized; as such, the administrator may serve as a role model to the rest of the staff.

Regardless of an administrator's bibliographical skills or forte as a role model, there are instances in which you cannot help the user; the fact or document or text or figure is beyond the library's collections. These instances serve as flags for the administrator working the reference desk because they flesh out—in terms of the disappointed information seeker—the unfulfilled need for library materials, i.e., our failures. Better (or worse) yet, the quest may lead the reference librarian/administrator to conclude that the collection is weak in the subject area generally. When our habit of finding an acceptable alternative source fails, what else can one conclude? Quite frankly, it is also helpful for the administrator to have to face the user when the collection (or the institution, if you will) has failed him.

An important component of the strength of the library's collections is the adequacy of the bibliographic tools and finding aids. The purchased indexes and tools are essential, and it is necessary to have some measure of their strength. Of critical importance, however, is the use and benefit of the locally-developed tools: the on-line/COM/card catalog, the periodicals printout, and the Faxon Linx system for example. Because of the cost involved and the dependence placed upon these tools, the administrator at the reference desk has a singular opportunity to observe the tools in use — and to use them as he/she walks a library user through the paces.

SOME DISADVANTAGES

I will lose my credibility forever if I do not admit that there are some drawbacks to an administrator's working the reference desk and some warnings which should be posted for those who consider such a course of action. First, do not be drawn into the mindset of guilt: "I must pull my share of the load with the desk schedule." Usually, the administrator is the highest-priced and least skilled reference librarian in the library. Do work sufficient hours to provide your desired insight and viewpoint, but no more. I'd recommend 1 to 3 hours per week on the average.

In addition to an acknowledgement that the administrator will not "shore up" the desk schedule, be prepared to admit ignorance and to seek help from more experienced reference staff (most of whom may be younger than you, to boot!). I find it humbling to plead ignorance when facing a friend on the teaching faculty, but I am more terrified at the consequences of bluffing and being discovered. It has been my observation that most people extend good humor and some camaraderie when you admit that you don't know something, but will seek to find out immediately.

IS IT WORTH IT?

Is the time spent on the desk and away from administrative duties worth it? Yes, yes, a thousand times yes! The foregoing list of reasons I advance for reference desk service for administrators skirts one overarching but seminal reason for doing it. That, quite simply, is that the reference desk service is what libraries are all about. Much of what we, as administrators, do is the means which lead to the end. The reference function is the end: the delivery of *something* to the library user. Automation, circulation control, bibliographic control, collection development, stacks maintenance, fund raising, staff development, personnel — all assist and lead to that ultimate act: the juncture of user and information/document.

If you have an interest in gaining some new insight, for strengthening relationships with staff and users, and for refurbishing your perspective, work that reference desk! Find out "how you're doing!" As a friend of mine once said, "After all, Ralph, you may need to go back to work some day!"

Unobtrusive Evaluation:
An Administrative Learning Experience

Patsy J. Hansel

SUMMARY. In 1985, the Cumberland County Public Library & Information Center conducted an unobtrusive study of its information services. The author provides some background on that study and shares some of what the library's administrators learned from the process. The author concludes that unobtrusive evaluation of a library's services is a painful but productive process, and one that library administrators ignore at their peril.

In the fall of 1985, the Cumberland County Public Library (CCPL) & Information Center (IC) conducted an unobtrusive self-study of its information services. I use the broader term than "reference" service because for our study we did not target the reference desk or the reference staff. All public service desks, all staff, all telephone lines were fair game. The purpose of the study was not only to determine whether the answer to a question was right or wrong, but also to find out whether questions directed by the patron to the wrong desk, the wrong telephone number, the wrong staff person, or the wrong library location were referred correctly by staff. In this article, I will attempt to share some of what some of the administrators of the library system learned from the experience.

Patsy J. Hansel is Assistant Director, Cumberland County Public Library & Information Center, 300 Maiden Lane, Fayetteville, NC 28305.

BACKGROUND

For years, the head of information services and I had been talking about coming up with some sort of method for evaluating reference service at CCPL&IC. We really wanted to do it, but since it wasn't absolutely necessary to keep the library running, other things always took priority. What finally made us move evaluation to the front burner was one of those items that organizations seem to have a never-ending supply of: a personnel problem. We had had a reference librarian whose accuracy at the reference desk was not good. This person's reference log sheets indicated that wrong answers were given and inappropriate sources were used more often than we thought permissible. However, when you get right down to it, what standards for individual reference accuracy can libraries support? I think we would all agree that we could not accept the performance of a person who answered every other proffered question incorrectly; yet the unobtrusive studies reported in the literature tell us that libraries overall don't do much better in reference accuracy.[1] Think about it: if a library decided to dismiss an employee based on an accuracy rate of no better than, say, 60%, would the employee have a valid appeal based on these studies indicating that the profession at large doesn't perform any better? Our personnel problem didn't make it that far, but our raised consciousness did convince us that it was time to find out just how good our reference service was.

As we discussed how to set up the evaluation, we decided we could not study only the reference function and get an accurate picture of what kind of service the library system's average patron received. At the time of the study, for the purpose of the library's quantitative reports, 80% of the "reference transactions" for the system occurred in the branches; and at that time, for all our branches we had one professional position, and it was vacant. Any evaluation of information services could not ignore the large number of reference transactions occurring in our reference librarian-less branches. We decided that what we had in our system was an organic structure of information services, and we could only evaluate that service on a systemwide basis.

So, the fundamental question for our evaluation became what kind of service could a patron contacting the library at any point expect to receive. If the person called the reference desk at Headquarters, would the question be answered correctly or referred correctly to another source. If the person called a branch, would the question be answered correctly from the branch's resources. If the branch didn't have the resources to respond to the question, would the patron be referred to the correct department at Headquarters. If the patron called the wrong number at Headquarters, would he be referred to the correct department without a lot of runaround.

The next problem became, given what we wanted to know about our library's service, what was the best way to find out. For us, the answer was obvious: an unobtrusive study. To get an accurate picture of interactions between patrons and staff on a daily basis, we felt we had to use interactions that staff did not realize were part of a study. What was obvious to us, we realized, is not obvious to the profession as a whole. As Alvin Schrader concluded, "Crowley and Childers' unobtrusive procedures have not yet become a component of the standard methods for evaluating library and information service performance."[2]

When administrators of a library system decide to do an unobtrusive study of their own services, they discover a number of articles in the literature based on studies that researchers have done; none detailing the methods employed by practitioners. The closest we could come at the time of our study were the statewide studies in Illinois and Maryland. We decided to use many of the questions asked in Illinois, and borrowed that form with a few local adjustments. All of this was coordinated by our then head of information services, Joanne Gilmore. As proxies for regular library patrons, Joanne chose regular library patrons. Some were friends of the library, some were friends of friends, we even had a couple of volunteers from the library board.

I have included two illustrations summarizing the results of our study. I will not describe the study in detail, because that has already been done.[4] (See Illustrations 1 & 2.) What I would like to do is to share some of what we learned from the process.

Results of Unobtrusive Study of Reference Accuracy - CCPL&IC - 10/85

Location	Total Responses	Correct Responses	Correct Referrals	% Correct	Transactions Incomplete=Incorrect Staff offer of follow-through not accepted by patron	Transactions Incomplete=Incorrect Patron asked to call back	%	Transactions Inadequate=Incorrect Unnecessary or incorrect referral	Transactions Inadequate=Incomplete No offer of follow-through	%	Wrong answers=Incorrect	%
HQ1	22	9	7	72.7	1	2	13	2	1	13	-	-
HQ2	28	21	-	75.0	1	1	7	-	1	3	5	17
BR1	26	13	3	61.5	1	-	3	3	1	15	5	19
BR2	22	15	2	77.3	-	-	-	2	-	-	3	13
BR3	17	7	5	70.6	1	-	5	-	1	5	3	17
BR4	15	12	-	80.0	-	-	-	-	2	13	1	6
BR5	19	13	2	78.9	1	-	5	1	-	5	2	10
BR6	13	8	4	92.3	-	-	-	1	-	7	-	-
System	162	98	23	74.7	5	3	4	9	5	8	19	11

Illustration 1

Results of Unobtrusive Study of Reference Accuracy - CCPL&IC - 10/85

Location	Total Responses	Correct Responses	Correct Referrals	% Correct	Friendliness "good"	Competence "good"	Patron Satisfied	Patron would recommend
HQ1	22	9	7	72.7	81.0	90.5	95.0	95.0
HQ2	28	21		75.0	96.2	96.2	88.9	100.0
BR1	26	13	3	61.5	100.0	70.8	83.3	87.0
BR2	22	15	2	77.3	90.9	100.0	100.0	100.0
BR3	17	7	5	70.6	82.4	88.2	82.4	100.0
BR4	15	12		80.0	85.7	100.0	92.9	100.0
BR5	19	13	2	78.0	100.0	87.5	87.5	100.0
BR6	13	8	4	92.3	100.0	84.6	91.7	91.7
SYSTEM	162	98	23	74.7	92.2	89.4	90.1	96.6

Illustration 2

WHAT WE LEARNED

1. We learned that we can do a study with value to our library without spending an inordinate amount of time trying to ensure the strict precision required for a research study. In the process of developing the study and evaluating the results, we were a little intimidated by the articles on unobtrusive evaluation that had appeared in the literature. All the ones we could find were studies done by professional researchers, not by practicing librarians, and sometimes we thought we were a little out of our depth. However, we persevered. After it was over and we could reflect on the process, we decided that some of the things that might be perceived as making our study less "rigorous" in some ways also made it more "authentic."

Our proxies were all already users of this library system, some did not attend the training session (although all did receive copies of the written instructions), and they were encouraged to deviate from our list of questions and devise questions of their own. These questions were not always factual, and as a result they made our "grading" of the results more complicated. However, they were certainly authentic, and were an undeniable reflection of the types of questions that patrons of this library system ask. And by using our own patrons, we did not run into the problem of having the staff recognize them as outsiders, which we know has occurred in other studies.[5]

2. We learned that our "non" professional branch staff do an excellent job with the resources they have. I have had many arguments (professional discussions?) with reference librarians at every level about how much reference we can expect non-MLS staff to handle. I believe this issue affects all sizes of public libraries, regardless, in most cases, of the relative wealth of the libraries. Most public libraries do not have enough degreed staff to refer all questions to them, although I do know of libraries that try. In our system, we try to offer as much reference training for staff as possible, with the general goal of having staff learn when they can handle a question using the resources that are available to them, and when to refer the question to a staff person with more training (or more specialized training) or to a library location with more resources.

Our study gave us some assurance that this strategy is working. Most of our branch staffs were able to handle the questions that their branch collections could support, and to judge when to refer questions that were more appropriate for another library location to handle.

3. We learned that accuracy alone was not what we were measuring. When we started this study, our objective was to determine the odds of our library's patrons' questions being answered or referred correctly. As we read the returned forms, we often found that as well as an accuracy rate, we were also receiving invaluable feedback on some questions about library service that we hadn't known to ask. For example, in one complicated series of events, a patron had to make three tries to contact the specific staff person she had been referred to for the answer to a question. In this case, we counted the library's response wrong each time since although the patron ultimately got her answer, the transaction, involving several different staff, was not handled well.

In another case, a patron called just as the library was closing. The staff person who took the call listened to the question, then told the person to call back in the morning. We gave ourselves a wrong, rather than an incomplete on this one. Joanne and I both felt that if the staff person had the time to listen to the question, he could at least have taken the name and number and called the patron back in the morning, rather than have the patron contact the library again. These were both judgment calls, but we made them based on what we felt the best handling of the questions would have been. However, this is the sort of local wrinkle that would make our study less directly comparable to other unobtrusive studies, even if you trust our methodology otherwise.

4. We learned that, in spite of everything, CCPL&IC seemed to do a little better on its accuracy score than other libraries in other studies. I have already mentioned the emphasis we place on training. I think another of our strengths is having a very visible, very effective information and referral component to our information services. I believe this may make us less susceptible to a weakness one of the earlier studies noted: "The dependence on infrequently revised books to the virtual exclusion of more current sources of information suggests a serious shortcoming in library information service."[6] This is a shortcoming that I also

have observed in libraries over the course of my career. We are trained to have a certain reverence for the printed word, and a myopia that limits our vision to the resources resident in our own libraries. This makes us reluctant to admit that contacting another library or another agency is the best way to get the patron his answer. I have seen staff spend hours trying to track down an answer in the library's reference collection when a quick call could have saved them and the patron a lot of time. Part of this may be some sort of errant professional pride that requires us to find the answer in those collections that we have so painstakingly built. Perhaps the advent of on-line databases is helping librarians get out of this mode. At CCPL&IC I still see it on occasion, but I think having information and referral as an integrated part of the library's services has helped.

ACCESS Information and Referral was started as a federal project in 1980, and in the past year has become fully integrated into the Headquarters information service. Currently, three positions have as their primary responsibility collecting and updating the information for the I&R files, but everyone who works the information desk is trained in using the files. The ACCESS staff have always been big users of the telephone to track down information, and I believe their example has helped some of our more traditionally trained reference librarians be less shy about going beyond the reference collection for information.

Given the emphasis on current information that ACCESS helped the entire library system develop, it was a little galling to learn that one of our proxies had received an incorrect answer to a question, and the answer had come from one of the lists of rapidly changing information that had been provided from Headquarters to the branches. The branch that received this question should have received an updated list, but was using a dated one. So our study reminded us that we can't just collect this information, but that we must also make sure that all the procedures are followed to get that information into the patron's hands when he needs it.

5. We learned that our best people aren't perfect. Unlike similar studies, we did ask our proxies to get the name of the staff person they were dealing with whenever possible, and frequently they did. In at least one case, our suspicions about a poor per-

former were confirmed. What we weren't prepared for was the less than perfect performance of some of our stars. We all know intellectually that we don't always do our best at the reference desk—fatigue, too many patrons, annoying patrons, just being in a bad mood can affect the service any of us gives. However, seeing such lapses illustrated in stark black and white on a survey form can come as quite a shock. The errors our good people made tended to be ones of carelessness or not paying sufficient attention to the quality of the interaction with the patron rather than using a dated source or misunderstanding a question. This was a reminder that all of us who work public services desks must continually be aware of the quality of service we are giving, no matter how smart we are or how many obscure sources we have mastered.

As an administrator who works public service desks on a regular basis, this study has made me more keenly aware of the service I give on a day-to-day basis. Over and over in the course of an evening's reference work I ask myself, if that patron had been part of an unobtrusive study, what kind of rating would my answer have received. I'm not always pleased with my response. However, I am very pleased that I participated in this study and developed that extra little edge on my information service conscience that I never had before.

6. We learned that patrons' expectations aren't necessarily the same as ours. As Illustration 2 indicates, although we gave correct answers only 74.7% of the time, our proxy patrons were satisfied with the service they received in 90% of the cases, and were prepared to recommend the library to others following 96.6% of the transactions. There were instances in which the patrons did not seem to understand that the information that they had received was not correct. Sometimes they were impressed with how hard we tried even when they did not get an answer (my favorite comment: "not discouraged—young lady was polite and sincere"). Unfailingly, they were impressed when a staff person "knew the answer without looking it up," a practice that we discourage. These sorts of reactions are further evidence that we cannot depend on our patrons to keep us honest; we have to take an active role in the evaluation of our services.

7. We learned that effective follow-up to this sort of study is a

difficult and never-ending task. Beyond obtaining some feedback on how CCPL&IC information services were operating, we wanted to use the results of this study to improve those services through training and staff development programs. We now have monthly reference training sessions hosted by Headquarters staff and open to all staff; reference training occurs regularly at branch head meetings; the two branches with the largest staffs have regular reference training sessions; and the current head of information services (Joanne left us for greener pastures in Columbus, Ohio) is working on a reference orientation program for all new staff.

However, the quality of day-to-day feedback that individual staff receive on their performance varies greatly depending on the management style of their supervisors; and it is that day-to-day feedback that is so crucial to improving performance in any area of work. We will always be working on that.

CONCLUSION

8. We learned that this can be a painful process. Reading survey forms telling you that your library gave the wrong answer to a question, or that one of your staff displayed a lousy attitude in dealing with a patron, can be excruciating. Even though our percentages were better than those of libraries in some of the other studies, we found that based on this study, 25% of our patrons can expect inadequate service. This is horrifying. As librarians and library administrators, however, we must be prepared to face such facts and use the information to improve our services.

Bill Katz used strong words when he wrote that perhaps "one reason librarians suffer the ignominy of low salaries and even lower community respect is that they do so badly at their work."[7] Improving the performance of the individuals who work in libraries is the only way to improve the performance of libraries; and that cannot occur without the serious commitment of library administrators. This should be the foundation of everything we do as library administrators. However, that does not appear to be the case. My conclusion is the same as Alvin Schrader's was in 1984, and I can't say it any better:

The problem of lack of commitment to reference service excellence will neither go away nor be resolved by the kind of passive approach which has so far characterized our efforts. Researchers, educators and practitioners must, first and foremost, acknowledge the existence of problems with respect to reference service accuracy. This acknowledgment has not yet occurred on a wide scale. Until it does, until our community is prepared to take seriously the call for reference service accuracy, unobtrusive performance measurement will remain as the next frontier for library and information services. As of now, we are still in the age of misinformation.[8]

NOTES

1. Terence Crowley, one of the pioneers of unobtrusive research in libraries, surveyed the research in the fall 1985 *RQ* "Half-Right Reference: Is It True?" pp. 59-68.

2. Schrader, Alvin M., "Performance Standards for Accuracy in Reference and Information Services: The Impact of Unobtrusive Measurement Methodology," in *Evaluation of Reference Services*, edited by Bill Katz & Ruth A. Fraley, New York: The Haworth Press, 1984, p. 208.

3. See Gers, Ralph & Lille J. Seward, "Improving Reference Performance: Results of a Statewide Study," *Library Journal*, 1 November 1985, pp. 32-35 (at the time of our study, we had a draft of their results); and *Illinois Library Statistical Report*, Springfield, IL: Illinois State Library, 1983-.

4. Hansel, Patsy J., "Unobtrusive Evaluation for Improvement: The CCPL&IC Experience," *North Carolina Libraries*, Summer 1986, pp. 69-75.

5. In conversations with librarians from several libraries involved in another study, I heard similar stories of the library staff knowing when the "proxy" arrived because the research team's van, clearly marked, pulled up in front of the library so that the proxy could hop out and come in to ask his question.

6. Crowley, Terence & Thomas Childers, *Information Service in Public Libraries: Two Studies*, Metuchen, NJ: The Scarecrow Press, Inc., 1971, p. 55.

7. Katz, "Why we need to Evaluate Reference Services: Several Answers," p. 4.

8. Schrader, p. 210.

Reference Service vs. Work Crews: Meeting the Needs of Both During a Collection Shift

Susan L. Seiler
Terri J. Robar

SUMMARY. In the General Reference and Periodicals Department of the University of Miami, the Abstracts and Index collection had traditionally been arranged alphabetically by title. In 1985 and 1986, all of these serials were cataloged. In June of 1986, with the cataloging finished, it was time to rearrange the collection into call number order.

The authors developed a methodology which allowed them to drastically disrupt and rearrange a highly used collection while maintaining high standards of service and accessibility. A collection of over 7,000 volumes was shifted in less than four days with very little manpower and no interruption in reference service. This article takes the reader step-by-step through this methodology.

In the Otto G. Richter Library of the University of Miami, we have traditionally maintained the abstracts and indexes (A&Is) as a separate collection. In the past, this collection has been arranged alphabetically by title (as is the main periodical collection). Many of us in the General Reference and Periodicals Department were concerned that the most appropriate index was not always being used simply because people did not know it existed.

We felt that much of this trouble could be avoided if the A&Is

Susan L. Seiler is Associate Reference Librarian at the Otto G. Richter Library, University of Miami, Coral Gables, FL 33124. Ms. Robar is Assistant Reference Librarian at the same institution.

were grouped by subjects. In order to do this properly, however, the collection would have to be cataloged and classified. This proved to be a monumental undertaking which began in 1985 and eventually involved many librarians and other staff from several different departments.

The final step of this project was to rearrange the A&I collection into its new order by call number. Traditional methods of shifting would not have worked well in this instance. As the supervisors of the project, we developed a new methodology. This method proved to be so accurate and so successful that we were able to reorganize more than 7,000 volumes in less than four days with a minimum of staff.

This method will work with any type of shift dealing with a serials collection. We were rearranging the books but, if you are moving your collection to new shelves or just expanding by a few ranges, this method can help.

CATALOGING THE A&I COLLECTION

When doing a project of this nature, it makes things easier if you get off to a clean start. We found that we had to do several things before we could start cataloging. The following is a list of the major preliminary steps.

1. Make a firm decision on what should be in the collection.
2. Remove from the collection everything which does not belong there. (For example, we removed ceased titles and all volumes which had been superseded by a cumulation).
3. Add to the collection any titles which should be there. (We transferred items from both the reference and periodicals collections).
4. Have an accurate list of the contents of the collection in their current order which can be easily updated throughout the project.

We found step four to be vitally important both during and after the cataloging phase of the project. The A&I lists were all kept on a microcomputer so they could be easily updated and manipulated.

We started with a list that we called the *A&I Alphalist.* This gave all of the titles in the collection in alphabetical order. It also included all of the former titles of the indexes.

During the project, we developed what we called the *A&I Shelflist.* We started with a copy of the *Alphalist* and added the call numbers as they were assigned. These finished titles were then rearranged into call number order on the list. If an index had several title changes and all received the same call number, then we made only one entry on the *Shelflist* for that number but listed all of the title changes in chronological order.

The objective of the cataloging project was to group the A&Is by subject within the LC classification system. Our corollary was that as few titles as possible were to receive the somewhat ambiguous A or Z classifications. These were used primarily in cases of multidisciplinary coverage.

When we examined the collection at the beginning of the project, we found that some titles were already cataloged (because they had once been part of the reference collection) and all of these had A or Z call numbers. We divided the entire collection into four parts: Previously Cataloged, Reclassification, Uncataloged, and Inventory. Table 1 shows the relative size of each of these categories.

The category Previously Cataloged contained those titles which were already cataloged and which would retain their A or Z call number. The Reclassification group were those which were already cataloged but which would have the call number changed, usually to something other than an A or Z. The Uncataloged and Inventory categories were both made up of titles which

Table 1

Category	# of Titles	# of Volumes
Previously Cataloged	30	614
Reclassification	47	2,070
Uncataloged	170	2,320
Inventory	11	2,272
Totals	258	7,276

had never been cataloged but the Inventory ones were the extremely large titles which had to be handled in a special fashion.

When the cataloging was finished after 18 months, the *Shelf-list* provided us with an accurate, detailed list of the A&I collection in call number order. The actual books, however, were still on the shelves in alphabetical order. It is best not to rearrange anything until you are ready to rearrange everything. Maintaining a two-tiered and constantly changing collection over a long period of time is too confusing for both patrons and library staff.

INTRODUCTION TO METHODOLOGY

The authors had been involved in other projects which required shifting large collections of books. We were familiar with techniques which worked and with the problems that could arise. We knew that this shift would have unique problems stemming from two causes: (1) the order of the books would change drastically but (2) the collection would continue to occupy the same set of shelves.

It would be virtually impossible to just start at one end and shift the books in order. Too many volumes would have to be moved out of the way and we had very little displacement shelving available. We needed a plan which would allow us to shift at any point in the collection where space could be found.

Such a plan was possible because we were dealing with a serials collection. The space occupied by each title could be measured and its future growth could be estimated. This meant that its new location could be determined exactly if we had these measurements for every single title.

The following pages describe the methodology which we developed. By following these steps and formulas, you can apply this same strategy in your own library.

Data Collection

The first step in planning for the shift is to gather certain information about each title. This information should be organized on 3 × 5 index cards which will be referred to hereafter as the "work cards." One card is needed for each call number in the collection except in the instance where two call numbers exist for the same index because of a title change.[1] Each card should contain the following data:

1. The call number.
2. The present title and all previous titles.
3. The number of shelves the title occupies now.
4. The number of shelves the title will occupy in five years.[2]
5. The height of the tallest volume in the series.
6. The present location of the title.
7. The new location of the title after the shift.

Both old and new titles are listed so that if a member of the work crew is sent to fetch a certain title, he will know to bring all of the title variations.

When recording the number of shelves, always round up to the nearest half shelf (1.5, 2.0, 2.5, etc.). This serves two purposes: (1) it allows for easier computations and (2) it allows a little extra growth room in case the title grows faster than you anticipate.

We chose five years of growth room as our goal. You should select the figure that best suits your needs and situation. If you are uncertain, you may want to measure for two different goals. For instance, we determined both three and five years of growth because we were not sure at the time which amount we wanted to leave.

The height of the tallest volume is needed in order to determine the spacing of the shelves. The locations (items 6 and 7) are designated by means of a special code which will be explained later. Items 6 and 7 should be added after the final planning is finished.

Compiling these work cards is the longest part of preparing for the collection shift. It takes approximately four minutes to fill out each card. To determine the amount of time it will take to fill out the cards, use one of the following formulas, where A = the number of cards to be filled out.

$4 \times A$ = the approximate number of minutes it will take to fill out the cards

$A / 15$ = the approximate number of hours it will take to fill out the cards

We had 240 cards to fill out.[3] It took us approximately 960 minutes (4 × 240 = 960) or 16 hours (240 / 15 = 16) to fill out our cards.

Shelving

The next step is to determine the amount of shelving needed to accommodate your collection while providing the desired amount of growth room. First, you must calculate the total number of available shelves presently in the collection. In order to do this, you must collect three measurements.

B   =   the number of 12″ shelves in the collection area (a 12″ shelf being one that can hold any book up to 12″ tall)[4]

C   =   the number of single-faced sections of 33″ counter-height ranges (if used in your collection)

D   =   the number of shelves currently occupied by titles taller than 12″

C should be calculated only if you have counter-height shelving as part of your collection. We found that counter-height shelving will hold only two 12″ shelves but will hold three 11″ shelves. We found that about two-thirds of the time, the books were short enough that we could sneak in the extra shelf.

If you have titles over 12″, you will find that you lose one shelf per section for every shelf of tall books. D represents this loss.

Let E = the total number of available shelves presently in the collection. E can now be calculated by the following formula:

$$E = B + (2/3 \times C) - D$$

In our specific instance, B = 636, C = 66, and D = 11. Therefore, we had 669 available shelves (E = 636 + (2/3 × 66) − 11 = 669).

Next, you need to determine the total number of shelves which will be needed to accommodate your collection in its new configuration and how this total differs from what you now have. In order to do this, you need to determine the following values.

F = the total number of shelves which will be needed to accommodate the present collection along with five years of growth room for each title

G = the estimated number of shelves which will be needed to accommodate new titles which will be acquired during the next five years

On your work cards, you have already calculated how many shelves each title would occupy in five years. Add all these calculations together. Let this sum be equal to F.

You also need to allow space for new A&I titles you expect to acquire in the next five years. Be sure to investigate whether you might be purchasing some extra-large sets. Otherwise, a general rule of thumb is five new titles per year for a medium sized library and 10 new titles per year for a large sized library. Let this number of titles be equal to G. The equation doubles the value of G to allow two shelves for each of these new titles.

Let H = the difference between the number of shelves which are available and the number of shelves which are needed to accomplish this goal. H can now be calculated by the following formula:

$$H = E - F - 2G$$

In our specific instance, E = 669, F = 683, and G = 50. Therefore, H = 669 − 683 − (2 × 50) = −114.

If H is a positive number, then go ahead and continue with your plans! You have all the space needed to make a successful move.

Most people will arrive at a negative number. This is the number of additional shelves you will need to add to the collection in order to accomplish your goal. In our case, H = −114 so we needed to add at least 114 shelves to our collection to handle five years of growth.

If you arrive at a negative number, it is now time for a decision. Either less growth room can be left or more shelves will have to be added. Our immediate supervisor decided that it would be better to add more shelving and an order for the shelving was placed.

We added more than the 114 shelves we needed in order to maintain the symmetry of the collection. These extra shelves were spaced throughout the collection. If you decide to order the additional shelving, it is important to decide where that additional shelving will be located. This must be done before you continue.

Planning the New Locations

You can now begin planning for the move itself. Our planning was done with copies of the *A&I Shelflist* which lists the titles in call number order (the order they would be in after the move). Make sure you begin your planning with a list which gives your titles in the order they will be in after the reorganization.

First, write beside each title the height of the tallest volume and the number of shelves needed to accommodate five years growth room (or however many years you are planning for). This information is on your work cards.

The following calculations are very important and have to be accurate. As a safeguard, have your calculations double-checked by someone else.

Using your *A&I Shelflist* marked with the height and growth room information, determine the final location of each title. Mark down this location by means of the following code. This code designates the exact range, section, and shelf where the title will start as well as the number of shelves it will occupy. The first title on the list will be located on Range 1, Section 1, Shelf 1. Each following title will begin where the previous one left off. An example of this would be:

1-1-1-2 (Range 1, Section 1, Shelf 1, 2 shelves used)
1-1-3-6 1/2 (Range 1, Section 1, Shelf 3, 6 1/2 shelves used)
1-2-2-3 (Range 1, Section 2, Shelf 2, 3 shelves used)

While figuring these locations, keep in mind the following points:

1. Remember the spacing that you have decided to use between shelves. For example, a full-height section will hold seven shelves of 12" books or eight shelves of 11" books; a counter-height section will hold two shelves of 12" books or three shelves of 11" books.
2. If you have added new shelving, remember where it is and use it in your calculations.
3. You have some unassigned shelves, such as those added for future titles, which should be spread throughout the collection. An extra shelf or two added here and there can prevent a title from being split between two ranges or around a corner. Extra shelves can also be used to prevent a small title from being split between the bottom shelf of one section and the top of the next.

Start at the beginning of your *Shelflist* and work straight through to the end. Your final list will show where each title will start after the extra shelving is added and a final shift is made. Make a working copy of this list for each work crew supervisor. On each of your work cards, mark the present and final locations of each title. These cards will also be used during the move.

Reference Service

This may seem like an awful lot of work up to this point but the rewards are worth it. These location codes will keep the work crews aware of where everything is and where it is going. The codes can do the same thing for the reference librarians.

At the reference desk, we kept a drawer of catalog cards for the A&Is which were arranged alphabetically by title. These can be copies of the actual catalog cards for each title or they can be handwritten index cards. There has to be one card for each title in the collection. Each card should have the title, the call number, and the code for the present location. These cards will be referred to hereafter as the "drawer cards."

Make sure your ranges are clearly numbered. If you do not have permanent numbers, use temporary ones made from construction paper. Label both ends of every range. The primary reason that everything needs to be clearly and accurately marked is that the librarians at the reference desk need to be able to service the collection. They have to be able to find any title at any time to assist the patrons. To make sure that each librarian understands the system, hold a special training session.

Our meeting only lasted about 30 minutes but it proved to be time well spent. Show each librarian how to read the location codes. Explain about the drawer cards and show how they will be updated several times a day. Ideally, these cards should be updated every hour. Less often may result in misdirecting a patron. It is essential that these cards are updated as frequently as possible in order to keep reference services running smoothly.

Remind each librarian that the work crews will be there to reorganize the collection while the librarians at the reference desk should provide the service. This is an extremely important point to keep in mind. If the work crews are interrupted, they cannot make the most efficient use of their time. Patrons looking for a specific title should be sent to the reference desk for help.

The Move Itself

The primary problem with our move was that the order of the books would be changed but they would still be located on the same set of ranges. One small counter-height range was the only temporary displacement shelving we had available. This essentially meant that nothing could move because everything was in everything else's way.

This is why we did the detailed planning. The final location of every title was known before the move started. It was not necessary to start at one end and move every title in order. That would have required a tremendous amount of temporary displacement shelving to hold the thousands of volumes that would simply have been in the way.

The first step was to fill any space that was empty. These "small areas," as they shall be referred to in this article, could range from one shelf to several sections. They held the relatively small titles as opposed to the large inventory titles. When working on these small areas, the work crews were constantly shifting throughout the entire A&I area.

Basically, the ideal process with a small area was as follows:

1. A set of shelves would be selected (e.g., one side of a counter-height range).
2. As many of these titles as possible would be lined up on the countertop (if you are not using countertop shelving, you will need displacement shelving equaling approximately 10% of the anticipated size of the collection).
3. The work cards would be changed to show the new location of each title. If they were on top of counter range five, for example, they would be marked with the location code '5 Top.'
4. The shelves would then be filled with new titles according to the final location plan.
5. The work cards for these titles were marked to show that they were in their final location. These cards were then removed from the pile of work cards and set aside.
6. The drawer cards were changed to reflect all of the above changes.

This ideal scenario for a small area was repeated many times and was often going on in as many as four places at once. There had to be one person whose primary duty was just keeping track of the work cards in order for this system to work well. Once several of these small areas had been done, it was possible to start on the next step.

The next step was moving the big titles such as the inventory titles. Before *Chemical Abstracts* could be moved, for example, its destination area (a total of 73 shelves) had to be cleared. For the sake of the librarians at the reference desk, we had decided whenever possible to always move an entire title and not just part of it.

The ideal scenario went as follows:

1. Many of the titles in the destination area had already been moved because some of the small areas were done first.
2. Another small area might be started by another work crew because it would take several more of the titles out of the big title's destination area.
3. The tops of nearby counters would be filled with titles from the destination area.

4. The few remaining titles would then be moved out of the way to the temporary displacement shelving.

With all of the shelves in the destination area cleared, the big title could now be moved. Once a big title was moved, its former location could then be filled in.

These ideal scenarios will often need to be modified to accommodate the peculiarities of the collection or the number of workers who are on duty. The modifications, however, are usually both minor and temporary.

The entire reorganization of our collection was accomplished with two 2-man work crews, plus two supervisors. The supervisors not only directed the work crews but also handled all the paperwork. The total number of man-hours required for the move was 85.

Supervisors: Ms. Seiler 24

Ms. Robar 24

Work Crews: 37
                                  —————
Total 85

As you can see by the figures above, this system of reorganization requires very little manpower. Many librarians are faced with this problem. This system enables one to use what little manpower one does have in the most efficient manner.

Each supervisor worked six hours a day and each 2-man work crew worked two and a half hours a day. Once the work crews had caught on to the system, they were able to go so fast that we had to limit the time they worked. As supervisors, we needed those extra hours each day to update the work cards, update the drawer cards, double-check the work that had been done, and decide what areas would be done next. The physical move (including the paperwork) began at 8:00 a.m. on Monday, June 9, 1986 and ended at 4:00 p.m. on Thursday, June 12.

CONCLUSION

Our library has done several projects in recent years that required shifting books. Based on these previous experiences, every reasonable estimate projected that this A&I shift should have taken at least two to three weeks. We finished it in only four days.

We feel that what made the difference was this new methodology. It enabled us to avoid many of the usual pitfalls. We could accurately determine the amount of shelving we needed so we did not run out at the end. We knew precisely where every title was going so we never had to reshift. We actually turned down help because we needed so little. Most important, we were able to continue the regular use of the collection even during the move.

The most important consideration in a reference department is to maintain high standards of service regardless of any disruptions to the normal routine. This methodology allows the reference librarians to continue assisting the patrons while allowing the work crews to do their job without interruptions.

NOTES

1. For example, *Library Science Abstracts* was continued by *Library & Information Science Abstracts*. For technical reasons, each has a different call number but are located side by side in the collection. No growth room was needed for *Library Science Abstracts*. Therefore, both call numbers and titles were listed on the same work card.

2. Record the total amount of space that the title will occupy in five years, not just the growth space. This eliminates having to stop and add the present space and the growth space while doing the calculations.

3. Remember: we had 258 titles but only needed to fill out 240 work cards. See footnote 1.

4. A single-faced section of 88" high shelving will hold either seven shelves of 12" books or eight shelves of 11" books. This latter instance is not likely to occur except in the case of a title which is extremely long in length but short in height. We had no such title in our collection even though we are a large research library.

A Scenario of the Reference Librarian in a Small University Library

Beatrice E. Flinner

SUMMARY. The purpose of this paper is to give a panoramic view of a number of issues relative to a reference librarian in a small university library. From the personal point of view, a pleasant personality is a desired asset. From the professional point of view, being the proud "owner" of a Master of Library Science degree is a requirement; but these two statements only touch the tip of the iceberg. What are the traits and attributes which should either be possessed or sought after diligently? What comprises the "hidden agenda" which falls under the responsibilities and duties of a reference librarian? Is it possible to be both idealistic and realistic, or must an academic reference librarian be resigned to a life of professional reality? These questions and others will be considered in this paper.

Reference librarian, what is the story of your professional life? How would you explain the quest to your present position? In your very young years, did your mother take you to the public library, thus instilling in you a burning desire to some day be a librarian? Or, when you were struggling to pay college expenses, did the job-placement center give notification of the availability of a student-assistant job in the campus library — and you just happened to be the one individual who was best suited for the opening? It could be that you worked in the college or university library while your spouse was a student, thus helping to balance

Beatrice E. Flinner is Coordinator of Public Services, R.T. Williams Learning Resources Center, Southern Nazarene University, Bethany, OK 73008-2671.

the family budget. Or, perhaps you always loved to read and work with books, and simply "flowed" into your present position, with an abundance of hard work, of course. Whatever the reason, you are now a librarian; you are privileged to be a reference librarian.

Hopefully, you are now experiencing a bit of "library paradise." If you thoroughly enjoy your job, you may feel that your utopia has been reached. Your work will be so exciting and rewarding, that even the much-used term of today will not penetrate your mind—"burnout." (This term will not even be discussed, although there may be readers who are suffering from this malady).

For a few moments, let us conduct a self-evaluation. Are we doing a satisfactory job? Are we being ideal reference librarians—or at least seriously working towards that goal? Or must the admission be made that some dreams will never come true, so we have settled back to a life of day-to-day reality in the library world? Can we not live in both worlds to a great degree? I believe we can. Obviously, with our human limitations, most of our professional life must be in the realm of reality; but we can surely try to spend part of it in an idealistic world of reference librarianship.

The purpose of this article is to present a panoramic view of a number of issues relative to a reference librarian in a small university library. From the personal point of view, a pleasant personality is a desirable quality to possess. From the professional point of view, being the proud "owner" of a Master of Library Science degree is a requirement. But, this is only the tip of the iceberg. The second part of the article will relate not only to the basic responsibilities of a reference librarian, but also to the "hidden aspects" of being an efficient one.

Reference librarians have an ongoing responsibility and privilege, both personally and professionally, to operate on a continuum for the purpose of constantly becoming more competent and skilled in work performance. There is no place to rest on one's laurels in this important position; rather, there must be a continuous striving for excellence.

PERSONALITY TRAITS

While some may disagree, the majority of clientele will wholeheartedly concur that a reference librarian should have a pleasant personality, and should also evidence certain attributes that will enhance contact with the public. Such traits as tact, patience, warmth, an even temper, charisma (though certainly not a universal trait by any means), and a pleasing appearance both in dress and personal hygiene are valuable assets. The list could go on at length. We must be alert, approachable and capable of making the patron feel at ease as he nears the reference desk, thereby establishing good rapport.

What frightened or intimidated freshman is not going to feel just a little uneasy when he approaches the reference desk for the first time, but fearing that in one brief moment he may reveal his ignorance by asking a very simple question. Granted, there will be a few exceptions—but not many. A courteous, enthusiastic, knowledgeable, encouraging, efficient reference librarian will take every necessary precaution to ease the situation.

A positive self-image projected by the reference librarian will have a pleasing effect on the patron; this also helps to establish the credibility of the former. The individual with whom we are working will quickly recognize our willingness, or lack of it, to be a good listener.

PROFESSIONALISM

Regardless of negative attitudes which may be exhibited on the part of a frustrated and disgruntled patron, we must keep our composure. Hopefully, it will not take long for him to recognize that we are a trained, caring, communicable, persevering, non-prejudiced, motivated, conscientious and flexible individual who really is concerned that the patron's library needs be met. While this is not a complete list, even though it is rather extensive, two more very important requirements must be added: (1) the ability to keep one's trend of thought no matter how busy we are, and (2) the ability to keep one's objectives clearly in mind.

Considering the fact that we may be working on several questions at the same time which will probably fall in completely different, unrelated areas, this is truly an art. There is probably not one of us who can measure up totally to all of these attributes; in fact, we may fall shockingly short. However, there is not one of these that should be deleted. Students and faculty deserve our very best work.

THE REFERENCE INTERVIEW

A patron approaches the reference desk for the first time, and the exciting moment is at hand when the reference interview is about to take place. It would not be surprising if the reference librarian is just as intimidated as the student, especially if the former is new in the reference field. Actually, the interview had already begun before the patron arrived at the desk, and unless his fears were alleviated as he approached, he may begin by saying "You'll think this is a stupid question, but . . ." The response to that statement is of utmost importance. Quickly dispel the patron's fears and timidity, and reassure him that no question is stupid or dumb; then you are ready to continue the interview.

That awkward situation could have been eased significantly for the patron had the reference librarian been wearing a name tag, which is one of the most effective ways of breaking the ice. The patron has a right to know to whom and with whom he is speaking; everyone has a name — we are not just faces. This helps the librarian to feel comfortable, and it gives the patron the feeling that he knows the person behind the desk. It really can make a difference.

There is another situation which occurs all too frequently, and although it cannot be helped, it must be handled wisely. In our library, we do other work while working at the reference desk, carrying out further duties and responsibilities — which is definitely my preference. While there may be library policies that prohibit working at the reference desk other than waiting for patrons to approach, I personally would feel guilty and would become bored if that were the situation with my position. If we are to earn our salary, there is much that we can do at the reference desk in between patrons; and we can still make those approaching the desk feel comfortable, knowing that they are top priority.

However, tact and good common sense must be put into practice if we are to be approachable, even though our heads may be down because we are reading or writing. When a patron says "I'm sorry to bother you, but . . . ," his anxieties must be quickly dispelled. Help him to understand that he is not bothering you. In fact, on the bulletin board, directly behind the reference desk I have placed these words: "Students! Please interrupt! You are 'top' priority." There have been some very favorable comments to that positive invitation and assurance.

We must never convey the impression of being too busy to help a client; he should not have to apologize for asking a question. If we are too busy, it is time to leave the reference desk and ask for a backup librarian.

Jargon and Acronyms

Another area in which librarians need to be careful is that of using library jargon with patrons. They may not always understand the language of librarians, such as "tools," "stacks," "spines" and "docs." One of the university professors mentioned in class that we live in a world of acronyms, is this true more often in the field of librarianship than in any other profession? Bauer refers to it as "alphabet soup."[1]

It is not always necessary to avoid the acronyms, but if they are used in the presence of a patron there should be an explanation given; this is especially simple to do when giving individualized assistance.

Terminology

An embarrassing situation may evolve when a student interchanges words such as "reserve" for "reference," "biography" for "bibliography," "microwave" for "microfiche," etc. Poise must be evidenced on the part of the librarian when this happens.

Resource Knowledge

It is the responsibility of the person(s) working the reference desk to be familiar with both titles and contents of the reference collection, as well as the other resources in the library. We need to become familiar with new subject headings, because new editions of publications are utilizing them. It does not take one long to realize that a number of older terms are being replaced by new terms, especially in thesauri.

Technology alone has introduced numerous terms-coming to us from the media, recent periodicals, workshops, seminars, conferences and professors who have recently received degrees in higher education. Our vocabularies and our knowledge must be increased in all disciplines to avoid being caught off guard by the patrons. We interpret the library collection to the clients; this is our responsibility.

Words of Caution

One of the areas in which a reference librarian must become quite adept is that of cultivating the ability to stop quickly what he is doing, and then be capable of returning to the project at hand successfully. It must be remembered, however, that no two librarians are alike; nor do they carry out reference work in the same manner. Each one will conduct a reference interview in his own unique way, hopefully. If this were not true, creativity would be squelched and robotic-like characteristics would prevail.

When it becomes evident that a question is not a directional one, it is a good idea to stand during an interview; and perhaps in many situations it will be wise to step out from behind the desk. This will avoid the necessity of a patron having to lean over the desk, and it will also allow for better eye contact.

Be thorough, but know when to stop searching; otherwise, the client may leave with a terrible case of "overload." On the other hand, he should not leave empty-handed and frustrated. The reference librarian should know when it is time to refer the patron to another librarian who may know information about the problem/question; or, perhaps it may be necessary to make a referral to someone off campus. One word of caution if you are not successful in helping a patron, simply allow the patron to know that you do not know the answer to his query. Honesty is the best policy, and if you do not care to admit your lack, the patron will discover it anyhow.

THE PATRON

Dependent or Independent?

To a degree, it is understandable that a professor expects his students to have knowledge of specific research tools in their major area of study. However, not everyone who takes a particular course is majoring in that discipline; this means that for some, the area of tool-expertise may lie in an unrelated subject area.

How many times a professor has said to the reference librarian, "You shouldn't have to help the students with their assignment; they are supposed to find the materials themselves." Where would a student begin who has the assignment of finding out "how much water there is in a tennis shoe?" In fact, where would the reference librarian begin? I had that question. Telling a student to start with the "Reader's Guide," then leaving him alone to find his way through the maze of additional indices is inexcusable. True, the "Magazine Index" or the "Education Index" might be discovered during his search; but what about the numerous resources of which he has never heard? That approach simply does not always work. This is where the ideal changes quickly to reality because not every patron has the same background knowledge in a subject. There may not even be a grasp of the assignment, or perhaps the student's capability for carrying it out does not exist; thus, at this point, he is a dependent patron.

If frustration takes over, there is more damage done than there would be if the reference librarian would have helped the patron to get started. It might be necessary to guide him through the process of locating the needed material. Allowing a patron to flounder just does not seem acceptable. If our clients were all independent users there would be little need for professional reference librarians.

While David Isaacson is not opposed to students learning how to work independently, his personal theory takes the opposite viewpoint:

> As an academic reference librarian I believe I have a responsibility to assist students, formally or informally, directly or indirectly, to gain confidence in their use of the library. I hope my motive in offering library instruction is to

> help students, rather than to make things easier for our staff or to challenge a professor's library assignment.[2]

To the reference librarian, what could possibly take priority over making sure that the patron leaves the library with the material required to complete his assignment? Obviously, the clientele will be highly diversified, which will necessitate a quick evaluation each time an individual approaches the desk. The patron may be a freshman, a graduate student, a community senior citizen, a faculty member or a high school student. But the reference librarian must be capable of making the right decision relative to treating that person as a dependent or independent library user. Each situation and question must be assessed carefully and wisely.

Service to Patrons

Have reference librarians lost sight of their purpose? According to an article by Miller and Rettig, the answer would have to be "Yes." They quote S.R. Ranganthan's Fourth Law of Library Science: "Save the time of the reader."[3] From an article written by Jeremy W. Sayles comes the following statement: "A discerning reference librarian has properly noted that too many of us are teaching students how to be librarians rather than fulfilling our more realistic function of using our training to aid students in their search for information."[4]

It is true that frequently a patron will be successful in locating what he seeks, and will leave with a pleasant countenance. But did he find only "surface" information? Did he locate the information necessary for an academic paper or project that could have been his if the reference librarian had given him adequate guidance? But, again, this situation reverts back to the reference desk (and obviously relates to the reference interview) where the initial decision had to be made as to whether or not the reference librarian had a good grasp of the question.

It really goes without saying that the reference librarian cannot work on an individualized basis with each patron, since there could be a number of people in the queue. This does happen frequently, so quick and wise judgments must be made to get each person started on his search; and the decision must also be considered as to which person(s) will merit a follow-up, and whom will be given priority. This is the ideal — to simply help everyone, one-on-one. Unfortunately, reality takes over again and it becomes impossible to get back to each patron; this is discouraging to the librarian and the patron.

THE REFERENCE DESK

Location

The reference desk should be located as close to the entrance of the library as possible and feasible, in order for patrons to approach that area first. There should be a well-placed sign indicating the reference area. There can be a potential crisis when a student approaches the circulation desk and pours out his need to the individual on duty; and after a lengthy request he receives a smile and the statement, "You'll have to talk with the reference librarian." Have you ever heard a patron emit a big sigh? I have. The lengthy, and perhaps uncertain, request must be stated again, but it can get even worse if the reference librarian cannot leave the desk, and must tell that frustrated patron to go to another part of the building and ask the same question again. This could be a sure way of sending that person right out the door — and perhaps right to the door of his professor's office.

This just must not happen. Nothing should keep us from doing our best to see that the clientele get help needed. Should our goals relate to a statement made by Vincent, when he said that "One-on-one reference service, of a sophisticated nature, remains absolutely essential?"[5] That would be the ideal.

COMMUNICATION

Good communication skills are essential at the reference desk, and must be present throughout all reference transactions. These include both verbal and nonverbal communication. In William Young's article, he includes a behavioral checklist developed by Rebecca Kellogg who lists five major skills in which are included behaviors that comprise reference desk standards: "Communication style with users (verbal and nonverbal)"; "user interaction at the reference desk''; ''co-workers interaction at the reference desk''; ''knowledge of collections''; and ''personal qualities/ traits exhibited at the reference desk (towards users and co-workers).''[6]

Glogoff believes that communication skills are so vitally important that he made the following statement: ''The negotiation of reference questions, in fact, can be considered one of the most complex acts of human communication.''[7]

POLICY MANUALS

Need and Basis

A policy manual must be based upon the goals and objectives of each particular library, and consideration must be given to the clientele to be served. If your library has a policy manual, does it list the responsibilities of the reference librarian as follows: conduct reference interviews; assist patrons in locating information; compile and update bibliographies; conduct library tours and perhaps do bibliographic instruction? These are positive guidelines, but they are not enough. What is really involved in being an effective reference librarian? What does your policy manual indicate?

It is this author's contention that a reference librarian's policy document should be drafted in the form of an extensive manual. The standards must closely relate to the individual library and its unique needs. However, some such policies simply highlight broad areas, rather than getting down to the details of what is encompassed in the title of ''Reference Librarian.''

Obviously, everyone who works the reference desk on a part-time basis will not be able to carry out all of the responsibilities; however, the Head Reference Librarian should make every attempt to follow the manual. For instance, everyone who works the desk will not necessarily do bibliographic instruction, nor relate closely to the faculty. But there needs to be a printed policy to which reference librarians can refer when necessary, giving consistency to the position. In all fairness, it must be noted that to list every detail relative to reference would be an impossibility;

but that does not preclude the need for a thorough document to be consulted when necessary.

Why is it necessary to have a policy manual? From the Reference Service Manual of the University of Massachusetts-Amherst comes the following statement: "The purpose . . . is to state guidelines for providing reference service in order to insure a uniform standard of service of the highest possible quality consistent with available resources."[8]

Checklist

A possible alternative to a policy manual could be a checklist which might prove to be a better guide because it provides in-depth criteria for not only responsibilities, but personal traits as well. Remember, an MLS degree does not automatically bring about the creation of a qualified reference librarian.

RESPONSIBILITIES

Hidden Agenda/Flexible Schedules

Unfortunately, the assumption cannot be made that a policy manual is all-inclusive, even though that would be the ideal. There is no way of knowing that a teacher from the public schools is going to call and ask for a library tour for her class of 35 students. What about the unexpected reports which must be filled out by a certain deadline, or special correspondence that requires immediate attention? Your policy manual may say nothing about committee work, since committees are usually voted on annually; thus, the membership may change from year to year. If so, there will be unexpected meetings if you happen to be elected to serve. Perhaps a professor drops by (for which I personally am quite appreciative), and conveys to you the message that an assignment has been made which will require some special preliminary work on the part of the reference librarian. New books appear at the reference desk and must be given your attention so they can be sent quickly to the appropriate area for shelving. Be prepared for the unexpected.

Database Searches/Bibliographic Instruction

If the reference librarian does the actual computer searching, or works with the interviews, these must be worked into the schedule. The interviews can be quite time consuming; they must be carried out carefully and thoroughly.

A reference librarian who does bibliographic instruction knows that it is sporadic as far as scheduling is concerned; consequently, there cannot possibly be a rigid schedule set up for this purpose. There may be two or three presentations in one day, which will involve considerable time; this does not even include the time involved to get ready for the presentations.

Government Documents

Do you work with government documents? If so, you are very much aware that one question may involve an hour's search, which must be squeezed into that already tight schedule. If there is any chance that you will be working with documents, it is important that you know how to do so, because many students work under time pressure and do not have extra time to wait until the librarian learns how to use the tools.

Marilyn Moody is concerned about government document usage, and has made the following statement: "Librarians are often much more concerned with selecting, obtaining, classifying, and shelving documents than with showing people how to access and use the documents already in our libraries effectively."[9]

Unit Teaching/Term-Paper Clinics

Every time the opportunity arises to teach a unit, I do so because it is an excellent way of helping students and faculty to get into the tools in more depth than usual. Obviously, preparing for and teaching a unit requires considerable time.

I would welcome term-paper clinics, but as yet have not had the privilege of working in this area.

Problem Assignments and Other Requests

If there is evidence of a problem relative to an assignment, it is sometimes best to make a call to the professor in order to clarify the request. It is amazing how many times students feel that the librarians have the answers to such questions, and this may be true; however, clarification is the only way to handle some requests.

It is not uncommon for a student to ask a reference librarian to proofread a paper and make necessary corrections in the punctuation or changes in grammar or sentence structure. These responsibilities (?) are only part of the "hidden agenda," which necessitates changes in our scheduling. Care must be taken not to allow these types of activities to become problems; they must be kept to a minimum.

BIBLIOGRAPHIC INSTRUCTION

Bibliographic instruction should be carried out by those who are familiar with the resources of the library. For the sake of continuity, the teaching should be done by those who will be working with the students after the lecture sessions. Also, students feel more comfortable with someone they have met and heard lecture for one or two class periods. Only the bibliographer knows what was presented in the lectures, unless some of the other staff members were present—which is advisable. It is my belief that the reference librarian who will be working with the students throughout the semester should be the one who selects the materials for presentations and prepares any necessary handout items; this includes bibliographies. By following these procedures, there will be continuity for the students as they pursue their research.

It must be remembered that everyone who does reference well is not necessarily qualified to teach. In fact, many librarians do not care to teach, nor work with the public in any way. The reverse may be true; that is, a good lecturer in a classroom setting may not be able to think quickly when working with reference questions.[10]

Benefits

Bibliographic instruction can be quite successful when used in conjunction with subject areas such as psychology, biology and fine arts. It is always best to correlate presentations with the professor of the class, but this is especially true when covering specific disciplines. Also, it is an excellent idea to have worksheets if the professor approves. Admittedly, bibliographic instruction in a classroom setting is only a partial solution to helping students become aware of the vast amount of materials and information that are available.

As quoted by Jeremy Sayles in Vincent's article, the "reservoir of experience which we possess as reference librarians cannot be taught in the form of library instruction."[11] It takes prompt service, bibliographic instruction, individualized instruction and patient explanations; in other words, we must put into practice our education, training, common sense and knowledge.

ON-LINE VS. MANUAL SEARCHING, OR TECHNOLOGY VS. REFERENCE LIBRARIANS

One of the most important aspects of an on-line search is an effective and thorough interview, which is vitally important because of the high cost of on-line charges. This is the time for clarification of the topic and in-depth manual searching of the indices and thesauri for the appropriate subject headings; the computer cannot do this. Studies have shown that these two procedures complement each other; one without the other leaves much to be desired.[12] Certainly on-line searching makes more information and materials available to the patron; this is one of its strong points. Also, it is much quicker than manual searching. There is no doubt that computer searching is here to stay.

Will technology replace the reference librarians in the future? No, there will be room for both. Reference librarians know that there are hidden questions that evolve as the interview is conducted, and these may be the major clues to locating the desired information. No computer will be able to provide this type of service. One of the most important aspects of the interview is knowing what questions to ask, and this can only come about via human interface. Also, the reference librarian is needed to provide the necessary subject headings to be used in the search. This need will always be evident; so actually, the reference librarians of the future will be more involved with computer searching. "In particular, the growing field of artificial intelligence will need a great deal of librarian input."[13]

There is no intent to question the value of on-line literature searching, or even the bibliographic searching of one's own library holdings. However, "the ability to browse among the book and journal collections or to chance across additional sources in the reference room is a vital element in the creative process."[14] But, patrons will still need reference service.[15]

EDUCATION: FORMAL AND INFORMAL

A Master of Library Science degree is required to be a professional librarian, but this should not be the end of formal education. One needs only to read a few classified sections in library periodicals to become aware of the fact that at least one additional Master's degree in a subject area is required. A broad educational background is invaluable to a reference librarian. Those who are privileged to take courses on their own campus, whether graduate or undergraduate, will benefit greatly; not only by new knowledge learned, but they will have a much better understanding of the materials covered by the professors as well as the assignments and library requirements relative to the courses.

Continuing education is important even if a second graduate degree is not being sought. Because of new technology, new concepts in librarianship and even the need of additional hours for the purpose of promotion or salary increases, it is imperative that librarians continue with their education.

Workshops and seminars are offered in specific areas of interest. Although many of these do not carry academic credit, they are beneficial in helping to keep the librarians up-to-date on library information and tools.

The broader one's base of knowledge, the more capable and qualified he will be as a reference librarian. In addition, because he is familiar with so many subject areas, it will be possible to generate enthusiasm on the part of the patron; and this is really necessary at times.

Reference librarians have an on-going responsibility, both personally and professionally, to strive to become more competent and skilled in their work performance.

EVALUATION OF REFERENCE LIBRARIANS

Evaluating the performance of reference librarians is extremely difficult; thus, the best approach is to evaluate what they do and how they perform their duties.[16] This can best be done by the faculty and students with whom the librarians work. A survey would be an excellent method of doing this project.

Evaluation of reference librarians is an area of study which does not yet carry much validity, even though there is a significant amount of literature on the subject. However, the entire issue of *The Reference Librarian*, edited by Bill Katz and Ruth A. Fraley is devoted to the subject.[17]

COLLECTION DEVELOPMENT, EVALUATION AND WEEDING

None of these activities should be carried out without input from the reference librarian(s) who becomes much more familiar than anyone else with the needs of students and professors, as well as the materials needed to cover the current topics that are being studied. Even though professors should be involved in all three activities, they still are not always aware of the numerous and varied topics being researched by the students, except as they relate to each professor's class assignments.

Traditionally, public services personnel work more closely with the individual patrons than the other librarians; therefore, they must work very closely with the selection process and any other services relative to the public. From these ties it becomes possible to "obtain knowledge of the trends, goals and objectives of users. It is easy then to determine what the library's long-range plans might be to meet the needs expressed by users in their day-to-day interaction with the collection."[18]

Reference librarians should be involved also in the circulating collection building, as well as the weeding of the collection — and even in the addition or deletion of periodicals, if they work in that area. There is not anyone on the staff who could have a better knowledge of what should be kept and what should be discarded than the people who work with the collection constantly; that is, the reference librarian(s).

One area which must be considered very carefully is that which comprises the literature books which may be listed in collections, or anthologies. If the books are discarded because they are old, this certainly makes the indices to collections of much less value; but, it does happen. For the same reasons given for development, reference librarians should be heavily involved in the evaluation and weeding of the entire collection.

CONCLUSION

Being a reference librarian does not mean simply sitting at a desk answering questions, or directing people to certain tools or sections of the library. One must possess certain qualities, have a broad academic background of knowledge and possess much wisdom and tact; this is the ideal. Also, a reference librarian must be capable of coping with the constant revelation of "hidden" agenda, which probably never ceases entirely. This is one of the most important keys to being a successful (and happy) reference librarian — facing the unknown and the unexpected, and being willing to be challenged each time a patron approaches the reference desk. This keeps one alert and deeply interested in his work.

Being a reference librarian is a continuous learning process, as well as a helping service. I can think of no other profession that lends itself to this type of satisfaction, because the learning comes from all disciplines.

The literature abounds in articles relative to every subject covered in this article, plus many more. The author's idea was not to write just another article; rather, the purpose was to "chat" with each person who reads the article, and who is either a reference librarian currently or is anticipating serving in that capacity some day.

Regardless of the many unexpected "surprises" and responsibilities, being a reference librarian is the most rewarding position in an academic library. It means working with and serving people; and it means job satisfaction. If an individual loves people and thoroughly enjoys his job, there will be no such thing as "Burnout."

NOTES

1. Bauer, George R., "Conflicts in reference service: A personal view." *The Reference Librarian* (12), Spring/Summer, 1985, pp. 73-81.

2. Isaacson, David, "Conflicts between reference librarians and faculty concerning bibliographic instruction." *The Reference Librarian* (12), Spring/Summer, 1985, pp. 117-128.

3. Miller, Constance & James Rettig, "Reference obsolescence." *RQ* 25(1), Fall, 1985, pp. 52-58.

4. Vincent, C. Paul, "Bibliographic instruction and the reference desk: A symbiotic relationship." *The Reference Librarian* (12), Spring/Summer, 1984, pp. 39-47.

5. Ibid., p. 44.

6. Young, William F., "Methods for evaluating reference desk performance." *RQ* 25(1), Fall, 1985, pp. 69-75.

7. Glogoff, Stuart, "Communication theory's role in the reference interview." *Drexel Library Quarterly* 19, Spring, 1983, pp. 56-72.

8. Easley, Janet, "Reference service policies." *Reference Services Review* (13), Summer, 1985, pp. 79-82.

9. Moody, Marilyn, "Government information." *RQ* 25(1), Fall, 1985, pp. 39-45.

10. Brody, Ellen, "Reference librarians as teachers: Ego, ideal and reality in a reference department." *The Reference Librarian* (14), Spring/Summer, 1986, pp. 159-171.

11. Vincent, "Bibliographic instruction," p. 45-46.

12. Kent, Eben L., "The search interview." *Online searching: The basics, settings & management* (ed.), Joann H. Lee, Littleton, CO: Libraries Unlimited, Inc., 1984, pp. 34-40.

13. Surprenant, Thomas T. & Claudia Perry-Holmes, "The Reference Librarian of the future: A scenario." *RQ* 25(2), Winter, 1985, pp. 234-238.

14. Bonta, Bruce D., "Online searching in the reference room." *Library Trends* 31(3), Winter, 1985, pp. 495-508.

15. Ibid., p. 508.

16. Young, "Methods for evaluating," p. 69.

17. Katz, Bill & Ruth A. Fraley (eds.), "Evaluation of reference services." *The Reference Librarian* (11), Fall/Winter, 1984, entire issue.

18. Futas, Elizabeth, "The role of public services in collection evaluation." *Library Trends* 33(4), Winter, 1985, pp. 397-416.

Marketing the Library in a Time of Crisis: Rewriting Public Policy Statements

Ruth E. Turner

SUMMARY. As the 1980s draw to a close, libraries are again contending with the problem of budget cuts in a declining economy. In the light of this situation, it becomes necessary for librarians to return to the drawing boards to revise public policy statements. How to cut services without destroying the traditional role of libraries in society, whether or not to invoke user fees under a "free access" philosophy, and how to increase the productivity and level of performance of librarians are some decisions that have to be made.

INTRODUCTION

With the budget cuts in the early 1970s, libraries found it necessary to trim staffs, discontinue additional new services, and to implement fees for certain retained services.[1] As the 1980s draw to a close, libraries again find themselves in similar predicaments, if not worse than were experienced in the 1970s.

Utah is one of the states where academic libraries are placed in that kind of dilemma. During the current fiscal year, 1986-87, institutions of higher education have been required to absorb a cut of 4% in their budgets. For libraries this has meant a cut in materials, student assistance, and hourly budgets. The latter two items are very important to the maintenance of proper records

Ruth E. Turner is Associate Professor of Library Science and Head of Government Documents/Reference Librarian, Stewart Library, Weber State College, Ogden, UT 84408-2901.

and back-up personnel for public services. In addition to the fore-going, state owned colleges and universities were asked by the Governor of the State, that the next fiscal year budgets reflect a 94% level of the present budget, in other words a 6% cut, and has caused deep cuts to be made in programs and personnel budgets, resulting in a $15.4 million reduction in the higher education budget. Consequently, 102 programs and services had been identified for elimination; 130 programs and services have been recognized for reductions; 20 programs or departments have been consolidated; 444 faculty and staff positions have been scheduled for elimination. This reduction in personnel alone surpasses the whole faculty of Weber State College. Each institution was to retain 100% of the 94% left to strengthen those departments, including libraries, that remained.[2]

As the Utah Legislature dismissed for this current year 1987 term, a return of close to the 100% of the 94% was granted, however, another 1% cut must be absorbed between now and June 30, 1987, when the current budget fiscal year ends.[3]

LIBRARY POLICY STATEMENTS

What does a situation like this imply for the policy statements of academic libraries such as Weber State College's Stewart Library and others under similar circumstances? It requires a return to the drawing boards for a look at what services can realistically be offered, to what extent, and to what standard they can be maintained.

In this day and age with the proliferation of information available, in a number of different formats, in an effort to be all things to all people, an academic library reference/information service may have a tendency to spread the personnel too thin in order to accomplish all of the desired services. In so doing, perhaps a disparity in reference services may develop rather than having a unified equality of service to all patrons.[4]

I believe that most professional and paraprofessional librarians have the desire to give the best possible assistance within the parameters with which they have to work. It is possible that when librarians are expected to reach beyond what is a logical expectation to accomplish all the services outlined in an unrealistic policy statement, they may well become frustrated. Perhaps with the tightening of budgets, libraries will be compelled to create a more rational policy statement which before, in some cases, might have been a reflection of an idealistic situation rather than a practical one.

In Utah, citizens have been rebelling against increased taxes for adequate revenues to be used for public schools and higher education. Some proclaim they have not seen any or enough improvement in education for all the monies that have poured into it over the past years. In preparing new public policy statements, perhaps a statement emanating from the Board of Regents or whichever governing board is over the colleges or universities, delineating just what "public" academic libraries are expected to serve, would be appropriate.

However, state owned institutions are financed a great deal through tax dollars from the general public, which may lead citizens to believe there is an obligation to the public from academic libraries beyond their own immediate student and faculty community.

At Weber State College the only fee that has been charged to patrons beyond the college community has been for WSC IDs to use the library's material for checkout, no charge for in-house use or librarians assistance in research has been instigated. The cost for WSC IDs has been just $5.00 to the general public or to those who are not part of the campus community, but this will have to go up to $15.00 in the near future. To this point charges for database searches have been only the direct cost incurred with computer connect time and telephone long distance charges. No surcharge has been issued, indirect costs have been sustained by the library. This has been the case not only for the campus immediate community, but also for school districts, community business people, as well as students from the universities' graduate programs. The charging of indirect costs of this more sophisticated service may have to be invoked in the near future for categories of users other than our own students and faculty.

Beyond the direct benefits for the library, preparing a realistic policy statement that will let librarians know exactly what is expected of them in these times of crisis, it will also provide a document that may be shown to taxpayers to indicate how their money is being spent in a more frugal manner and what has been done to use the tax dollars to the best advantage.[5]

Another problem that faces libraries in this retrenchment of policymaking, is the fact that many contributions in the form of money and materials have been enjoyed by librarians in the past through the personal contact and attention given by librarians to people from outside the academic community. In fact it might be said there has been a real romance between librarians and donors. If this kind of attention has to be confined to the academic community only, compounded by the certainty that credit for contributions has nearly all but been deleted from the new income tax law, librarians may come to suffer from lack of revenue from still another source.

Goals, Priorities, and Standards

In redrafting a reference public policy, certain components need to be included which reflect what pragmatic goals and objectives the library must consider feasible in a crisis situation, and maintain such until better times once again appear over the horizon. An academic library needs to set priorities as to whom it can continue to serve and to what extent. In keeping with the new goals and priorities, an explicit reference policy would be necessary. A reference policy statement creates a criterion for service, to include to what level it can be rendered, as well as to what restraints must be placed on service, such as shortened hours, or the need to have only two reference personnel at a time where there may have been several before.

The next step would be to develop an articulate and effective procedures policy that could easily be followed by each reference person in order to offer consistently high quality service even within limited parameters. Such a document would provide good training too for new staff members as well as give reference personnel clear guidelines to fall back on in the event that a certain act of a librarian might be challenged. These standards and guidelines also provide an instrument by which the efficacy and proficiency of a performance may be measured.[6] Another value of this kind of document is that it may be used to guide librarians in the appropriateness of answering certain types of questions. If a telephone request were to arise that involved interpretation of legal, medical, or statistical matters, referring to the policy, even the newest one on the reference desk, would know how to handle such a situation.[7]

CHARGING FEES

When the question of fees to be incorporated into a library policy statement arises in academic libraries, several questions need to be asked as well as the need to consider different possibilities. Where should charges begin? Should they begin with new services or should they also be applied to existing services? Is it possible for the paying group to be segregated from the non-paying patrons? Can services be quantified in order to properly prorate these charges? These are not easy questions for a library to answer, however a division between basic services and augmented services has been tried by some libraries in the incorporation of fees.[8]

Libraries in colleges and universities may propose one price for their primary users consisting of students and faculty or no fee at all, but for secondary users such as business, industries, or the public at large, it is becoming customary to consistently charge fees.

There are several ways fees may be determined. Sliding scales based on different categories of customers might be considered. A library may decide to work into fee charging gradually by moving from free service to partial subsidizing to total charges. However, the least problematic method and perhaps the most common is the flat rate or fixed charge. In many cases patrons who require specialized information would be willing to pay a reasonable charge for the convenience.[9]

In the consideration of moving into fee charging, there are four characteristics listed by the Advisory Commission on Intergovernmental Relations for determining user charges which libraries might find useful as a barometer to follow:

1. A user charge might be employed if the purpose is to restrict the demand for a limited service.
2. What is the essence of the benefits derived from the service? Would a charge on this particular service dissuade users from taking advantage of it and, therefore, the benefits that might have been gained from it will never be realized.
3. If the cost of administrating the collection of a fee is greater than the revenue from it, then it best be forgotten.
4. Is charging a fee equitable? Does the fee deny the service to those who would benefit from it but could not afford the cost? However, a fee would allow individuals to pay for only those services they would choose to use.

In summary the most vigorous arguments for fees would be if substantial waste would be the consequences if services were free, if advantages accrued basically for the user, if the fees could be easily collected, and if costs were believed to be equitable.[10]

On-Line Searching Fees

One of the most common areas in reference service policies where fees beyond direct costs are charged is in the on-line searching. For a library to implement on-line searching it is fairly costly to start up. A library of comparable size would probably need two or three computers with all of the components necessary to actuate such a service. As technologies improve, new models are often purchased. Software packages for accessing are usually a onetime expense, as long as all the hardware remains compatible for the selected software. The basic training unless it can be done in-house is not cheap and in order to keep up-to-date and maintain expertise in subject searching it becomes necessary for searchers to continue to attend workshops on different vendors or different database files. To help defray these incurred expenses, some libraries have a graduated charge for on-line searching, depending on the category in which a patron falls. An important element in determining public charging policy has been how well a library can assimilate the searching costs within its own operating budget. Placing a charge to help recoup indirect costs for the library increases the cost to the requestor and consequently the demand for such services may drop.[11]

At Weber State College when a grant of $4500.00, which provided free subject searching for students for seven quarters, ran out, and the direct costs had to be transferred to students, the demand dropped dramatically. Based on past experiences, one might project that if it becomes necessary to assess indirect costs to users, the demand for this service may completely fade away. Along with a depressed budget period, students' tuition at Weber State College has been going up constantly so that many students have little money left over to pay for the more sophisticated services and tend to prefer to do their own manual searching. Perhaps for smaller colleges a discontinuance of the on-line searching may be in order for the time being until budgets take an upward swing.

With the introduction of indirect costs to patrons comes the greater liability for librarians to obtain correct and germane information in doing subject searching. This may place the librarian searchers in a more stressful situation. Incorrect information may not be observed by the patron before he/she leaves the library and thus a difficult situation may ensue with a disenchanted patron. Some statement concerning where the responsibility lies between the user and the librarian for obtaining accurate information, perhaps should be included.

Interlibrary Loan Fees

Another area where fees have been installed into reference public policy as part of the reference services is for interlibrary loans. This has been the case with many academic research libraries.[12] This charge, compounded by on-line searching costs, may make it too expensive for patrons to do research projects. If the library doesn't have adequate backup sources, whether the research is done by computer or manually, the cost to obtain copies of articles remains the same. How far a library is liable to patrons for weaknesses in collections is hard to determine. Selection policies affect the ability of the reference personnel to effectively help users find the materials they need. Complaints are often voiced by students when titles of magazines are not available in the library, and books the same way. The burden of extra time and costs is placed on them when interlibrary loans have to be initiated.

Traditionally small libraries have depended on larger ones to supplement their collections through interlibrary loans. But small libraries are perhaps finding, increasingly so, that substantive fees are being placed on the borrowing of books by a number of libraries and of late the charge per page for photocopying has also started to rise. We have found this to be true at Weber State College, especially when it becomes necessary to make requests outside the state. It might be well in the revision of policies to make a statement about the rising costs of this service to users.

LIBRARIAN PERFORMANCE

When budgets are short and personnel on the decline, a situation is created which places greater demands on the performance of reference librarians. With decreased opportunities of getting new and plentiful resources to add to the library's holdings, librarians must become more innovative in using what the library has to offer and become more familiar with all ways of answering questions in order to offset the shortages in new and updated materials. If not before, now is the time for public policy statements to include uniform standards by which librarians are expected to discharge their responsibilities.

Merrily Taylor, Librarian at Brown University during her presentation at the Dekalb Symposium stated that the library on her campus she felt had a singular position which gave the librarians an angle different from others at the University, regardless of how sophisticated the others' knowledge might be.

1. Librarians are privy to how information is employed by students and faculty in day-to-day research surroundings.
2. Librarians recognize how needs and use of information vary from discipline to discipline.
3. Librarians understand reality versus theory when it comes to making plans for the future.[13]

Perhaps Ms. Taylor's description of the library and librarians at Brown University are constant with libraries and librarians on most academic campuses. With this kind of inside knowledge, librarians should make excellent mediators between information in the library and those who need to access it.

A study done in 1983 by the Public Library Branch of the Division of Maryland State Department of Education found that only 55% of the time users of the libraries obtained correct answers to moderately hard questions. As an outgrowth of this study some suggestions were made on how librarians might improve.

1. Evoke the precise question from a user.
2. Indicate interest in the question.
3. Be alert and concerned for the patron's question.
4. In concluding the reference interview inquire of the user if his/her question has been fully answered.
5. If giving an answer to a question, cite the source or identify the answer.
6. Understand the type of information that comes from basic reference sources (ready references) and, when proper, use these as they provide quick answers to certain questions.[14]

Although this study was done with public libraries, the results would be applicable to academic library reference services. The suggestions for improving the performance of public reference librarians in response to users might well be incorporated into the policy standards of librarian performance in the college/university environment.

CONCLUSION

In rewriting public policy statements and standards of performance in academic libraries, even though under an atmosphere of declining economy, perhaps librarians should not be too impetuous in making radical changes without giving considerable thought to the impact these changes may have on their public. Librarians need to stand in awe of the traditions and responsibilities of what libraries have meant to society. They have housed the recorded history of mankind, the culture and thoughts of mankind that have emanated from prehistoric times, through the classical period of Greece into the 20th century. The evolution of science may be traced through books contained in libraries. Libraries have provided sources for the enlightenment of the masses through the conceived idea of free access to information in a democracy.

On the subject of free versus fee-based access to information, an English Librarian, John Smith, FLA has this to say:

> Access to the culture is a right, and the exercise of that right should not be restricted to those who can pay. Access is a freedom and a responsibility for all. I would define culture as that which causes growth. In other words, the library network is the resources of the past, used in the present, causing the aspirations of the future to materialize; a manifestation of the aspiration of our society. Therefore if a society is to be mature, if a society is to achieve both individually and collectively its potential, it needs to maximize the opportunities inherent in every individual, and so purely economic values of ability to pay should not dominate that freedom or destroy the responsibility of choice that free access to the culture implies.[15]

Libraries faced with the need to make tough decisions, walk a tightrope, balancing between an attempt to maintain their traditional values for society, and facing the reality of faltering budgets.

NOTES

1. Nancy Kranch, "Fees For Library Service: They are not Inevitable," *Library Journal*, 105, (May 1, 1980), 1048.

2. Fred Stringham, Member of the Board of Regents, "Regents Back Taxes for Schools," *Salt Lake Tribune*, (Feb. 14, 1987), A3.

3. Dawn Tracy, "Higher Education's Budget Holds at $257 Million," *Salt Lake Tribune*, (Feb. 27, 1987), A5.

4. Alice Driscoll, "Back to Square One: The Writing of A Reference Policy Statement and Procedures Manual," *Southeastern Librarians*, 31, (Fall, 1981), 109.

5. Alice Driscoll, *Southeastern Librarian*, 110.

6. Janet Easley, "Reference Service Policies," *Reference Services Review*, 13, (Summer, 1985), 80.

7. Janet Easley, *Reference Services Review*, 13, 81.

8. National Commission on Libraries and Information Science, *The Role of Fees in Supporting Library and Information Services in Public and Academic Libraries*, (Washington, DC: U.S. Department of Education, 1985), 16.

9. National Commission on Libraries and Information Sciences, 18-19.

10. Nancy Kranich, *Library Journal*, 105, 1050.

11. Mary M. Huston, "Fee or Free: The Effects of Charging on Information Demand," *Library Journal*, 104, (September 15, 1979), 1812.

12. Herb White, "Who Pays for Peripheral Services and What Are They Anyway," *American Libraries*, 13, (January, 1982), 40.

13. JoAn Segal & John Tyson, "The Library's Charging Role in Higher Education," *Library Journal*, 110, (September 15, 1985), 44-45.

14. Ralph Gers & Lillie J. Seward, "Improving Reference Performance: Results of a Statewide Study," *Library Journal*, 110, (November 1, 1985), 32, 34-35.

15. John Smith, "A Conflict of Values: Changes in the Publicly Funded Library," *Journal of Librarianship*, 13 (January, 1981), 3.

Letter to the Editor

William Katz
School of Library and Information Science
Draper Hall
State University of New York
Albany, New York 12222

Dear Professor Katz:

I am writing in reference to an article that appeared in the Winter 1986 issue of *The Reference Librarian*. In the article, "The Myth of the Reference Interview" (pp. 47-52), Mr. Robert Hauptman makes sweeping generalizations and applies them to the entire library profession based on what he calls "informal surveys." Informal surveys are not to be discounted since they often serve as starting points for more structured empirical research. I would argue, however, that the "informal surveys" conducted by Mr. Hauptman are not worthy of even that lowly term, and have been used inappropriately by the author to make damaging, possibly fallacious statements about reference service.

As a library staff member at one of the institutions visited by Mr. Hauptman, it might be assumed that comments from this source will be biased. Indeed, they are biased. However, this bias originates from a deep concern regarding what passes as research in the library profession. If our goal is to be accepted as professionals within a "science," we must be concerned about the quality of research that is being conducted in our field. Like other professions, we should set high standards for research, especially if we plan to draw generalizable conclusions from our research and disseminate these conclusions through the professional literature.

371

During Mr. Hauptman's visit to the University of Minnesota, I questioned him about the methodology he was employing for his "informal survey." Frankly, his answers appalled me. His methodology was flawed in numerous respects. The time lag between Mr. Hauptman's visit to our institution and my current letter does not affect the accuracy of my observations, as I am referring to in-depth notes I compiled on the day of Mr. Hauptman's visit.

Observation periods varied from institution to institution, each ending when Mr. Hauptman had had, in his own words, "enough." Enough what? No clarification was forthcoming from Mr. Hauptman. In a footnote within the article, Mr. Hauptman details the time he spent at each of the eight institutions, with observation times varying from 30 to 90 minutes. One wonders why Mr. Hauptman bothered at all with these visits, given the insignificant amount of time he spent at each institution. Also in question is the number of staff Mr. Hauptman could have observed during his abbreviated visits. Assuming double-staffing of the eight service points, it is probable that he observed no more than 16 librarians. It is ridiculous to claim that 16 academic librarians' actions are indicative of the thousands of reference librarians who currently staff all varieties of reference service points. Using the University of Minnesota as an example, I am compelled to point out that it is impossible to draw any conclusions about even this single institution after spending merely one hour out of a total of 143,438 annual service hours, observing two staff members out of a total of 408FTE, at only one of the 55 service points on the Twin Cities campus.

Another troubling aspect of Mr. Hauptman's "informal survey" was his failure to adequately define what comprised a reference interview. He informed me that he was looking for "long, intense interactions between the patron and the librarian." How long? Once again, no clarification was forthcoming from Mr. Hauptman. In all practicality, is length of the patron-librarian interaction a true indicator that a reference interview has taken place? A few well-chosen questions posed and answered in a few moments may be as effective a reference interview as a prolonged set of queries occurring over 30 minutes. How can Mr. Hauptman claim to have examined the reference interview when he is unable to define it in measurable terms?

A third, and very serious flaw in Mr. Hauptman's methodology, was his procedure for observing reference staff. How many reference librarians conduct an entire reference transaction, including an interview, from behind the reference desk? In my own experience, not unlike that of my colleagues at the University of Minnesota, I have found that the major portion of the transaction, including the interview, takes place away from the physical confines of the desk. Mr. Hauptman neglected this entire aspect in his observation at our institution. He stationed himself on a stool located four feet behind the desk and didn't leave this position a single time during his observation, in spite of the fact that the reference librarians were away from the desk assisting patrons for most of his observation period. I can't imagine why Mr. Hauptman chose to proceed in this manner. In most cases, he was completely out of earshot during the larger portion of the transaction. In his article, Mr. Hauptman states that, "... I decided to observe a diversified group of reference librarians at work. I, therefore, visited eight libraries in order to learn just how one should utilize the reference interview effectively. I learned very little." I'm not at all surprised, given the fact that he was an inattentive, ill-prepared student.

Upon questioning Mr. Hauptman as to how he chose the libraries for his survey, he informed me that they were all located close to Interstate 80, and therefore convenient for him. Although I can appreciate his desire for ease of access, I have grave doubts that eight academic libraries located near a particular freeway are representative of libraries in general. (It is difficult to determine exactly who comprised Mr. Hauptman's population. He speaks grandiosely of "libraries," implying public, school, and special libraries; yet the libraries he observed were, without exception, academic libraries.) Whether or not the author actually did bias his results is secondary to the strong suspicion that this was highly likely.

These are serious flaws, and they invalidate any data gathered by Mr. Hauptman. The author has inconsistently and whimsically gathered incomplete information from which he has proceeded to draw inappropriate, unsubstantiated conclusions about the library profession as a whole. I am disappointed to see such a poor and possibly false representation of the library profession appearing in our professional literature. Certainly, Mr. Hauptman is allowed his opinions, and opinions about the profession do have a place in the professional literature. However, when these opinions masquerade as empirical truths, and are purveyed as such, we do our profession a serious disservice and undermine its credibility.

In conclusion, I would suggest more rigorous screening of future authors' methodologies. We cannot afford to let spurious investigations such as Mr. Hauptman's diminish the integrity of our profession.

Sincerely,

Kathleen L. Gorman
Assistant to the University Librarian
University of Minnesota
Wilson Library
Minneapolis, MN 55455

Response to Preceding Letter

Kathleen L. Gorman has a prodigious memory. In late 1984, I spoke with her briefly and spent a total of 60 minutes observing the reference process at the University of Minnesota. Nevertheless, almost three years later she is able to recall virtually everything that transpired except the color of my shirt. I think, however, that she protests too much. Her response to my admittedly informal survey is extraordinarily overreactive. Part of my essay is merely personal observation extrapolated to some fair generalizations. (And that is precisely what reference interview proponents do as well.) I am not condemning the observed nor reference librarians nor the profession. I am only indicating that based on my limited experience, a reference interview frequently does not occur. Apparently some professional leaders at least found this interesting, since of the 23 articles contained in that thematic issue of *THE REFERENCE LIBRARIAN* only "The Myth of the

Reference Interview" was chosen for lengthy summary in "AL Digest" (*AMERICAN LIBRARIES*, June 1987, p. 486).

Let me briefly clarify six points:

1. *My* goal is not to be accepted as a professional within a science. Library service, like so many other pretentious disciplines, is not a science and only masquerades as such. All of the pseudoscientific methodologies and paraphernalia used by "researchers" in their surveys and observations will never change this.

2. My objective at each institution visited was to spend approximately one hour in observation, and this is precisely what I did except in two instances. The amount of time was not insignificant; eight hours allowed me to overhear 229 questions (with no interviews taking place). Furthermore, Gorman completely ignores my own experience: 101 hours and 1074 questions (with only six interviews).

3. I disagree. Indeed, one *can* draw conclusions, not about a specific institution, but about a process based on librarians' attitudes, *immediate* answers, and inaccurate information conveyed.

4. I indicate that a brief counter-question or two does not comprise an interview. A full and complete interview requires paralinguistic observation (kinesics, haptics, proxemics, etc.) and a complex series of interchanges through which the librarian discovers the hidden, the real, the true need of the patron. It does not have to last 30 minutes or even ten. Time is not the key factor here; complexity is. (Isn't Gorman familiar with the literature?)

5. Once again, I disagree. At the University of Minnesota and at all of the other institutions visited, I observed and overheard virtually *all* of each interaction. In some cases, I *did* follow the librarian and patron to another location. That is why I did not include the phone interchanges: I could not hear what was being said. In most cases (even at the University of Minnesota), I was *not* "completely out of earshot during the larger portion of the transaction."

6. I did not inform Gorman that the libraries were located close to Interstate 80, which runs East/West. I stated that they were in the proximity of Interstate 35 which runs from Texas to Minnesota and right past Gorman's own University.

I agree with Gorman that much library research is questionable, but that in itself does not invalidate my findings. I also sincerely appreciate her lengthy response to my essay. It is her right to disagree and her duty to articulate her thoughts. But taking my comments as a personal attack, and reacting in language that borders on *ad hominum* argument ("I'm not at all surprised [that Hauptman learned very little], given the fact that he was an inattentive, ill-prepared student." or "We cannot afford to let spurious investigations such as Mr. Hauptman's diminish the integrity of our profession.") is unfair, unprofessional, and unconvincing.

Robert Hauptman
Assistant Professor
St. Cloud State University

For Product Safety Concerns and Information please contact our EU
representative GPSR@taylorandfrancis.com Taylor & Francis Verlag GmbH,
Kaufingerstraße 24, 80331 München, Germany

Printed and bound by CPI Group (UK) Ltd, Croydon, CR0 4YY
08/05/2025
01864408-0004